FLYING THE LINE

AN AIR FORCE PILOT'S JOURNEY

FLYING THE LINE

AN AIR FORCE PILOT'S JOURNEY

VOLUME TWO,
MILITARY AIRLIFT COMMAND
1981-1993

Lt. Col Jay Lacklen,
USAFR, retired

MCP Books, Maitland

MCP Books

2301 Lucien Way #415

Maitland, FL 32751

407.339.4217

www.MCPBooks.com

ISBN-13: 978-1-63505-490-3

LCCN: 2016955561

Distributed by Itasca Books

Printed in the United States of America

Dedicated to soldiers who die young:

Tombstone inscription

"For the wife I will never see
For my children who will never be
I trust my legacy to Thee."

Jay Lacklen

NOTE ON VOLUMES

Consider this a thousand-page memoir divided into three chronological books of just over 300 pages each.

Book one took me from college, though pilot training, Vietnam, and the Strategic Air Command from 1970 to 1979, all on active duty.

This second volume will cover my brief excursion into civilian aviation from 1980 to 1982 and my return to military aviation flying the C-5 for the Air Force Reserve from 1981 to 1993.

Book three will commence in 1993 and carry me to my 2004 military retirement. This 1993 demarcation between book two and book three is defined by my return to Dover AFB, DE from Westover AFB, MA and the command's name change from Military Airlift Command (MAC), to Air Mobility Command (AMC) in June 1992.

Each of the books carry the primary title of *Flying the Line, an Air Force Pilot's Journey*, with subtitles differentiating the volumes, as follows.

Volume I subtitle: *Pilot Training, Vietnam, SAC, 1970-1979*.

Volume II subtitle: *Military Airlift Command, 1981–1993*.

Volume III subtitle: *Air Mobility Command, 1993–2004*.

NOTES ON BOOK ONE

There are several errors in book one.

First, the draft lottery affected only those not in college. Since I had graduated, I was prime fodder for the draft. However, I incorrectly stated current students were vulnerable, but they were not.

Second, my initial Arc Light tour was from August to October 1973, not March to May. The final bombing halt in August came after my two Cambodian bomb runs. I apparently transposed my third tour dates in 1975 to my first tour.

Third, my final Arc Light tour ended in early June 1975, not late May, when I led the last Arc Light cell out of U-Tapao AB, Thailand.

I regret these errors and thank those who gleefully pointed them out to my Facebook audience.

CONTENTS

PROLOGUE

WHERE THE AIR FORCE LIVES

I've always wondered where the real Air Force lives.

Congress lives in the Capitol, the governor lives in the state capital, Microsoft lives in Seattle, the football Cowboys live in Dallas, a family lives in their home, but where does the Air Force live? Where is the essence we call the Air Force to be found?

The quick answers do not satisfy. The Pentagon has lots of Air Force generals, but it has generals from other services too. Texas has many Air Force bases, and many pilots, including me, took basic training there. This might have made Texas my default location for the Air Force home, but as I moved around the Air Force system, Texas did not seem unique. California has lots of bases, too, including a huge composite wing at Travis AFB with several types of airlift aircraft. Then there are the super bases such as Wright-Patterson AFB in Ohio. It also seems every Air Force major command has its separate headquarters which disperses the Air Force home to a half-dozen different locations, such as Langley AFB, VA, and Scott AFB, IL. In the face of such widespread activity centers, the Air Force seems more an extended family spread across the country and the world rather than a family unit located in one home.

I have vivid, varied memories of Air Force life that defy the concept of a specific home, yet still define the place the real Air Force inhabits.

In northern Maine I remember climbing into the seat of my B-52 bomber one early morning and finding the windscreen beautifully covered with a latticework of snowflake-shaped ice crystals that shimmered first silver, then gold, as the sunlight illuminated them. The artistry of nature placed upon the surface of a stark metal war machine. Then, along with the marvelous winter view, I felt the icy shock of the cold-soaked, flexible rubber oxygen mask as it gripped my face when I made a radio call to the command post. Did the Air Force live here in far northern Maine, I wondered? It seemed to at the time, but was this its home?

During Vietnam, Saigon seemed the Air Force home. There were no ice crystals in Nam. Vietnam had the Central Highlands, a long chain of small mountains that ran down the country as a dragon's spine shrouded in misty clouds that only sporadically revealed its vertebrae in their dense tropical greenness. It also had oppressively humid heat that could only be fought off with whirring, ever-present window air conditioners that became the predominant sound I remember from the time. In an operational sense, the Air Force lived in Vietnam from 1965 to 1973. That must have been the Air Force home, I thought. Yes, the Cold War was still being tacitly fought in Europe, but the action and the Air Force essence was in Nam, or headed there, or coming back from there, or planning to go there. Surely that focus of activity made it "home"?

But Nam was for a previous generation. Today's generation lives in the Arabian desert, where the overwhelming heat is dry and the denizens often adorned in flowing white robes rather than black pajamas. This seems to be the new home of Air Force essence, the primary going-to and coming-from location where much of the service lives or plans for.

So is the Air Force home a perpetual vagabond that shifts its abode to the current hot spot? Is there no permanent home for the service?

Yes, there is.

One night just a few days into Operation Desert Shield in 1990, five C-5 crews from our Westover AFB, MA, reserve wing would cover the ramp at Dhahran AB, Saudi Arabia. We flew planes from a variety of C-5 bases, but we were all Westover crews. We exalted at our leading edge position in the war as we discovered each other. I moved down the ramp visiting each cockpit to enthusiastically swap mission stories and gossip with my compatriots, all of us giddy to be in a war and doing wonderful, manly things in an exotic Arabian desert.

It was during this ramp interaction, and during the flight to Dhahran, that I found the Air Force home.

My route to Saudi Arabia from Ramstein Air Base, Germany, ran south through eastern France (where we kept asking questions of Air Traffic Control just to hear the female controllers croon to us in their melodious French accents). Then we flew down the length of Italy, south and east down the coast of Greece, and finally south across the Mediterranean toward the mystical realms of Egypt and other stark deserts where the war awaited. Turning south toward El Daba, Egypt, we overtook another Westover C-5 crew at sunset. Their strobe light flashed to us in repetitive sequence, a mobile airborne lighthouse signaling its position in the darkening sky.

I recognized the voices as they checked in with Cairo Air Traffic Control as a Westover crew flying from Torrejon AB, Spain, outside Madrid. They were headed to Dhahran as we were; however, I sensed something wasn't right. Why were they flying so slowly and allowing us to catch them? I asked the questions, sensing there were several "somethings" that were not right with them.

Who was on the crew, I asked? The pilot mentioned only one other pilot. Whoa, I protested, do you mean you only have two pilots? Aren't you on an augmented crew day [24 hours] that requires three pilots? He responded that this was how it turned out, the mission had to go, and they had to fly it. I suspect they wanted to keep going, and didn't admit to the command post they were a basic crew (16-hour duty day maximum). As I later discovered, they flew a thirty-two-hour "basic" day from the States, to Spain, to Dhahran, and back to Torrejon with only two pilots, a task that would have exhausted a full crew.

I knew that later, but coasting into Egypt I wondered why they were poking along a .74 Mach instead of the standard .77. Reluctantly they told me they were short on fuel and had to fly at .74 for maximum fuel efficiency. They had 15,000 pounds less fuel than we did at this point, and we eventually landed with 15,000 pounds, 5,000 below minimum landing fuel. When I later asked them their landing fuel at Dhahran, they refused to answer, and I didn't really want to know. I was just glad they made it.

This encounter over the Nile haunted me over the years. Here we found a fellow Westover crew in the darkness over Egypt where the bright strip of gold and silver lights along the Nile River wound starkly and narrowly through the utter darkness of the landmass below. We discussed in professional tones the operational problems we would later chatter about excitedly on the ramp at Dhahran. After our consultations on each other's problems, my aircraft slowly pulled away from the other crew due to our greater speed, and lost contact with them over southern Egypt.

All this occurred as we sailed through an invisible dark blue air ocean above exotic lands that left us gazing silently at the beauty we saw. Alas, we are but pilots in a poetic realm we can marvel over, but are often unable to describe. The points along our journey mesmerized—Cairo, Luxor, Gassim, Alkir, Tabuk—as we flew an American war chariot to the front lines while passing over the home of the pharaohs and Ali Baba. These would be such marvelous feelings to share, if only we had the words.

I walked back through the C-5 crew compartment toward the galley. Some of the off-duty crew slept in rear compartment seats collapsed in a bizarre parody of war dead frozen in rigor mortis, mouths slackly agape and faces pale in a desperate weariness that no amount of such sleep would cure.

Others worked at their duties, either on the engineer panel or at the crew table toward the back where they planned downloading, uploading, and landing data for the arrival. A poker game raged amid mixed gleeful and disparaging shouts as cards slapped emphatically against the table. These never-ending, eagerly sought-out games of chance bind all military generations and are played as intensely at 33,000 feet as the Roman legions must have played during the heady days of the empire.

I later realized that this is where the Air Force lives. This is its home: on the line, in the air, and on the ground, in a thousand different locations around the world. The essence of the force resides at the action points where the mission is accomplished. In this instance it was in banter between two kindred crews randomly brought together over magical lands, where difficult decisions would be made, various problems pondered, and two missions accomplished.

**

Generals keep a terrible secret. While they "fly desks" at plush, extensively decorated headquarters back in the States, they yearn to be with us, flying at 33,000 feet over Egypt on the way to a war zone. That is why they must be provided with enhanced perks, pay, and crisp salutes from everyone on base. If they did not get these perks, none of them would trade a war chariot on a mission for that gilded desk.

After retirement, generals are eager to remind everyone they wore stars. Yes, general, you carried the rank, but we were there, at Mogadishu, Saigon, Dakar, Darwin, Mombasa, Islamabad, U-Tapao, Kunsan, Trondheim, Misawa, Jubail, Balad, and Tegucigalpa. While you commanded at headquarters, we possessed the Air Force soul and dwelt in its home, on the line, where the mission is accomplished, the essence revealed, and where you may get to embrace a brother crew in the dark skies over the Nile.

Liftoff. Sound track accompaniment, *Kyrie*, by Mr. Mister.

Chapter One: The Civilian Side

Dole Presidential Campaign

After my Air Force exit at Castle AFB in June 1979, I drove cross-country from California to northern Virginia for a six-month stay with my uncle Charlie and his family, living in their basement while I sought a job.

During that search I did volunteer work for the "Robert Dole for President" campaign, the first, little remembered, attempt at the presidency for the Kansas senator. I performed as president of the National Volunteers for Dole Committee, a group of which I was the only member.

This brief foray into national politics provided a heady glimpse of Washington political society. Our offices in a posh area of Alexandria, with bistros and boutiques around every corner, made going to work for Dole an exciting proposition.

Speaking of which . . . one of my two coworkers was Miss Kansas from the Miss America pageant a decade before. We had a few lunches together, although usually we dined as a threesome with Dole's daughter, Robin, who was about our age in our early thirties.

At one of these lunches with only Miss K, she suggested she cook dinner for me at her nearby apartment that Friday night. I thought that a friendly gesture and imagined we might hit a few bistros and bars afterward. I apparently had missed the signals. After dinner she suggested we watch a movie on TV. Once the movie started, she approached the couch on which I was seated, paused, and then curled up on the floor with her head on my feet. It soon became obvious that, after the meal, I was dessert.

Unfortunately, I initially suffered my first bout of erectile dysfunction. When it became obvious I had a problem, I apologized and said this had never happened before, and it left me profoundly embarrassed. If I couldn't get it up for Miss Kansas, I might as well retire from such activity! Something about being manhandled by a former beauty queen had wrecked my standard process. I was supposed to be in charge! Maybe I subconsciously feared I could not measure up to her standards, but I had no explanation.

She smiled knowingly and said not to worry about it, it happened sometimes, but perhaps there was something she could do about that. There was, she did, and the rest of the evening went well.

As a volunteer, in addition to licking hundreds of envelopes, I also answered calls from Kansas constituents. I had driven through Kansas while driving cross country from California, but otherwise knew nothing about the state except what I had gleaned from the movie The Wizard of Oz.

One call came from an elderly woman who seemed short a marble or two. She had great concern about some problem and could not be convinced that I was not Senator Dole. So, finally, I decided to become Senator Dole and told her I would get right on that problem. She praised me (Sen. Dole) effusively and hung up.

In December it became apparent Dole was going nowhere in the Republican contest for the 1980 election, and the campaign team, all three of us, disbanded.

HENSON AIRLINES

Photo by Thomas M. Lewis

Henson Airlines Shorts 330 Commuter Aircraft

In January, 1980, I had been told a commuter airline in Salisbury, MD, Henson Airlines, was advertising for a management position. This fit with my career scenario, get with a commuter flying props and guide them into a jet operation to contest the uncompetitive larger airlines. I hoped my jet experience would fit well with this plan.

Dick Henson had made his fortune as a test pilot in his twenties with Fairchild Aircraft Corporation. He had formed a commuter airline flying Beech 99s and Shorts 330s out of Salisbury and Hagerstown, MD, two towns about a thirty-minute flight from Washington, DC, and Baltimore, with Hagerstown to the northwest and Salisbury to the southeast. When I arrived in late 1980, the company route map included Washington, Baltimore, Philadelphia, and Newport News, VA, at the mouth of the Chesapeake Bay. By the time I left in 1982 it had expanded to Pittsburgh, PA, Shenandoah Valley, VA; and Richmond, VA. They had also added the de Havilland Dash 7 to the fleet to cover the expansion.

The commuter flew as a subsidiary and feeder for US Airways during my tenure, although this converted to Piedmont Airlines shortly after I left.

I contacted the operation in Salisbury and got an interview on the same day of the famous U.S. vs. Russia hockey match in the 1980 Olympics. On the two-hour drive from DC to Salisbury, I honed my Ayn Rand, free-market philosophical arguments, something I correctly believed would resonate with Henson. In the interview I sang his song and he grinned and hummed along as I pontificated about free markets and the nefarious danger of unions. His body language and the twinkle in his eye when I finished told me I had knocked the interview out of the park and that a job would soon follow.

Henson is one of the most remarkable personalities I have encountered. He was about 70 years old when I met him. Mostly bald with a gray moustache and dapper attire, he resembled the capitalist rogue on the front of a Monopoly game. His temperament could careen from cheerful, cordial amicability and earnestness to eye-bulging, spittle-flying histrionics if he were tired or encountered any of his nemeses, airline unions or other liberal constituencies. He was old-school conservative and a no-nonsense manager who demanded the same of those he employed. He could be deft in personnel decisions, however. His euphemism for firing someone, or moving them to another position, would be "*I don't think this position is their cup of tea.*" This avoided condemning the person or deprecating their ability, only observing their unsuitability for their current task.

As I drove back to Washington that night, I listened to the hockey game with increasing interest as the Americans, against all odds, were handling the favored Russians. In the final period I sensed they could pull this off, as did the announcers who had become breathless and ebullient at the prospect. As I neared the beltway, the game ended with an American victory and desk-pounding cheers from the announcers. This pick-up American team had bested the invincible Russian team that was professional in most respects, the equivalent of the Boston Bruins used to pounding the daylights out of true amateur teams from other countries.

A few months later, however, I had a more somber view of the victory as I recalled the American basketball team losing to the Russians in the 1972 Olympics. That game ended in controversy as the international referees called repeated fouls on the Americans on the final inbounds play by the Russians, who trailed by one point. Finally, on the third try, the Russians completed a full court pass to their center, who caught the ball, somehow, with two American players draped on him. He then turned and made the winning basket. The Russians had beaten America at their own game and they rushed the court in exaltation much as the American hockey players would eight years later in Lake Placid.

The aftermath of the two upsets would not play well for America, however. The U.S. basketball team, in rage and embarrassment, boycotted the award ceremonies, and did not accept their silver medals in protest of what they considered tacit cheating by the officials to give the Russians multiple chances to steal the victory. This was a continuation of mayhem that erupted from the American players at the end of the game, a shouting, screaming, towel-throwing tantrum at having lost, and bombast at officials and international fans who cheered their demise.

Days later I saw the hockey footage of the American victory and wondered if the Russians would throw a royal tantrum as the Americans had earlier. The parallels were multiple. Both teams had lost in a sport they had owned, and had invested significant national pride in. Both had suffered disputed calls against them during the final moments of each contest and each felt they had been robbed. Both teams would suffer severe recriminations for having lost.

After several minutes focusing on the American jubilation, the camera finally turned down the ice to the Russians. They stood, dejected and morose, but they took it in silence, heads bowed and leaning heavily on their sticks. The American team and fans shouted, waved American flags, and spun around in ecstasy in front of the defeated Russians, and they stood and took it. Their home commissars would blister them, as would the Russian sports world, but they stood and took it. Then they stood stoically on the award stand to accept their silver medals. They took it like men while the Americans petulantly boycotted their ceremony over an equal adversity.

Both teams had suffered crushing, dispiriting losses, but the Russians won the contest of losing well and keeping their composure.

Two days later Henson's secretary called to offer me the job, starting as a pilot and a crew scheduler, and later, potentially, to be chief pilot. I packed up and moved to Ocean City, MD, a beach resort with many empty hotel rooms in the winter off-season.

My hiring class of four included three other pilots who had come up the hard way, paying for their own tickets. If they held any animosity toward me for having the military pay for mine, they did not show it. Maybe they realized I paid for mine by going to Vietnam. We all trained on the Beech 99, a twin-engine turboprop that carried 15 passengers. The company offices, classrooms, and maintenance hangar were in the same structure, so lots was happening when I went to work.

The civilian aviation regime had a marvelous feature the military realm did not, flight attendants. I saw them as a libidinous smorgasbord selection for pilots who only secondarily served passengers. The flight attendants had what pilots were looking for and vice versa, although not specifically the same features.

The B-99 did not have flight attendants, but I mixed freely with them in the crew break rooms around the system. So many alluring targets, I had died and gone to heaven. Some were so staggeringly attractive I had trouble forming sentences while speaking with them. Peggy, Pam, Kathleen, Charlene, aaaaaah! Sensory overload! No more sweaty old enlisted guys bringing me coffee. When I moved up to the Shorts 330, I had curvaceous Cinderellas in the cockpit cooing in my ear to see if there was anything I needed. Ooooooh, yes, Cinderella! Let me recount the list!

There were warnings in the crew room and among pilots, however. One parable told of the senior airline captain who made $300,000 a year but lived in a trailer because his four ex–flight-attendant wives and kids got all his money in alimony and child support. Also, once you married a flight attendant, she would know what transpired on the road and would be eternally suspicious of you, perhaps with good reason.

On the downside, performing as a B-99 copilot had its struggles. As the passengers entered by the rear, left-side passenger door, I would take their carry-on luggage to place in the rear cargo compartment, Mr. Step-and-fetch-it. I was used to ordering around lower ranking officers and enlisted crew members, and now I found myself at the bottom of the steps literally and figuratively while performing for half my military pay. I was invisible to the passengers, a bag boy unworthy of a second glance.

One episode from my days as an SD-330 copilot remains prominently in my mind. The passenger cabin had ten rows of seats. Each row had one seat on the left of the aisle, and two on the right. One day at Newport News, the flight attendant (Charlene, oooooh!) came to the cockpit, gagging, and told me someone had barfed against the right sidewall of row eight.

I couldn't order some airman to clean up the mess; I had to do it, another un-marvelous feature of being a copilot. When I got to row eight I began gagging also. Clinging, and slowly dripping, down the sidewall was something that looked like half a peach, except it was red, and wasn't a peach. I don't know what it was and didn't want to know. I headed out the back passenger door for a bucket and scrub brush from crew ops.

We were approaching takeoff time and the passengers were waiting just behind the stairs. As I started down the three-step ladder, a matronly older woman in an expensive suit glared at me.

"Why are you making us wait? This is unacceptable! Why can't you stay on time?"

I was tempted, sorely tempted, to say: "*Why, Madame, you are entirely justified in your angst. Please allow let me seat you myself at this very moment in seat 8C.*" But I didn't. I got the bucket and scrub brush, held my breath, and did my duty.

Airline pilots had another laudable feature in their work day; when they parked the airplane at their last stop, they were done. There were none of the military's additional duties, professional education, or bag dragging a ten-man crew's bags to a bus to find the billeting office. Hotel transport would be waiting for you, and maybe the flight attendants would want to have a drink in the bar.

I did have an additional duty, however, as crew scheduler. We launched four planes per day out of Salisbury, two B-99s and two SD-330s. The first B-99 left at 0600 followed at hourly intervals by another B-99 and then the two SD-330s. The planes stayed in motion until 2200 or so with a crew change in early to mid-afternoon. We had 15 crews, so eight were in motion every day, seven days a week.

In the last week of the month I would fly my scheduling desk and hand-carve a schedule for the following month. I was about at the capability limit of hand-carved schedules and we would eventually publish lines of flight assignments, and the crew members would select the one they wanted by seniority. But initially I would get day-off requests and try to mesh them to meet the schedule requirement. I not only had to meet the schedule, I also had to even out the scheduled flying hours, a demanding task in the early days of computers. (I had a Tandy Model One in my apartment. I remembered wishing for an upgrade to 14/15/16, a 14.4 modem, a 15-inch screen, and 16 MB of RAM.)

I immediately found out who was flexible about changing schedules or volunteering to fly on a scheduled day off, and who was not. Those who were not, who were usually senior, would fly into a rage when they thought they had been crossed. The sense of entitlement and grandeur rose exponentially with one's seniority. I called the senior flight attendant "Queen Bee" and would not dare ask her for a scheduling favor. The senior pilots were even more insufferable and inflexible. Most crew members would not answer their phone in the morning, suspecting it was me trying to assign them to fly for someone who had called in sick. I once drove the twenty miles to Ocean City to pull two flight attendants off the beach, since I knew precisely where they would be, to cover an afternoon flight. They never frequented that spot again to foil any further such attempts.

Everyone got 15 or 16 days a month off, and often had to fly weekends. Holidays were a madhouse where members junior in seniority were almost guaranteed to be flying on holiday eves, the busiest travel days of the year.

One day I had returned from lunch at the grill in the terminal and settled in to engage with the tedious task of making sure everyone had about the same number of flying hours. I knew several of them would closely inspect the numbers to make sure I wasn't screwing them. As I began the task, one of the secretaries brought me a note.

"You had a call from a mister...ah...Lyon. Here is his number, it's local."

I barely looked up, took the note and went back to my task. A few minutes later I picked up the phone to make the call. As I sat back and raised my eyes to the room, I recalled later, but did not think of it at the time, that the women in the office were looking at me out of the corner of their eyes.

The phone rang, a woman answered: *"Good afternoon, Salisbury Zoo, can I help you."*

"Yes," I said, *"I'd like to speak with Mr. Ly...."* I caught myself just before falling into the trap. *"Ah, I'm sorry,"* I said, my voice rising in faux indignation. *"I seem to have the wrong number!"*

I shot a glaring look at the secretaries. Each had their hand closest to me covering the side of their face, but their shoulders were shaking in silent laughter.

9

I suppose if I had said "*There is no Mr. Lyon there?*" they would have leapt in to say "*Oh, wait, I think it was actually Mr. Giraffe; no, wait, maybe it was Mr. Aardvark, bwahahahahaha!*"

Ah, well, a nice diversion from having senior crew members stalk up to my desk to ream me for giving two fewer hours flying for the next month to one of their pals.

My copilot time in the B-99 was largely uneventful, and in a few months I moved up to Shorts 330 copilot. The plane seemed underpowered and very susceptible to crosswinds with its twin vertical stabilizers and broad flat sides. Once the number of seats went beyond 15, the FAA required a flight attendant on the crew, so the Shorts, at 30 seats, had one, much to my delight. I had eye candy the entire day, and the flight attendant made all the passenger announcements, something I was required to do in the B-99. I also generally didn't have to deal with irate passengers unless the flight attendants couldn't handle them.

Management Boys' Club Boorishness

Mr. Henson hired a woman to join the management team in 1981, Beth. Tall, slender, and attractive, she presented herself as knowledgeable, thoughtful, and diligent toward her task, which, if I remember correctly, was flight attendant hiring and supervision. Always well dressed in business attire, she seemed a positive addition to management ranks.

In the early 1980s, the issue of women's role in the workplace did not yet have the prominence it does today. There were no lawsuits demanding fair and equal treatment and opportunity for women. The glass ceiling seemed a foot thick and few could penetrate it.

Mr. Henson, in his forward-thinking style, brought Beth on because it seemed the right thing to do, to have a woman managing the women on the crew force. As always, he didn't give a damn about conventional wisdom, he did what he thought was right.

Initially Beth blended well with the boys' club, as I'll call us. But as the airline had begun expanding, pressure had risen on the management team that had led to some carping and back-biting among us. We occasionally vented on each other to the detriment of cohesion and good order.

One day the venting cannon turned on Beth. Five or six of us were upstairs in the main building discussing various management issues. This group included John Pressburg, airline route and scheduling manager, Chuck Wintermoyer, chief pilot, Beth, me, and one or two others.

Beth was speaking about flight attendant indoctrination and used the term "dog and pony show."

Immediately Wintermoyer broke in: "*Ah, Beth, you do know what a dog and pony show is, right?*"

Beth, somewhat flustered at the interruption, responded, "*Well, yes, you hire a dog and pony to do tricks at a children's birthday party, for instance.*"

I saw what was coming and cringed.

In a somewhat patronizing manner, Wintermoyer took his pipe out of his mouth, pointed the stem at Beth and said: "*Well, that's half right, Beth. The dog and pony turn tricks all right, but they do them with women, it is X-rated, and it is termed pornography.*"

This was meant to embarrass Beth in front of the peer group, a zinger aimed at the only woman at the table. It had its intended effect. Beth's face turned purple in either anger, revulsion, embarrassment, apoplexy, or a combination thereof. After a few seconds, she stood, gathered up her papers, and left.

In the awkward silence that ensued, the rest of us shot disbelieving glances at Wintermoyer. This seemed a needless and destructive bit of sophomoric humor.

"*What?*" he said defensively. "*What!*"

"*Oh, all right, I'll apologize to her later,*" he finally said.

I don't know if Beth reported this to Mr. Henson, or if Wintermoyer ever paid a price for his boorishness, but Beth soon moved onward and upward to Pittsburgh with US Air. I presume she did well.

EIGHT-MILE-HIGH VACUUM CLEANER

In the late summer of 1980, as a Shorts copilot, I encountered the grim reaper again. I thought he might lay off me since I wasn't in a combat aircraft, or in a combat zone, but here he was, empty eye sockets and all, watching over my shoulder.

The final mission leg one night took us from Baltimore-Washington International (BWI) to Salisbury, MD, with a 2100 takeoff time with a full load of 30 passengers. The weather briefing had been ominous with severe thunderstorms forecast, but takeoff and departure toward the Chesapeake Bay Bridge had been clear. Shortly after crossing the Bay, however, we picked up a dire radar depiction in the vicinity of Salisbury, a bright red return with a narrow yellow perimeter indicating a powerful storm. It was about ten miles from the Salisbury Airport but seemed headed in roughly that direction, southwest to northeast. We approached from the northwest.

As we reached 30 miles from the field, the storm had moved to within five miles of the airport. I considered that we should return to Baltimore because it would be a very close call on beating the storm to Salisbury. But, this was the last leg of the day, Salisbury was our domicile, and get-home-itis suggested maybe we should give it a shot. As a relatively new commuter copilot in the Shorts 330, I asked the captain, Deano, if we might consider returning to BWI.

"*Naw,*" he said, "*we can make it.*" With that he pushed up the throttles and the race was on.

With more than ten miles' visibility we could clearly see the runway and airport as we lined up on a nine-mile final. It looked like we had it made.

The storm, a towering black column with crackling lightning, seemed about two miles on the other side of the runway, but it was obvious we would get there before it did and land with clear visibility.

Thunderstorms are impressive creatures. They can develop as eight-mile-high vacuum cleaners violently sucking up the ground air around the storm base and propelling it upward violently until it spews out the top of the column. As the low-level air is sucked off the ground, it must be replaced, usually from the air several hundred feet above it. As this air above the ground air is pulled downward toward the ground, it too must be replaced, usually with some of the ground air rising into the storm. This creates vertically circular eddies swirling around the storm at irregular intervals.

Just as I declared to myself we were home safe on about a one-mile final, we encountered one of the violent, vertically circular vortices in the clear air just ahead of the storm. This is termed the frontal gust that, if observed from the ground, displays trees with branches thrashing and bending back and forth in the strong wind. We had a fifty-fifty chance of getting an updraft or downdraft.

Had we hit a downdraft, we would have all been dead in the cornfield off the approach end of the runway in about three seconds. But my guardian angel saved me and we caught an updraft.

Suddenly we were not in control of the plane. I felt as if a giant invisible hand had scooped us up and raised us into the sky, a sensation similar to a rapidly rotating Ferris wheel after you pass the bottom of the circular arc and begin to rise rapidly.

Deano pulled the throttles to idle and shoved the nose downward in a futile attempt to descend to the runway that had begun to pass under us. Despite idle power and 15 degrees nose low attitude we rose at 1,500 feet per minute. The power of this force made me later realize we could never have recovered if the air column had been going down instead of up.

Finally, as we neared the departure end of the 5000-foot runway, the upward force released us and left us 1,500 feet above the ground and gasping in terror. But we were back in control of the plane. I'm sure the passengers sensed our plight. We raised the gear and flaps and sped away from the mayhem we had just encountered. A few miles from the airport we did a large 180-degree turn to appraise our chances of getting back to the field. The sight as the airdrome location came back into view sucked all the air from my lungs.

The storm had moved on to the field, blocking our return. Further, in its mass to the southwest and threat of moving to the northeast, it had blocked any possible return to BWI with our current fuel load. Behind us was nothing but the Atlantic Ocean. Except...

Twenty miles away and five miles from the shoreline lay the Ocean City, MD, airport with 5000 feet of runway. Unfortunately, it was closed for the night, no lights, no tower, nothing. Further, although we had visual conditions, we didn't know exactly where the field was located and had nothing to guide us there except an educated guess from the road network leading to the resort.

Again we went to full power to reach Ocean City with the storm roiling up behind us. We made our guess on the airport location and illuminated our landing lights, turning to and fro trying to sight the runway. Finally, there it was, all 5000 beautiful feet of concrete. We configured with gear and flaps and headed straight for it. We had no idea which way the wind was blowing and didn't care, we were putting it down immediately regardless of the wind.

The frontal gust had not quite arrived so the winds seemed near calm. We landed, and as we rolled down the runway, the passengers broke into applause and cheers. We turned off at the end of the runway and began taxiing back toward the terminal. About the time we arrived at the gate area, the frontal gust arrived and then the storm with rain as heavy as I have ever experienced with the wind rocking the plane on its landing gear.

While this segment of the episode was over, there were more segments to come. Salisbury sent a bus to pick up the passengers so they could return to that airport that arrived about an hour later. Thirty minutes after that, the storm had passed over the area and we took off for the ten-minute flight back to Salisbury.

I felt like a zombie at this point, tired, drained and not enthused for this final leg. It was my turn to fly and I thought about asking Deano to take it, but Deano wasn't looking so hot either. So I took control after he had lined up the plane on the runway.

Visibility was about five miles in mist and fog from the thunderstorm aftermath. I lined up on final at Salisbury and had the VASI approach lights in sight. Both were red. I had to fly at the minimum descent altitude (MDA) until the top one turned white and then fly down the visual glide path maintaining white-over-red.

While I waited for the top VASI to turn white, my mind glazed over in fatigue. I wasn't paying attention to my instruments because I was in visual conditions and was depending upon the VASIs to indicate when I should begin my descent. Unfortunately, in my physical lassitude, I had begun to sink slowly below the MDA. The VASIs would not save me here, they would stay red/red until I got to the glide path or hit the ground. Finally, about 200 feet above the ground, Deano recognized the impending disaster and took the airplane, tersely telling me I was 100 feet low and sinking. This startled me awake and left me wondering what had happened. I had relaxed for a moment and spaced out at just the wrong time. Three cheers for two-man cockpits! Today's planes have warning systems that would have warned me "Too low, terrain!" and snapped me out of it. These were developed after many episodes of pilots doing what I had just done.

And, still, the saga was not over. The next week, the FAA launched an investigation of our flight to see if our errors had caused the near catastrophe. They called and asked us for a written explanation for why we landed at an unscheduled field.

Deano contacted an aviation lawyer since, as the pilot in command, they were primarily after him. That lawyer wrote a letter to the FAA saying we requested any information the FAA had so we could respond. The lawyer told us to say nothing, that in these nebulous cases, the FAA will give up unless you convict yourself in writing.

He was right, the FAA did not pursue the incident. The only questionable call we had made was trying to beat the storm to the field, and nine times out of ten we would have. However, the local FAA office in Baltimore was not happy. We wouldn't give them any statements they could use to hang us, but they could exact a penalty, and that was that I would not be approved as chief pilot.

DOVER CONTACT

Serendipitously, shortly before this incident, I received a call from an Air Force recruiter at Dover AFB, DE, asking if I had any interest in flying C-5s for the Air Force Reserve. Dover had a dual wing, one active duty, and one reserve. Each wing had two flying squadrons and the reserve wing needed pilots. I have no idea how they found me, but they did.

I had left active duty to escape another northern tier assignment that I felt sure would follow my Castle tour. But the reserves were different. You could select your base of assignment and never be moved unless the unit closed, a rare occurrence. So I could pick my airplane and my location and not have to worry about being moved around every four years. This put things in an entirely different light and I was interested.

I interviewed with the 709th Airlift Squadron and liked what I heard. I would get three months to attend C-5 school in Altus, OK, and then a three-month "progressive" tour on active duty. My pay would rise to the level of Henson's most senior pilots, about $40,000 a year.

By government regulation, Henson Airlines would have to take me back at my previous position and allow me fifteen days of military leave per year. The company would not be happy, but I felt I needed the added income and an alternative to an airline career, if necessary. I already had ten years' active duty so I was only ten short of a minimum retirement.

HAGERSTOWN

As I mulled this over for a few months, I upgraded to B-99 Captain and moved to Hagerstown to fill a position there. The town seemed stuck in the 1950s but lay in the picturesque mountains of western Maryland. I spend the spring and early summer of 1981 there rooming with Phil DeCarlo, who had also transferred up from Salisbury where we had also roomed together.

Phil had a manic personality and seemed tightly wound most of the time, usually good-naturedly. His idiosyncrasies were legend. He slept on a mattress on the floor and kept only enough clothes to be able to pack in five minutes to leave for his "real" airline job with a major airline when he got one, his prime objective in life.

Previously, in the Salisbury apartment we rented from senior pilot Jesse McCormick, Phil had been on an overnight and I slept alone in the apartment. About midnight I heard what sounded like someone walking up the stairs from the first floor. I marveled at how stray noises in a house can make it seem someone was really there, when actually they were not. But then the door to my room opened.

I momentarily felt as if a lightning bolt had shot through me. A Caucasian man, perhaps 25, stepped into the room. My first survival instinct asked: can I take this guy if I have to? He was apparently unarmed, rather paunchy and about my size. I decided I could take him if I had to.

"*Ah, who the fuck are you?*" I demanded. The man jerked around, apparently surprised someone was home. He seemed somewhat confused and spacy and proffered that he must have the wrong house, and that he was high on drugs, which might explain his confusion.

I jumped out of bed, not exactly a terrifying presence clad in nothing but my underwear, and started toward him. He partially cowered and apologized again. I grabbed him roughly by his upper arm and began leading him downstairs. He kept apologizing as I dragged him down the stairs, stumbling. I opened the door and shoved him out.

I walked back to the dining area and found my wallet lying open with the $20 or so it had contained missing. It seems he was not very confused when he encountered my wallet. Apparently I had left the rear sliding glass door unlocked and the stray cat walked in.

My primary memory from Hagerstown was the overwhelming aroma of honeysuckle in June. This provided marvelous ambiance that demanded Copeland's "Appalachian Spring" symphony play in the background over the verdant green hills and valleys of the area. Every time I have encountered honeysuckle since 1981 I have thought of Hagerstown in June.

A second memory is the presence of Mack trucks in town. A saying I remember growing up was "built like Mack truck." But something happened about this time; Mack seemed to have lost its luster and reputation but I don't know why. People hardly know what a Mack truck is today with its bulldog mascot. It is a rarity for me to see a Mack truck on the road.

That summer, after moving back to Salisbury, I decided to join the 709th reserve squadron. They got me a September class date for Altus and I broke the news to the company. They were not happy, but I continued to manage the schedule and to fly as a B-99 captain out of Salisbury.

Only one incident arose before my departure for my military stint. The Baltimore hub became congested as we added aircraft to the fleet, in this case de Havilland Dash 7s, a four-engine turboprop that put the rest of the fleet to shame. It had new technology, upgraded comfort and smelled like a new car. Henson was becoming a "real" airline.

In an attempt to manage the traffic at the end of the "B" concourse, the Baltimore operation hired ground marshallers to park the aircraft more tightly. Great idea, but it quickly blew up on the Baltimore operation, and on me.

I pulled in early one evening to a tightly packed ramp area. One of the marshallers waved me to the lone empty spot between a Dash 7 and a Short. As I approached the terminal, the marshaller began waving me into a sharp left turn deep within the parking spot. What we all learned next was that the marshallers did not understand the concept of "tail growth" in a turn. While the fuselage of the '99 could make the turn successfully, the tail could not. My tail fin whacked the left wing of the Dash 7, bringing us to an abrupt halt and causing damage to my aircraft but not to the Dash 7.

I mention this because a similar C-5 incident fifteen years later brought this issue up again. The current Henson chief pilot, my entry class compadre Doug Trimper, investigated the incident. He said I would have been in big trouble had I done this on my own, but since I had responded to direction from the ground marshaller, I was off the hook. This established my thought pattern for such situations that got me in deep trouble in 1998 at Cairo West airport in a C-5. That will come up again in the middle of book three.

RETURN TO HENSON

In September 1981, I left for six months' military duty with the Air Force Reserve. I'll skip forward to my return to Henson the following April, 1982.

I resumed as a B-99 captain in Salisbury. The system had added Ocean City, MD, by the time I returned, and one bright morning I landed there for the first time since my emergency landing in the thunderstorm over a year before.

As I taxied up to the gate area I saw a woman with marshalling wands ready to guide me to parking. I recall noticing her auburn hair and pleasing profile. She began waving me forward, with rapid arm motions initially, then with slower motions as I approached the final parking niche. She aimed the wands at the ground and slowly raised them over her head crossing them smartly, indicating I should stop.

I could not know it then, but I had just been guided to parking by the future mother of my children.

I deplaned and arranged for fuel, then wandered into the terminal. The woman who had parked us was now busily checking passenger tickets and assembling baggage for the flight. She went about her task smoothly and competently and seemed to be a one-woman operation. She did it all, tickets, baggage, and ground marshalling. I found this interesting and impressive and made a note to self to investigate this further on my next flight to Ocean City. We spoke on my next trip and I found out her name was Bea, she lived in an apartment in Salisbury and commuted to Ocean City every day. We would soon be dating. A few months later a US Air executive noticed her diligence toward her duties while he was flying out of Ocean City and hired her away from Henson to work at the airline's hub in Philadelphia.

About a month later I returned on a C-5 trip as a copilot and had a maddening incident while running the engine shutdown checklist. I reached the item "Seat Belt Light Off" and could not find the switch on the overhead panel to turn it off. I had been swapping airplanes for several months as a B-99 captain with Henson and a C-5 copilot with the reserves. This minor fiasco in the C-5 cockpit made me realize one of the jobs had to go; I was allowing one to degrade the other. I informed Henson management I would resign a month later in August 1981.

CHAPTER TWO: 709 MAS, DOVER AFB, DE

ALTUS AFB, C-5 COPILOT TRAINING, SEPTEMBER–NOVEMBER 1981

USAF Photo

Takeoff

In late August I loaded up my 1977 Honda Accord and drove to Altus.

I made Altus in two long days from Salisbury. I spent the first night in Memphis, TN, and completed the final segment of the trip to Altus the next day across Arkansas and the lower portion of Oklahoma. I thought I had reached the edges of Indian Territory in Lawton, but I still had 90 miles left to Altus.

The town lay just above Vernon, TX, and almost to the Texas state line near the Texas Panhandle and Amarillo.

In the early 1980s civilization had not completely arrived in Altus, but then a Pizza Hut opened up while I was there bringing the town somewhat up to date. Previous to that we had to make do with a Furr's buffet cafeteria on the main drag downtown, which was actually pretty good.

The Oklahoma fall weather was as clear, bright and comfortable as I have found anywhere on earth. The skies, like those of Montana, are "big" and stretch horizon to horizon across the flat plain of south Oklahoma. In retrospect, a more current song that seems to capture the ambiance of the area is "Amarillo Sky" by Jason Aldean. I also recalled the musical *Oklahoma* from the 1950s and revisited it, finding its songs and story a perfect fit for the actual place: "Where the wind comes sweeping down the plain."

The plain was mostly flat except for Quartz Mountain about twenty miles north of the base. This state park saw me, for the only time in my life, run a sanctioned road race, a 5-kilometer "fun run" up and down the small mountain roads of the park. I was terrified of not being able to finish without walking, so I planned to take it very easy. I lined up toward the back of the pack to avoid the embarrassment of being passed by everyone and found a female Air Force major in front of me when we started our trek. She had slightly large thighs with unfortunate cellulite evident. "*Well,*" I thought, "*I can at least beat her for sure!*" Except I could not. She passed me, going the other direction, a few hundred yards from the halfway turnaround point she had already passed that I had not. This so demoralized me I have never run another sanctioned race.

The training course ran three months, about a month of academics and two more of C-5 flight training. On the first day we were taken as a class out for a walk-around of the plane. I stood next to one of the nose tires that stood chest high on me, one example of the hugeness of all features of the Galaxy. I felt immediate trepidation about my upcoming task of learning the nuts and bolts of such a mammoth machine.

The C-5 is marginally larger than a Boeing 747. I joked that if the 747 guys would keep their "little" airplane out of my way, I'd keep my little wallet out of their way.

The C-5 had four engines rated at 40,000 pounds of thrust each and could produce hurricane-force winds behind the aircraft at high power on the ground. The wingspan of 222 feet is three-quarters of a football field wide. Max. gross weight takeoff was 769,000 pounds.

The cargo compartment encompassed the entire lower deck length of the aircraft. The rear doors opened wide and extended the rear ramp horizontally for rolling pallets into the cargo compartment from raised loading platforms (K-loaders). The ramp could also be lowered to the ground to allow vehicles to drive on to the aircraft. On the front end, the entire nose section could be raised above the cockpit to allow similar ramp action, horizontal or angled to the ground. For palletized uploads, long parallel strips in the floor could be turned over exposing rollers to allow pallets to be pushed and rolled the entire length of the cargo compartment. These strips could then be reversed to present a smooth floor for vehicular loads. Vehicles could drive on from either end, drive the entire length of the cargo compartment, and drive off the other end. This allowed rapid on-loads and off-loads of either pallets or vehicles.

One of the gee-whiz statistics of the plane's length was that the Wright Brothers' first flight could have taken place within it.

USAF Photo

C-5 Cargo Compartment

Above the cargo compartment, the crew area occupied front one-third of the aircraft length, and a 73-seat passenger compartment comprised the back two-thirds of the overhead area with seats facing the rear. Air conditioning ducting between the two compartments prevented transiting from one to the other.

The crew area had the cockpit with, originally, room for seven crew members, three pilots, two flight engineers, and two navigators, although the navigators got phased out fairly soon after I arrived in the unit. Walking aft from the cockpit there were two three-position bunk rooms on the left prior to reaching the rear crew area. This section had three seats facing aft on the left, a table on the right with four seats, and slightly farther back on the left, a latrine and a small kitchen area with a convection oven. Finally, a courier compartment lay just beyond the kitchen area with six rear facing seats in two rows on the left and two seats on the right. The front bunk room belonged to the pilots, the aft to the enlisted crew members, except we usually packed the rear room with carry-on equipment such as publication briefcases and helmet bags.

The C-5 "A" model began flying in the early 1970s and the almost identical "B" model joined the force in the mid-1980s. Seventy-six "A" models were provided and an additional fifty "B" models. The vastly improved "M" model (converted "B" models) would not arrive until 2005.

I had two fellow Dover reserve pilots in my class, Ed Poling and Paul Gillis. I would spend many happy evenings of drinks and dinner at the Gillis trailer with him and his wife Carol. I would be paired with Ed for flight training. All was friendly and cordial in these long-ago halcyon days, but it would not always be so.

I generally do not use specific names as I write, but I have an exception. Twenty years later during the anthrax inoculation disaster at Dover, the squadron, wing and Air Force would threaten me with a court-martial for refusing to take the anthrax shot. Those involved in that proceeding will have their names used when the time comes in book three, and two of the prime players will be Ed and Paul, especially Ed, as my squadron commander at the time, but also Paul, as his executive officer.

I place major blame for the anthrax abomination on high-level officers who threw their integrity overboard to save their careers, and at the expense of the troops entrusted to their care. I recognize officers at the squadron and wing level operated under tremendous, unfair pressure due to the failure of senior leadership, but they faced the same dilemma, save their careers or the save the health of those they commanded. With one exception, the Dover active duty wing commander at the time, Col. Felix Grieder, they all folded and saved their careers while disparaging resisters such as me as malingerers who were afraid to take any shot.

While I suffered at a great disadvantage at the time, performing almost solo against the entire military establishment up to and including Secretary of Defense William Cohen, I now hold the high ground since I can present the case I would be denied from making at court-martial. As Poling warned me in 2003, the only question allowed at trial would be: did you take the shot, or did you refuse? This would be a slam dunk against me for the court-martial with no opportunity for me to contest the shot itself. Soon, I will get my say, fifteen years after the fact, and readers can judge for themselves.

As a preliminary example of the issues, the anthrax shot arrived with a standing order that it must be taken, unlike any previous military shot. Why did they know this shot would require a military order to enforce compliance?

So eager am I to thrash out this issue, I almost wrote book three before book two, and out of chronological sequence, to satisfy my ire at the treatment of me and the rest of the troops. Hell will be paid for what they did to us. They got away with it, but they will not escape unscathed by history.

C-5 flight training proved unexceptional. The plane flew like any other plane except the landing picture resembled landing your house from the roof, which took some getting used to, especially since I had been landing a Beech 99 for the past two years. When I got back to the Beech 99, I swore I would rip the seat of my pants on the runway, so low did I have to go. Also, the cockpit seats were very wide apart compared to my previous military aircraft. On the B-52, I could reach over and tap the other pilot on his outboard shoulder. In the C-5, I could just reach his nearest shoulder. As we flew, it seemed we were flying the cockpit alone with no obvious comprehension of the massive aircraft following behind the cockpit.

USAF Photo

C-5 cockpit interior, Martinsburg ANG, WV, aircraft 60022

The main landing gear is a unique C-5 feature. To provide a wider gear footprint for taxiing and landing stability, and to spread the aircraft weight across twenty-four main gear tires, the gear goes through contortions to extend and retract. As the gear is raised, it rotates 90 degrees toward the aircraft, then slides upward and inward on metal tracks into the fuselage. Gear extension reverses this process as the gear slides outward and downward from the fuselage. Once down, it then rotates 90 degrees to align parallel to the aircraft centerline.

Usually the aircraft commander is in charge of everything in addition to being responsible for safely completing the mission. But there are exceptions. In the B-52, the commander transfers aircraft control to the radar navigator on the bomb run so he can release the bomb at the proper time on the proper track using his navigation equipment to steer the autopilot.

In the C-5, most of the aircraft systems are run by the flight engineer at his panel behind the copilot in the cockpit. The aircraft commander cedes some of his authority to the engineer to call the shots on system problems. One C-5 joke says, during an emergency the pilot asks: "*Damn, engineer, what do we do now?*" While pilots know the limitations and workings of the systems, they must depend upon the engineer to manage them and recommend actions during emergencies. This puts the engineer in partial command of the aircraft.

This sharing of command almost always worked well, and the times it did not were often my fault. My primary example from book one was taking an Operational Readiness Inspection bomb run away from a radar navigator who had the target locked. Oh, mama, did I pay for that one!

One time that things went awry in the C-5 was a nose gear indicator failure, to be covered later. I got bewildering information from a rookie scanner, but I had to accept what he was saying and consider it. Another time both the stan-eval engineer instructor and I missed that the student engineer had made a 100,000-pound calculation error on landing speed. Somehow I missed the error as the copilot briefed a 110-knot approach speed, ten knots below the standard approach speed. Usually either the pilot or engineer would catch such an error, but this time the two evaluators blew it.

The only mildly hilarious event during training occurred when Ed, taxiing out of the parking ramp, turned the potentially hurricane-force engine jet blast on a temporary wooden guard shack and rubber barrel barrier and sent them tumbling down the ramp.

On a positive note, Paul completed academics without missing a question. He bested a returning staff officer, a major, who predicted he alone would not miss a question in this second time through the course. To his deep chagrin and Paul's joy, he did miss one.

On the cool bright autumn afternoons, I would run a three-mile course on the perimeter road that ran parallel to the runway. This was also the heyday of the computer arcade game, *Ms. Pac-Man*, which I played addictively. After hundreds of games I had a pattern down to avoid the Pac-Men through four or five levels of the game. There was a Pac-Man arcade console in the back of the O'Club and I spent many hours there doing combat with the Pac-Men.

I noticed that an attractive dark-haired officer's wife also enjoyed playing the game on this console. Once, she arrived at my right shoulder as I slammed the control stick frantically side-to-side and up-and-down on level four in desperate flight from several Pac-Men converging on me from different directions. They got me. I turned partially toward her and noticed she seemed slightly too close. "*This game is really addictive,*" I said.

She smiled and said softly, "*I know.*" She paused momentarily, then left. I don't know if something else might have been in the offing, but it is just as well. I presume there was not.

The number one song during my stay was "Don't Stop Believing" by the group Journey. That song is still number one on my list of oldies hits.

RETURN TO DOVER

I drove back in November 1981 stopping, again, in Memphis. Arriving back in Dover I settled into the BOQ for my three-month progressive tour to cement my training and give me initial experience as an immediate follow-on to Altus instruction.

My first Unit Training Assembly (drill weekend) had a most unwelcome feature, an open ranks inspection. I had not suffered an open ranks inspection since Officer Training School, but now the reserves were going to inflict one on me! Not even SAC made me suffer such an indignity!

This apparently arose because the reserves were experimenting with allowing navigators to command flying squadrons, and I had a navigator commander when I returned from Altus. I presume he thought he would run a very tight ship to make up for not being a pilot. The uproar from this one inspection, however, made him quickly backtrack and forget all about such shenanigans in the future.

Dover, in the early 1980s, had Route 13 running north to south just east of the town and west of the base. This stretch of road is where most of the business were located. Two primary ones for those on base were the Brown Fox bar just outside the main gate, and Captain John's seafood restaurant about a mile north of the base.

I might have gone into the Brown Fox once, but I'm not sure. The "foxes" I generally sought were white, although I was an equal opportunity fox hunter! Captain John's provided a marvelous brunch for drill weekends, but I almost never went in the early years since, as a junior nobody, I had to play the game and remain on base and in the squadron building. The senior guys all signed in and then headed for Captain John's for breakfast.

FIRST C-5 MISSION

Soon after returning from Altus I departed on my first copilot line ride, a ball-buster air refueling enhanced mission direct to Dhahran, Saudi Arabia, thirteen hours of fun and frolic.

I had flown internationally in the B-52, but always to the Pacific and only once to Europe (Upper Heyford, England after losing an engine over the Atlantic). I enjoyed the exuberant enthusiasm of a first-time tourist on a new airplane. This fit well with the other pilots, who were only too happy to let me ride the cockpit while they slept. I think I was in the copilot seat for eleven of the thirteen hours and didn't mind a bit.

After observing the first two oceanic position reports sent on HF radio, I got the knack of it and did the rest of the reports on the crossing. Approaching Europe we had to fly the international air boundaries between Mediterranean countries because we didn't have diplomatic clearance for many of their airspaces. This would begin at Gibraltar at the entry to the Med. My eyes grew wide as the Gibraltar passage approached. On this clear night I could sense the outline of southern Spain and northern Africa, a spectacular panoramic view from my space ship. Then the oceanic controller directed me to contact Casablanca Center on a VHF radio frequency. *"Cool!"* I thought, *"Casablanca! Bogart and Ingrid Bergman at Rick's Café! Africa! The Sahara!"*

About an hour later, approaching Italy, I heard what would become a routine fascination in the airlift world, a Korean Air pilot trying to communicate with an Italian controller in English. I could hardly understand either one of them, but they seemed to understand each other, so it worked. As an aside, in the 1960s the international air conference voted on what the international air traffic control language would be. English beat out French by one vote. I felt sympathy for the Korean pilot and Italian controller. But for one vote, I'd have to communicate in French with possibly disastrous results. *Sacré bleu!*

More marvelous sights appeared, the Nile River at night, bright gold and silver lights winding narrowly through the utter darkness of the desert. Then, as the sun rose, it starkly displayed the deserts of Saudi Arabia in sharp detail with crystal clear air and almost blindingly bright sunlight. Finally, we arrived and the other pilots rejoined me for the landing on the long, multiple runway complex of Dhahran. We parked on a large ramp facing a small hill with the operations buildings on it.

We were billeted in the military compound adjoining the air base. It was possible to exit the compound to visit a nearby civilian mall, but I did not venture out on this first visit. Having not slept the entire trip, I hit the rack as the sun went down and slept blissfully…until.

Just as the sky was starting to lighten the next morning, I leapt out of my bed in a fright. A loudspeaker somewhere nearby blasted the area with what I eventually realized was morning Muslim prayers, but what I thought was jihadists coming over the walls for me.

"*Aaaa-oooo-aaaaa*," the liturgy began as my feet hit the floor, and then it continued in an Arabic morning prayer. Since I didn't see anyone running the halls in panic, I decided maybe this was something I would have to grow accustomed to. I would have to adjust my ear to a language style far different from Vietnamese or Thai. Many things would be far different from my B-52 and C-7 active duty period.

Later a movie on the compound TV showed my new multicultural world. A Clint Eastwood "spaghetti Western" played with Arabic voice-overs and English subtitles. So I had an American movie, shot it Italy, being shown in Saudi Arabia dubbed in Arabic with English subtitles—amazing.

On the return flight we crew-rested in Rota, Spain, a location I would see much of in the next twenty-three years. There I learned the rule that the billeting office would almost always give us the farthest rooms on the highest floor. As I lugged my trusty B-4 bag (a large satchel shaped canvas bag slightly larger than a large suitcase) up the stairs and down the hall, I developed a rhythmic swing with it to match my gait down the hallway. This was several years before wheeled suitcases replaced the B-4 bag.

Rota's Mediterranean climate on the Atlantic just above Gibraltar usually made it a marvelous crew rest location in all seasons except winter. Looking across the harbor at Cadiz, I learned that Columbus began his second America voyage from here and later read that Phoenician sailors from the eastern Med sailed through the Straits of Gibraltar to trade in Cadiz thousands of years before Christ, a thought I still find fascinating.

I reveled in this first mission and looked forward to many more voyages of my own to Europe and the mystical Middle East.

WOMEN ENTER THE COCKPIT, 1982

A significant change in Air Force culture began for me in 1982 when women entered the cockpit, in this case, as C-5 navigators. It began curiously for me.

On an early mission in my C-5 career as a copilot, two female navigators showed up on the flight. I'm not sure why we had two, but it caused a problem on the segment coming out of Dhahran, Saudi Arabia enroute to Frankfurt, Germany.

I know this was early in my C-5 experience because we still had the K-band weather radar that wasn't worth a damn. It showed dim spokes on its washed-out screen as it scanned the sky ahead and showed returns as ghostly, imprecise shadows with no color gradations to show intensity. Henson Airlines had far better ones, incredibly.

At this time, navigators were losing their mission. Inertial Navigation Systems (INS) had severely encroached on the navigator's space on the crew and would soon eliminate them as Flight Management Systems (FMS) provided almost all the information navigators had previously provided to the pilots.

But in the early 1980s, navigators controlled the weather radar and processed information from the triple (INS) setup. This trek across the northern portion of the Saudi peninsula, of all the hundred times I made it, had the worst weather I ever saw over this terrain. Thunderstorms were everywhere, some visible, some not when we flew into a cloud deck. This is when near-fisticuffs broke out between the two female navigators.

Sandy and Penny, both first lieutenants, seemed to be getting along well up to this point, but interpreting the K-band returns under pressure progressively led to a raging argument about which way we should turn the aircraft to avoid storm cells. Sandy, the pretty one, and Penny, the interesting one, hunched over the scope on the navigators' station behind the pilot. Their voices rose in volume and their tone turned argumentative and aggressive.

We pilots grew frustrated with the argument; we just needed someone to tell us which way to turn. We were flying blind as the argument behind us grew in intensity. Being of equal rank and crew qualification, neither seemed to be in charge. Finally, one of the women stalked to the back to check her forms to see who held the earliest date-of-rank between them. That finally settled who would call the shots. I can't remember which one it was, but we finally got information in a timely manner. Not an auspicious introduction to women in the cockpit as a cat fight erupts on my first mission with the fairer sex.

Another indicator that things had changed in the crew force happened as we checked into our rooms at the Rhein-Main hotel. Sandy and I shared the same bathroom that joined our two rooms, early shades of a unisex privy. True, each of us could lock the other's entry door, but doing so, noisily, announced that any of the various performances was about to begin. After a long flight, one of those would probably be one neither would want to share with the other, but would have to.

Unfortunately, while we were diligent in locking the door in such situations to avoid a potentially unfortunate face to face in the bathroom, we were less diligent about unlocking the other's door when we left. This could prove catastrophic in the middle of the night when you arose in dire need of relief only to find your bathroom door locked. You could pound on the door, or get semi-dressed and go out into the hallway to the other's room entry door and knock on that, dancing in the hallway trying to hold it (and don't forget your key!).

The true catastrophe arrived when the other person had locked your bathroom door and left their room. Now you were truly screwed and would have to use the public bathroom in the lobby, or find a housekeeper to enter their room and unlock your door.

And then, lascivious possibilities would arise in the mind. Such as, instead of locking the bathroom door, one of us would open it and step through instead, a rare possibility, I admit, but who knows what fantasy might lurk in Sandy's libido? Since she was married that limited the possibility even further, and she did not. But I had a string of such "limited possibilities" actually happen to me previously with Air Force wives, so who knows?

And, besides, Penny was the more interesting of the two, so if I got to choose, I'd have selected her. But as with 99% of such fantasies, none of these happened except in my mind. Just as well.

WILMINGTON AIR SHOW

One of my first stateside missions took me just up the road to Wilmington, DE as a copilot on an airshow crew. The C-5 aircraft commander, "Johnny Smooth," had a high powered job in Washington, DC, that paid very well. His job limited him to short duration missions and this would be one.

Except for combat sorties, air shows are the most dangerous missions crews will encounter. The danger rises not from difficult flying but from a lowering of caution by the crew. With their guard down, horrendous, embarrassing lapses in protocol can bring command wrath down on the unit and crew. The crew mistakenly assumes it is on vacation and no one is looking, but they are wrong. Everyone is watching to include military retirees who, as a group, keep close watch on currently active crews.

A sector of retirees feels they did things correctly while the current force has let discipline and order slip compared to the old-timers. They will closely watch crew actions and report any discrepancies they perceive as validation of their dim view of current military operations.

While the crew struts around to admiration from show-goers, old-timers subconsciously want to draw attention to their past glories by tagging current crew members for discipline lapses.

Johnny would provide a spectacular example of this air show syndrome before we even landed and would pay an embarrassing price for doing so. Years later, I would be a similarly hapless victim of the syndrome, but this day belonged to Johnny.

I had no inkling the syndrome was about to break out as we flew the fifteen minutes or so from Dover to Wilmington IAP about 40 miles north of the base. We had canceled our IFR clearance and contacted Wilmington tower for our VFR (visual flight rules) arrival. Johnny made the call to the tower himself.

"*Tower, MAC 4017, request high speed pass down the runway for a 5,000 foot right closed pattern to a full stop.*" Tower cleared him as requested. I should have suspected trouble when he asked for 5,000-foot clearance for the closed pattern, but I did not.

About eight miles out on final, Johnny pushed up the throttles and our speed rapidly increased from our 220 knot cruise speed. I thought he would stop accelerating at the 250 knot speed limit for flight below 10,000 feet, but he did not. Since neither he nor the tower had defined high speed, he defined it himself. As we descended toward the trees surrounding the airport our airspeed climbed to 300 knots. I looked down on tree-lined neighborhoods flying by in a blur with barely enough time for me to mentally register them before they were gone.

High speed at low altitude can be troublesome. The airflow across control surfaces is much greater than usual or expected and pilot actions can make over-controlling pitch commands a problem, resulting in a porpoise motion made worse by the pilot's efforts to control it. Fortunately, we did not experience this problem, but it should have been considered prior to accelerating to 300 knots. One misstep at that speed descending toward the ground could have been catastrophic.

Johnny pulled the throttles back as we approached 300 knots, mercifully, and we smoked down the runway at 200 feet in relative silence. That silence ended past the departure end of the runway as Johnny threw the throttles up to near maximum power and smoothly raised the nose to 15 degrees nose up with a right turn for our 5,000 foot closed pattern. Going through 3,000 feet, he then pulled the throttles to idle to slow the aircraft during the final 2,000 feet of climb. From there we made a normal landing. He said later that he wanted to provide an advertisement for the air show the next day.

Johnny probably would have gotten away with the excessive license he had granted himself for this maneuver except for one aspect. When he threw in the big power burst off the departure end of the runway, he did so over the house of newly minted congressman and future vice president Joseph Biden. Senator Biden was not impressed. A phone call to the Pentagon led to calls to MAC headquarters at Scott AFB, IL, then to the Dover wing commander to find out who the hell tried to take the roof off Senator Biden's house in a C-5. The phone was ringing in base operations before we had shut down the engines.

Johnny's punishment for the episode mimicked a Chinese Communist confessional where the culprit must publicly self-critique himself mercilessly for his error. Johnny therefore stood before the assembled drill weekend crowd, to include the wing staff, the next month to explain how he could have been such an idiot to have done such things.

TYING THE KNOT

Early in our relationship, Bea and I attended some sort of formal gathering where she had worn a particularly flattering red dress. After that, the song "Lady in Red," by Chris de Burgh summed up my feelings for her. The future appeared positive and hopeful.

After some months of dating in 1983, Bea suggested that, at age 37, if I wanted children I'd better get started. Things were heading that way, and I agreed. And so it would be! We tied the knot and bought a townhouse in New Castle, DE. This represented the approximate mid-way point between my job at Dover and hers at the Philly airport. We lived there for about 18 months, but the situation became untenable after first daughter Jessica arrived in 1984. Neither of us wanted her to grow up with babysitters while Bea and I worked. So Bea quit her job with U.S. Air and we moved to Dover. I had become a full-time pilot, GS-13, Air Reserve Technician (ART) and, once we moved, did not have to make the two-hour round trip drive to the base every weekday.

We rented out the New Castle townhouse and rented a brick farm house east of the base on Pickering Beach Road. In some ways this was my favorite house, with corn fields behind and a circular drive of apple trees in the front. The apple blossoms made Spring a marvelous event I miss thirty years later.

I remember watching the "Challenger" space ship launch on TV on base in 1986. Once the shuttle was in the air, I drove home for lunch. I was half way through this five-minute trip when the news came across the radio that the shuttle had blown-up shortly after launch. Everyone remembers where they were when they saw or heard the news of the disaster, and that is where I was, half way to the farmhouse.

BRIGHT STAR, 1983

After only a few copilot rides, I got to participate in a biyearly worldwide exercise, Bright Star, which provided my first around-the-world mission, flying east. We flew as a dual crew, two full crews who alternated legs, one flying, and one deadheading. We deadheaded to Ramstein, then flew the second leg to Cairo West airfield about twenty miles west of the pyramids in Cairo.

MONDO RONDO

One of my fellow rookie copilots on this Bright Star mission, Joe Rondinelli, provided unintended levity to the mission. On the first segment flying from Dover to Ramstein, Joe committed two sins for the ages. We had a MAC one-star general travelling with us who was accorded certain privileges, one of which was a white-collar bunk in the forward bunk room. But Joe, oblivious to heightened protocol, first transgressed by eating the general's box lunch, apparently believing the many box lunches were available for his selection instead of the specific one he had ordered. Having finished the general's lunch, he then went to the forward bunk room, marveled at the accommodations, and climbed into the white-collar bunk to sleep. This second act got noticed by one of the experienced pilots, who dragged him out by his ear and explained his rookie error. Soon the first sin was also recognized. The loadmaster who had ordered the lunches could not find the general's and went looking for it. Finally, he tracked down the culprit, Joe, who suffered another embarrassing rookie comeuppance.

CAIRO

History Channel Photo

Egyptian pyramids outside Cairo, Egypt

Mankind's first great city, Cairo, Egypt, remains perhaps the most essential human enclave.

Laying at the nexus of three great continents, this city has been at the center of human society since our first dim history was written five thousand years ago. Its rise under the pharaohs made it the center of the civilized world. While it lost that accolade long ago, it has remained the crucial crossroad of human commerce and social interaction.

The Nile River surges up from the depths of Africa, bringing a narrow four thousand mile long strip of jungle green to the shores of the Mediterranean Sea through the stark desert of Northern Africa, ending in Cairo.

The Nile also brought the first proto-humans north from our origins in Ethiopia perhaps 100,000 years ago. For nearly as long as there have been humans, there has been Cairo, where the first magic spark of creativity, imagination and ingenuity produced the initial city to hold the first great empire.

This first encounter with Cairo was sensual, not intellectual, however. Arriving at our hotel, the Mena House, near the base of Cheops Pyramid on the western edge of the city, I saw a pair of riders galloping across the desert dunes far in the distance as the sun set behind them in rich tones of red and gold. A silent stillness seemed to lie across the desert as the day came to an end.

The next morning, as I stepped out onto my hotel balcony overlooking a large rectangular courtyard, I sensed Eden. The sunshine was impossibly bright, and the air impossibly clear. The courtyard boasted grass that only abundant sunshine coupled with abundant water could make such a deep green. Flower gardens that surrounded the manicured lawn spoke of tropical Africa with their multitude of vibrant shades of red, yellow, and violet.

The air still held the last vestige of the cool desert night that would soon become overwhelming heat which would drive me back into my air conditioned room. But for this special morning interlude, the world could not have been brighter, more pleasant or more serene. When the world weighs on me, my mind returns to this morning in Cairo.

Later, a statue in the Cairo museum brought me the essence of Egypt. This simple work about 18 inches high shows a man of ancient Egypt standing erect, holding two poles in his hands, as if pulling an unseen cart. Beside and just behind him, a woman stands with her hand on his shoulder, facing forward with him.

I studied the pair, not initially grasping what they were telling me, but somehow knowing they had a message for me. Slowly it came to me. The man, larger, and in the foreground, initially seems to dominate. But the longer I studied the pair the more I saw the woman subtly begin to assume domination. She seemed to control the scene despite occupying a secondary physical position.

I gasped. Suddenly I saw the intricate male/female interplay the artist wanted to convey. I had received a sophisticated message of universal interpersonal relationships from an Egyptian artist 4,000 years dead, yet alive in his work to speak to me.

There are many cities more beautiful, more affluent, and more modern than Cairo, but there is no city more intricately tied to human social evolution and none more important to experience.

All this colorful splendor and security ended, however, as we stepped out the front gate of the complex headed for a pyramid tour with no real idea of what we were doing, or what we were in for.

A small swarm of boyish pitchmen accosted us just a few steps out of the gate. They wanted to provide us with horses to travel to the pyramids. We brushed them aside and sprinted for one of the taxis lined up on the street, glad to have escaped the hustlers, unaware even worse hustlers awaited.

After a short cab ride we arrived at a one-level strip mall of souvenir shops near the Sphinx. Camel rides commenced here to cross a mile or so of desert to the pyramids. We had no idea how much a camel ride would cost, but we soon got an offer, $10. Wow, that sounded reasonable, what a good deal! The pitchman seemed as familiar as a New York City con man, fluent in English and knowing exactly what we sought. He would be our hustler-guide.

The six of us mounted up, three on horses, three on camels. I got a camel, and a pretty decrepit one. Although, as it was my first encounter with such a beast, I had no standard to judge. Later I would see camels well-tended to and manicured as pets that put this first creature to shame. My mount ran green slime at both ends and had an attitude that matched his looks, angry, sullen and loudly uncooperative. When the hustler finally got my beast to kneel, I sat between his two humps on a colorful camel blanket. I felt fortunate I had not been bitten before I mounted.

The hustler mounted a pony to lead us, and away we went across the desert patch to the pyramids. We all grinned and laughed with joy with each other at our Lawrence of Arabia adventure striding across the dunes on our caravan animals. Unfortunately, this would be the high point of the excursion.

We dismounted at the pyramids and stared up at them, walking over to touch them, and walking to the one small interior room available to tourists. The room did not impress and had a faint smell of urine about it. We took pictures of each other standing at the structure's base and then mounted up, with our hustler guide's assistance, for the return trip. That is when trouble began.

"*For the ride back,*" our guide said, somehow with a smile, "*it will cost another $10 each.*" Ah, now the hustle had been revealed, but there was not much we could do. I wasn't walking that mile back across the desert, and the initial $10 did seem low, so we paid up.

Alas, about halfway back, the guide stopped us again "to rest." When we remounted for the final stretch, the guide said it would cost another $10. What? You freaking con man, we protested. But again, none of us wanted to walk the remaining distance in the desert heat, so again, we paid up.

In a final display of chutzpah when we finally dismounted at the concession area, our guide implored us to give him a tip for his service! Having no leverage on us, however, we told him he already got his tip on the return trip and he could pound sand, plenty of which was available.

Before we departed the area I decided I needed a souvenir, but not one from the shops. I wanted an authentic camel blanket, so I bought one off the back of one of the tourist camels. When I got it back to the States, the odor of the fabric sent my cat into hissing hysterics conjuring up a vision of what creature could have worn that blanket and provided that scent.

We took taxis back to the Mena House and walked briskly past the con men through the hotel gates to safety and serenity.

Since our aircraft had departed shortly after we arrived, we had to wait for the follow-on aircraft to arrive for us. There was a day delay, so we took cabs to the Egyptian Museum in downtown Cairo. I thought I had seen the world's worst traffic mayhem in Saigon and Bangkok. But Cairo rivaled those with swift moving rivers of vehicles flowing through the wide boulevards, horns blaring and paying no attention to traffic lanes.

The city concrete seemed covered with dust and grit but blossomed with tropical green while crossing Nile River bridges. This displayed the vivid contrast of intertwined jungle and desert that is Cairo.

BERBERA, SOMALIA

Our crew's second flying leg took us from Cairo to Berbera, Somalia for a quick turn, then on to the island of Diego Garcia in the Indian Ocean.

Berbera lies just below the point where the Red Sea enters the Indian Ocean. This area, to include the former French colony of Djibouti just to the north, is the most forlorn stretch of earth as I have seen. Djibouti seems to have had a tide of civilization sweep in at some time in the past, but that tide had departed and left the area bereft of any attractions. Former French architecture seemed unkempt and dilapidated, as if humans had departed a thousand years before and not returned. This also applied to Mogadishu farther south that I would visit ten years later in the aftermath of "Black Hawk Down." Civilization had departed and only barbarian tribes remained.

I deplaned onto the Berbera airfield tarmac with its 120°F heat and saw desolation in all directions. About a mile away toward the ocean I saw a row of corrugated tin warehouses of some sort with black men on top of them looking across the barren landscape at us. The vision of them wavered and danced in the rising heat waves, almost a mirage. I don't know what they thought of us, but I thought of them as denizens of hell wishing they could escape with us.

Darkness had fallen about an hour before our takeoff, which lessened the heat somewhat. We took off to the south flying across Somalia before crossing the coast to fly southeastward to Diego Garcia. This hour or so flying over the Somali landmass had an ominous feature to it: I could see no lights on the ground; none. I suppose herders might have had campfires, but who would light a fire in this heat? We could have been flying over the dark side of the moon.

DIEGO GARCIA

A British protectorate, the tiny island of Diego Garcia lies at the southern end of the Chagos Archipelago that runs south from India. It was still somewhat primitive on this, my initial visit, and we bunked in open-air, screened tent barracks about 30 yards in length. While this proved somewhat uncomfortable, even with cooler nighttime temperatures, we also had to walk down a gravel path to the bathroom facilities in a small nearby building. Unprepared for this terrain with no shower clogs or flip-flops, we had to move painfully slowly on the sharp pebbles to relieve ourselves.

The island was far less developed than it would become during upcoming Middle Eastern wars and had a rustic, shipwrecked ambiance to it. A small bar and grill looked out over a spectacular ocean view of white waves breaking on the coral reef a mile away.

The rest of the journey around the world proved largely uneventful, as we crew-rested in Okinawa and Hawaii on the way back to the States.

One wrinkle did occur, however, when we landed on Wake Island for a quick fuel stop. My crew was deadheading on this segment, and I sleepily deplaned onto the ramp on this tiny atoll for a few minutes. The sun was below the horizon but, since I was not familiar with Wake Island, and did not know which direction was east or west, I didn't know if the sun was coming up or going down. I gave up guessing and got back on the plane to sleep.

BEIRUT BARRACKS BOMBING

On October 23, 1983, I sat alone in my copilot seat flying west at 31,000 feet over Saudi Arabia while the other pilots slept. The rule said that, on the way downrange to Dhahran, any pilot could hit the bunk as soon as he wanted. However, whoever did so would get to fly most of the return leg to Europe. That is how I wound up alone as we crossed the Saudi desert, past the desert towns of Gassim and Hail, toward Egypt.

We had taken off before sunrise and leveled off as the sun rose above the horizon behind us, covering the desert in a soft morning light. Soon after level-off the pilot looked at me, smiled, and said, "You've got it, copilot, see you in a few hours." I settled in for a long haul.

Interesting features passed beneath on the desert floor. There were large circles of green on the tan desert landscape, agricultural farms drawing water from deep wells, which delivered their moisture to the plants through long metal irrigation arms that rotated around the circle. Most of these were near the coastal Saudi towns such as Dhahran. Passing Hail there were brown lines in the sand indicating rough corrals for desert livestock, probably goats. From 31,000 feet they appeared tiny. On the final segment across Saudi territory approaching the Red Sea and Egypt, I saw what appeared to be ancient volcanic cones with dark basalt fields surrounding them, probably flows from long ago. My guess is these volcanoes arose as the African tectonic plate encountered the one from Asia tens of millions of years ago.

Approaching the Wedj intersection on the air traffic control charts, located on the edge of the Red Sea, I had to switch from Jeddah control to Cairo. This area had weak radio reception in the early 1980s and meant repeated calls trying to raise Cairo westbound, or Jeddah eastbound. I would hear other aircraft calling Jeddah in a loud, high-pitched voice, rapidly saying "Jiddah, Jiddah, Jiddah!" Checking in on the standard VHF frequency over the Egyptian mainland, the Cairo controller always seemed to have a loud squeal in the background, and he'd always say "Calling Cairo?" as if he was surprised someone was calling him.

The autopilot turned the aircraft right, and north, over Wedj headed to Sharm el Sheikh at the base of the Sinai Peninsula. This would be the location of a near-midair in 1997 between a C-5 and a KC-10 refueling formation headed in the other direction. That near disaster would kick off a significant series of events which would put me on the CBS News program *60 Minutes* opposite the Air Force in 1998. But that was 15 years in the future and will figure prominently in book three.

I had followed my usual pattern of dialing up the British Broadcasting Company (BBC) on HF radio frequency 9410, my favorite method of keeping up with world news.

As the autopilot turned the airplane northward at Wedj, the BBC announcer, speaking in his standard slow, precise tones, began covering a breaking story, the bombing of the U.S. Marine barracks in Beirut, a city just up the road from where I was. This would be the tragic end to a noble but misdirected foray into Middle Eastern politics by the Reagan administration.

The American Marines had been sent to Beirut to cover the exodus of the Palestinian Liberation Organization (PLO) from Beirut after an Israeli incursion into Lebanon and southern Syria. The Marines were to enforce a 40-mile perimeter north of Israel to thwart rocket attacks. This disrupted the equilibrium between Sunni and Shia Muslims, as well as among Lebanon, Syria and Israel. This brought forth an action by a force now encountered for the first time, Islamic Jihad.

As explained in Wikipedia:

"*At around 06:22, a 19-ton yellow Mercedes-Benz stake-bed truck drove to the Beirut International Airport (BIA), where the U.S. 24th Marine Amphibious Unit (MAU) was deployed. The 1st Battalion 8th Marines (BLT), commanded by Lieutenant Colonel Larry Gerlach, was a subordinate element of the 24th MAU. The truck was not the water truck they had been expecting. Instead, it was a hijacked truck carrying explosives. The driver turned his truck onto an access road leading to the compound. He drove into and circled the parking lot, and then he accelerated to crash through a 5-foot-high barrier of concertina wire separating the parking lot from the building. The wire popped "like somebody walking on twigs." The truck then passed between two sentry posts and through an open vehicle gate in the perimeter chain-link fence, crashed through a guard shack in front of the building and smashed into the lobby of the building serving as the barracks for the 1st Battalion 8th Marines (BLT). The sentries at the gate were operating under rules of engagement which made it very difficult to respond quickly to the truck. Sentries were ordered to keep their weapons at condition four (no magazine inserted and no rounds in the chamber). Only one sentry, LCpl. Eddie DiFranco, was able to load and chamber a round. However, by that time the truck was already crashing into the building's entryway.*

The suicide bomber, an Iranian national named Ismail Ascari, detonated his explosives, which were later estimated to be equivalent to approximately 9,525 kilograms (21,000 pounds) of TNT. The force of the explosion collapsed the four-story building into rubble, crushing many inside. According to Eric Hammel in his history of the U.S. Marine landing force,

"*The force of the explosion initially lifted the entire four-story structure, shearing the bases of the concrete support columns, each measuring fifteen feet in circumference and reinforced by numerous one-and-three-quarter-inch steel rods. The airborne building then fell in upon itself. A massive shock wave and ball of flaming gas was hurled in all directions.*"

The blast killed 241 Marines, the worst one-day Marine death count since the battle of Iwo Jima in WWII. A second, similar suicide truck blast in the city killed 55 French paratroopers shortly thereafter.

The Marine guards not having loaded weapons, as a political consideration, showed our lack of appreciation of the new ground rules in the Middle East, a painful lesson in lack of preparedness.

Thirteen years later, in 1996, we would suffer a similar humiliating disaster when jihadists blew the face off the Khobar Towers military housing unit in Dhahran, Saudi Arabia. This led to relocation of our Air Force assets to Prince Sultan Air Base in the Saudi desert.

I felt a closeness to the event since I was passing through the eastern Mediterranean at the time, although I didn't get closer than about 100 miles to Lebanon. I marveled at the savagery of the act, our vulnerability, and wondered what changes would be wrought from this. There would be many.

President Reagan withdrew the Marines a few months later.

GRENADA INVASION

Also in October 1983, the day after I returned from the "Beirut" mission, the U.S. invaded the tiny island of Grenada in the southern Caribbean. A far-left political cabal had overthrown the somewhat left regime of Maurice Bishop and executed him and his inner circle. These events might not have resulted in a mini-war with the United States, except for the Beirut barracks bombing that had rocked the Reagan administration two days earlier. Desperate for a morale boosting event to take everyone's mind off the Beirut debacle, President Reagan ordered a full assault on Grenada, termed "Operation Urgent Fury," with 7,000 U.S. troops.

This little war was analogous to a professional football team finding a high school junior varsity team to obliterate to assuage a devastating previous loss, in this case, in Beirut. The standard alibis were rounded up: students at an island medical school were in danger, the American consul on the island had requested intervention—but his letter stating this was reportedly written in Washington after the fact and dated as a pre-invasion request.

This operation started a new trend of American military intervention around the world to be followed by Panama six years later (termed *Operation Just Cause*, nicknamed *Operation Just Because*) and multiple Middle Eastern adventures in the upcoming decades. As an obvious mismatch (the entire Grenada population numbered less than the stadium crowd at a Super Bowl), U.S. military forces descended upon mission planners as hungry wolves eager for heroic scraps of action. As many disparate units as possible were awarded missions so all could bask in this assured victory. After humiliating setbacks in Vietnam and Beirut, it seemed glory and medals had become available and everyone wanted action to validate their various missions. More than 50,000 medals would be awarded for the operation.

The impulse for cheap and easy glory, to say nothing of promotion-enhancing verbal fodder for future promotion boards ("singlehandedly won the Grenada war in exemplary and heroic fashion with one arm tied behind his back") brought forth wing staff members eager to fly support missions. They were far "too busy" to fly long exhausting routine line missions, but, by God, they were at the front of the line for short, glory missions! Most found it difficult to bag the two overseas sorties required every six months to maintain currency, so a quick Caribbean out-and-back would be a godsend for them.

Being at the end of my C-5 copilot tenure, I quick-turned after my Beirut mission to fly a Grenada mission with two such staff pilots, both evaluators who rarely left the home field. They suffered behind-the-back barbs among the line crews for being penguins (birds with wings that don't fly) or sea gulls (have to throw rocks at them to get them into the air), and I got two of them.

Our mission sent us to Homestead AFB, FL to pick up special ops personnel and equipment with a scheduled four-hour quick turn to fly to Barbados. This was the nearest island to Grenada with a large airport where smaller cargo aircraft could then complete the special ops force delivery requirements to Grenada.

The sea gull brothers flew all three legs in the pilot seats to pump up their currency. The four-hour "quick turn" at Homestead turned into an eight-hour fiasco as the glory-seeker line of units attempting to get in-theater had backed up and delayed us. With the sun setting and a long wait ahead, the brothers headed for the bunk room with the field grade navigator taking the third available bunk. That left me to finally attempt to take a nap on the ramp with my head resting against a nose gear tire.

When we finally got airborne, the brothers turned to me and told me I had the cruise portion of this segment and to wake them up thirty minutes prior to descent. They then dove back into the bunk room. The eastern sky had begun to lighten prior to sunrise when I had the flight engineer awaken the brothers for the landing.

The Barbados Bridgetown airport had descended into congested mayhem with the rush to get to Grenada by all the various services and units. We got downloaded in the tropical heat, filed for the trip home and just made our scheduled four-hour turn time.

(As an aside, I would visit Grenada again in 1986 to remove the port-o-johns from the runway location of President Reagan's speech commemorating the heroic invasion. That would be entangled with other command issues, to be covered later in "The Forsythe Saga." I awaited a "Grenada port-o-john removal" medal, but one never arrived.)

We leveled off at 35,000 feet enroute back to Dover. The left-seat sea gull called for the cruise checklist. That completed, he turned and looked at me in the jump seat. Having basically been awake the entire mission thus far, flown both cruise legs, and slept on the ramp while the brothers enjoyed the bunk room, I expected him to say *"Geez, Jay, you look like shit, why don't you get some sleep."*

But, nooooo. He grinned at me sheepishly, but with a certain entitled assurance in his glance, and said: *"Jump, I'm not feeling very well, so could you take the cruise portion home?"* Without waiting for an answer, the brothers climbed out of their seats and past me, headed for the bunk yet again.

The left-seat sea gull brother would get a just reward a few years hence when a copilot misaligned his INS. Due to his lack of proficiency he did not catch the error, making it necessary for him to make an unscheduled, embarrassing divert on a downrange mission. I will cover that in the "TACAN Mixing" segment below.

This episode provided one more reason on the list for me to bolt for Westover in 1987.

HIT-AND-RUN

Shortly after beginning my technician career at Dover, I decided to see what the civilian world might be offering. Airborne Express was conducting interviews in Raleigh, NC, near my mother's home in Greensboro, so I combined a trip home with an interview.

On the interview day I drove to Raleigh on a bright spring morning. I had to be there fairly early, 0830, and arrived in Raleigh with just about enough time to make the interview. I wasn't sure exactly where the site was, so I was a little anxious to beat the traffic to give myself something of a time pad.

I just got caught by a downtown traffic light at a busy intersection with two lanes going both directions and an additional left turn lane for each. I was first in line in my center lane and had a UPS delivery truck to my left in the left turn lane. The light sequence let all of us lined up together proceed at the same time, the left turn plus the straight ahead lanes.

I was driving my Honda Accord with a stick shift. From this compact car I could see nothing to my left but the truck that towered over me and was almost close enough to touch. I could just perceive the yellow caution light on the signal for the crossing traffic so I was prepared to leap forward when the light changed.

My light went green, I popped my clutch and leapt forward. What happened next took about two seconds and was over before I was fully aware it had happened.

As the car sprang into motion I suddenly saw the right-side profile of a 12-year-old girl directly in front of the car. Instantaneously my front end caught her at hip level and bent her onto the hood, causing her to strike it heavily with her right shoulder. Somehow, reflexively, and in a few milliseconds, my foot had found the brake pedal and the car dove to a stop. This motion catapulted the girl from the hood into the intersection as if shot from a cannon, school books and schoolgirl flying.

Dozens of cars were poised at the intersection aggressively awaiting a green light. While the intersection would soon have had an accelerating stream of vehicles after the light changed, all the cars, and the entire world, now froze as the schoolgirl tumbled into the intersection. For a long second, nothing moved, including me as I sat in a shocked stupor, eyes wide, fearing for a moment I had just killed someone.

To my relief the girl began picking herself up off the street. I cut the car off, leaving it in gear, and raced into the intersection to see how much damage had been done. The girl had large strawberries on her elbows and knees and one on her forehead but she seemed to be moving all limbs successfully.

"I'm sorry, I'm sorry!" she sobbed as she staggered around to collect her books and papers. She had tried to make it across the street before the light changed but only made it halfway, directly in front of me. The UPS guy had seen her coming but I could not have due to the truck blocking my view.

"Wait," I pleaded, *"I'll do that!"* I took her gently by the arm and guided her to the sidewalk. She was trembling and crying—and I was about to fall apart. It had been less than a minute since the light changed and still no cars had moved as everyone watched the drama. One minute before I could not have anticipated what the next minute would bring.

Once I had her off the street I quickly picked up her school items and returned them to her. I asked if she was OK, and she said yes, in a shaky voice. I told her to wait while I parked my car. Still, no car had moved. I took advantage and pulled across the right lane and into the school parking lot.

I took her into the school and asked for the principal's office. Once there I explained the situation to him and suggested he call the girl's parents and bring the school nurse to examine her. I didn't think we needed an ambulance, but I wasn't sure. He did both as the girl and I sat there. The nurse arrived and took the girl to the nurse's station to address her scrapes and bruises.

Now I had a dilemma. I was due at the interview shortly and things seemed to be beyond needing my care. I was sure I'd have to talk to the police, but I wanted to do the interview also. I handed the principal my driver's license and USAA number and told him I had an important meeting, but I would return later that morning to give whatever testimony might be required. He seemed satisfied with that and I left.

About two hours later I returned from the interview to find a police officer frowning and unhappy. *"Why did you leave?"* he asked. I explained my actions and he frowned some more. *"You are technically a hit-and-run driver,"* he said. That sent chills through me.

"I suppose so," I said, *"but I'm here now. There wasn't anything else I could do and I had an important interview."* It didn't occur to me he might have wanted to give me a sobriety and/or drug test, but he still could if he wanted.

He seemed satisfied that I was not under any substance influence and dropped the hit-and-run charge. We then discussed what had happened and he wrote up his report. He had all the information on the incident, and on me, and he released me with the promise to return if required.

The Airborne interviewer I met with told me my technician salary was far more competitive than what he could offer, so he feared I would leave after training and did not hire me.

About a week later I received a letter from the girl's mother saying she was OK and was sorry she tried to cross when she did. I said I was only happy she was not seriously injured and it had been quite a travail for me, too.

How quickly life can change in unanticipated ways.

TACAN MIXING

In the days before Flight Management Systems, where I had to work with three Inertial Navigation Systems (INSs), I developed a neurotic fascination with TACAN mixing the INSs, or adjusting their position calculation with information from TACAN stations on the ground.

INSs were marvelous contraptions. Using a set of internal gyros, these cube shaped black boxes about four inches on a side could tell you where you were on the earth at the moment in geographic coordinates, what your airspeed was, which direction the wind was coming from, and at what velocity, even doing 450 knots at 35,000 feet. And it did this with almost no outside-the-box information except for CADCs (central air data computers) that provided wind information. Other than that, they used only the information deciphered from the multiple gyros. The one piece of necessary information it had to have programmed into it was its present coordinates on the globe. Once it knew that, it provided all the other information, impossibly, to my mind. I still don't know how it could do that. PFM (pure fucking magic).

The individual calculations of the three cockpit INSs would drift off slightly during a flight and give slightly skewed information. For this reason, they triangulated among themselves to come up with a composite position.

Another method of checking the accuracy of the INS position was to TACAN mix, or dial up an available ground TACAN station so the INS could lock on to it and judge the plane's present position. Since it knew the exact geographic coordinates of the TACAN station and its distance from it in miles, it could compare that to its computed position. The most advantageous position for the TACAN relative to the aircraft was off one of the wings so its distance from the aircraft would stay relatively stable for some time. TACAN stations directly in front of, or behind, the aircraft would have distance changing rapidly and the INSs would not have sufficient time to recalibrate before the distance changed.

To provide even more precision, two TACANs could be brought up on opposite sides of the aircraft to give twice the reference points. I thought of this as a horse with two ropes around its neck from two different positions that held it tightly in one spot. Two TACANS provided the same for the aircraft position calculations.

On long overland legs, I would pass my time trying to TACAN mix as often as I could and savor the precision I would be creating in the INS, a truly neurotic fascination.

Two episodes highlight INS incidents on the road.

One involved the primary squadron "sea gull". Lt. Col. Sea Gull had to complete his two overseas missions in the required six-month reporting period, so he got on a downrange mission to the Middle East at the very end of the period. He demanded to command the mission (squawk, squawk!). But since he only needed two overseas legs, he only wanted to be in command for the first two mission legs: Dover to Rota, Spain, and Rota to Bahrain in the Persian Gulf. He loathed to expose himself to more than two legs in command. Who knows what might happen!

Sea Gull had another problem, however. Since he rarely flew, especially overseas, he sorely lacked proficiency in overseas procedures and with the INS system. To avoid disaster in the INS realm, he enlisted a senior copilot to program the "box" for him since he didn't know how to do it anyway. (That, ah, is why they made us go overseas twice each six months, for proficiency!)

But, dang the luck! Before takeoff from Rota, Spain, the copilot mistakenly programmed the INSs incorrectly by hitting "South" instead of "North" for the latitude position. This informed the INS it was somewhere in the South Atlantic off Africa, not in Spain. A technique I used to check the present position was to ask the INS to tell me the distance to the first flight plan "way point." I knew what it should be, and almost always the INS agreed within a mile or two. I had to make sure because, once you take off, you cannot reprogram the INS until you are back on the ground.

So when Sea Gull and crew took off from Rota and headed east, things began to go haywire immediately with their INSs. This was before the route could be programmed to show up on the weather radar, another way to check for correctness. When the copilot looked at the INS information, it informed him the first way point was 1,500 miles away (actually the distance from the false position in the South Atlantic). It was supposed to be 56 miles. They were screwed. If they tried to continue they would be in dire danger of violating airspace of countries they did not have a diplomatic clearance to fly in, to say nothing of getting violated by ATC for being off course.

Sea Gull had to admit defeat and land at Torrejon AB, near Madrid, to reprogram the INSs. Since he landed at an unscheduled stop, the commanders at MAC headquarters wanted to know why he had done that, and he had to tell them. Even though he had tried to protect himself by only flying in command for two legs, this leg was his and he owned it.

I had the second episode myself. I took off from Guam headed to Travis AFB, CA, a ten-hour flight across almost nothing but ocean. Just after takeoff, one of our three INSs died. That meant no triple mix position since we only had two INSs and no idea which would be closest to being right. What to do?

I looked at the flight plan legs painted on my weather radar and saw we would pass over the island of Saipan about twenty minutes after takeoff. I decided I would check positions as we passed over the Saipan navigation aid (navaid) and go with the INS closest to the mark. That turned out to be the #1 INS on my side. I decided to press on to California. Yes, this INS might drift off by some miles, but I couldn't possibly miss the west coast of the United States! Had I been flying the reverse course, I might have had other thoughts, because then I would have had to find a very small island in a very big ocean. We arrived successfully at Travis.

Skid Strip Gator

Every other year or so, I'd fly a C-5 mission to the Skid Strip at Cape Canaveral, FL, in support of the space shuttle program. Two features of the Strip stood out, the runway width, and the creature that lurked behind the parking pad.

The Strip runway is 300 feet wide, which is the widest I've landed on. Most runways are 200 feet wide. This extra 100 feet of width creates an optical illusion since, from experience, your brain still thinks you are landing on a 200-foot wide runway. This causes the pilot to flare high, thinking he is about to touch down when he is actually 50% higher than he thinks he is. That can cause the airplane to drop heavily onto the runway.

But the most interesting feature of the Strip was the creature—an alligator. He lived under a small bridge that spans a thin, ten-foot wide estuary, not more than a large ditch, that runs from the local bay to within about fifty feet of the rear of the aircraft parking pad.

As the loadmasters would start the download, we pilots would walk over to say hello to the gator, a reptilian monster about ten feet long from nose to tail. We would usually find him sunning himself on the near bank facing the airplane. While his body would not move at our approach, his eyes would track us, warily. My eyes would fix on him, too, warily. He seemed docile enough, but I would skirt him uneasily by twenty feet or so to reach the bridge right next to his sunning spot, from which I could look down on him from relative safety.

On one trip I saw validation for my instinctive wariness. A park ranger had come to greet us on our arrival and told us he had picked up a road-kill opossum that was in the back of his truck. He asked if we'd like to see him feed it to the gator.

Not wanting to miss this, we lined up on the rail of the small bridge. When the ranger held up the opossum, the gator moved slowly off his sunning pad and slid into the water about six feet below us, his head raised out of the water, aiming his snout at the opossum. He had apparently done this before. The ranger swung the dead animal back briefly and tossed it up lightly into the air over the reptile, where it paused on its upward arc and began to fall.

What happened next chills me still and haunts my dreams. The opossum descended about two feet to the right of the monster's head. Suddenly the gator's head had moved that distance to catch the opossum in its jaws... but I never saw it move. Somehow the two-foot move of the head was so fast it never registered in my brain, as if someone had cut and spliced a film to remove the motion.

The gator paused for a second or two with the opossum clamped firmly at the end of his snout. I think he did that to let the terror of his deadly quickness sink into my mind. Then he flipped his head upward, releasing the opossum, which turned one full rotation and descended into the now open jaws of the reptile. The jaws snapped shut as the animal disappeared down his throat. The opossum's tail hung limply from the gator's mouth at the jaw hinge as the reptile slowly slid back into the water. I remained motionless and speechless for several moments as a primal terror seized my mind.

I recalled this Jurassic moment years later when a spate of alligator attacks occurred around Florida ponds. In one, a female jogger had stopped to sit next to a pond when a gator suddenly thrashed out of the pond and dragged the woman underwater, drowning her.

Gators and crocs, mercifully, do not dismember their victims in the initial attack, while they are alive; they merely take them underwater and hold on firmly until the prey drowns. Then the terrible work begins. The reptile seizes a limb in its powerful jaws and begins rolling and thrashing to tear it loose to be consumed. Then it moves on to another limb, then to the head, then, finally, to the torso.

After this alligator display, I have an appreciation of how gators and crocs have survived since the age of dinosaurs. They are perfectly honed to their task, including a powerful tail that can knock down prey on land.

I never again went within forty feet of my reptilian friend in Skid Strip missions.

2:00 AM EPIPHANY

In 1984 our firstborn daughter, Jessica, came home from the hospital a few days after her birth and introduced me to fatherhood. One night I was on duty as the baby walker to try to put her to sleep, walking back and forth next to her crib. While she usually went quickly to sleep and stayed asleep, for some reason she awoke this night and needed to be coaxed back to sleep.

As I paced slowly, patting her back, I felt somewhat put-upon to be up at 2 AM. I recognized her mother bore the brunt of managing her, but I still felt grumpy about being up when I had to arise in a few hours to drive an hour to Dover for work. I indulged in self-pity. I'm doing this, I thought, and she will never remember my effort on her behalf and I will receive no thanks. Woe is me!

I continued pacing, but a few minutes later, stopped frozen in my tracks. It suddenly occurred to me that someone had done this for me when I was a newborn! Someone had sacrificed their sleep to tend to me, without me remembering or providing any thanks for their effort. They did it because they cared deeply for my welfare and freely sacrificed their comfort to ensure mine.

Now I felt terrible for my self-indulgent self-pity, and for never saying thank you to my mother and father for all their selfless efforts on my behalf when I was a child that I would never remember. They did all those things because that is what good parents do.

But then I thought that maybe this is normal. Children will grow up, have their own children, and, in the middle of some future night, have the same epiphany I did about their parents. They will realize their parents did it and didn't ask for any thanks, that they loved them and would do what was necessary on their behalf without demanding any credit.

I also realized, with chagrin, that as a young adult I had been angry with my parents a few times and said some unfortunate things I should not have that unfairly injured them. They, who had sacrificed for me for years and toiled silently on my behalf, stood there and took it solemnly and sadly. My revelation about their selfless efforts was years in the future, so the impact of my inflicted criticism, "sharper than a serpent's tooth," eluded me. They could have raged: "*How dare you!*" But they did not. I now rage at my younger self: "*How dare I have said those things!*"

I later shared this "2 AM" parable with my parents. They smiled, but said nothing; they still were not asking for credit, but I gave them thanks anyway.

I must also offer a thank you for those who may give me care in my final days, weeks, or months, when I may be unable to thank them, or perhaps not even to know they are giving me care. I thank you and bless you now in advance for the consideration.

Atlantic Night Crossing

The passage from Dover to Europe, almost always to Ramstein, Germany, usually occurred at night, since as reservists, we often took off after normal business hours and flew east in the darkness. We would often meet the rising sun over Ireland as we coasted in from the oceanic portion of the flight. We all came to know this night journey well, although conditions often varied depending upon weather conditions, visual or instrument conditions, and the time of year with long winter, and short summer, nights. Clear nights provided a spectacular view of the eastern seaboard from Cape May, NJ, to the oceanic coast out near Goose or Gander, Newfoundland.

As we got the gear and flaps up, set climb power and finished our checklists, we were usually over the dark Delaware Bay headed for the Sea Isle VORTAC navigational aid that would provide our backup TACAN radial (059) to maintain our prescribed navigation route. But that was in the early 1980s. We soon had triple INS guidance, where we flew between the GPS coordinates of the navaid instead of to the navaid itself. The navaids then performed as backups for the INS course. In the mid-1980s we also got a weather radar that provided a course centerline on the radar screen as further confirmation of our route. If the course line inexplicably headed off in the wrong direction it would warn us we had loaded an incorrect waypoint coordinate, a common error while punching in manual north/south and east/west waypoint coordinates that determined our route clearance.

We made the left turn at Sea Isle and headed northeast ten or so miles off the coast and paralleling it much of the way to the oceanic coast out. As we rolled out of the turn, Atlantic City, with its well-lit casino hotels aligned on the boardwalk, gave a colorful view of the city in its glory days of the 1980s and '90s. Next came the rest of the New Jersey shore leading up to New York City and Long Island. Further inland I could pick out the cities by their light concentrations: Wilmington, Philadelphia, Trenton, and Newark. Clear nights also allowed me to try to determine the various boroughs of NYC and to pick out the three major airports located there, JFK, LaGuardia and Newark. This God's eye view of the East Coast often left me wistful and contemplative about the human concentrations passing below me, how far they had advanced, and what lay in store for them in the future.

Flying south of Long Island and paralleling it, the concentration of lights diminished as we flew east. Long Island marks the southernmost reach of the glacial expansion during the Ice Age ten thousand years ago. It is formed from the moraine of rocks and soil pushed in front of the ice sheet and left behind as the glaciers retreated. At the far end of Long Island we'd begin to pick up the Nantucket VORTAC (identifier ACK) on our navaids that we could use to update our INSs if necessary.

Several times when the weather was not good, we found ourselves skimming the cloud tops at our cruise altitude and not enjoying it. While in the clouds the plane jostled about almost nonstop in the turbulence, and I would keep bugging the engineer to tell me when the performance charts said we could climb two thousand feet to escape the weather. (This is before FMS would allow me to see the data myself.) Sometimes I would request a climb from ATC before I had 100% capability and sacrifice speed just to get into the clear.

While surfing the cloud tops I would extend the wing lights to determine our relationship to the top of the cloud formation. The lights would swing into position from pointing straight down to forward and slightly down. When they rose and clicked into their extended position, they provided an instant sense of speed as the wispy cloud tops flew by us at several hundred miles per hour. At times the solid deck would open up below us to reveal huge cloud canyons many times deeper than the Grand Canyon before closing up again.

The ground lights became sparse after Nantucket as we passed by Nova Scotia and its few cities such as Halifax, where most of the survivors and victims of the Titanic were taken in 1912.

Traversing the mostly dark expanse of Newfoundland there were small towns and lights extending upriver from them ten or so miles toward the interior, where they petered out in the darkness. About an hour after crossing Nantucket, we approached coast out into the oceanic navigation routes, or NAT (North Atlantic Track System) tracks.

These parallel tracks, or highways in the sky, are redefined daily to ride on or near the jet stream. This swift moving river of air flows around the globe west to east and snakes around, moving northward or southward to conform to high and low pressure systems in the atmosphere below. Planners get the estimated jet stream position for the next 24 hours and place the parallel routes accordingly, usually four going east, Tracks A, B, C, and D. This allows aircraft flying from Canada or the United States to ride the jet stream express tailwind to arrive much more quickly at their European destinations.

The tracks were 60 miles apart in the 1980s and '90s but were moved closer together, to 30 miles, when more precise instrumentation better assured clearance horizontally and vertically. While this allows precision placement in the airspace, it can prove catastrophic if planes are inadvertently placed on the same track at the same altitude heading in opposite directions. In the 1980s this would result in seeing a plane pass a mile or two away at the same altitude, because flying TACAN radials were never very precise. Now, however, if a plane is at the wrong altitude, the chance of a nose-on midair is greatly increased because planes are exactly on course and altitude.

Westbound aircraft from Europe to North America naturally want to get as far away from the jet stream as they can because the sometimes 120 knot headwind would make their journey far longer than necessary. Westbound tracks are usually 100 miles or more north of the eastbound tracks and are labeled Tracks X, Y and Z.

At that time, about 100 miles from oceanic coast out, the copilot would contact Gander Radio on 127.1 (the frequency then) to get his assigned track and altitude for the crossing. Gander asks what time he will arrive at a pre-entry point, usually 50-degrees west, what altitude he can maintain, and his airspeed.

The copilot checks his estimated time for the point and estimates his optimum altitude to request. This altitude is the highest his performance charts show he can attain as well as maintaining the C-5's optimum cruise speed of .77 Mach. For comparison, the C-141 and C-17 maintain .74 Mach, and B-747 hold .84 Mach. Oceanic control parcels out assignments with these speeds in mind so B-747s are not running over C-17s on a particular track. On a Saturday night mission to Europe, we would watch as B-747s passed us, usually above us due to more powerful engines. The C-5M, which can keep up with large commercial aircraft, was still decades in the future.

After providing Gander Center with his request, the copilot would copy and read back the assigned track and altitude. "*Reach two-victor-seven is cleared Nat B, Flight Level 330, from four-eight north, five-zero west, flight plan route.*" During mission planning at base ops prior to takeoff, the copilot would obtain a current copy of the NAT tracks with a specific date and time; for instance: March 12, 2300Z. If the crew had that NAT message, they did not need to read back all the coordinates of the route to the controller. If they did not have a current NAT message, or in the early 1980s before the tracks were pre-printed, the copilot would copy the coordinates of the track points from Gander Center and read them back, laboriously, to the controller. Usually he had miscopied one of them and would have to start over, to the chagrin of all aircraft waiting their turn to obtain a clearance.

Once oceanic clearance was attained and the plane had coasted out over the water, the aircraft commander could turn the aircraft over to the copilot and/or first pilot seated in the jump seat, and retire to the bunk room until coast in to Ireland or England. Regulations dictated that the commander be in the seat for both coast out and coast in, so the three-hour or so oceanic portion was the only time he could sleep. When I was the commander, I would do that immediately on coast out. In the early 1980s, however, as a copilot, I usually caught the oceanic portion solo after the commander had departed for the bunk.

I would check in on the Oceanic HF (high frequency) radio to provide position reports to Gander Oceanic until we crossed thirty-degrees west latitude, where I would switch to Shanwick Oceanic in Ireland. I had to report every 10 degrees of longitude change, which usually occurred about once an hour. When doing so I would report the point I was crossing, estimate for the next point, and my flight level ("*Crossing four-five north, four-zero west at 0445Z; estimate four-six north, three-zero west at 0540, FL 330*").

Talking on HF radio is like communicating with Mars, or the afterlife, with strange bubbling noises, static, or bell-like tones sliding down the scale before disappearing. Since the signal bounces off the ionosphere high above and ricochets down to earth, you sometimes reach strange locations, depending upon the bounce. Coasting into Newfoundland one night I got Clark AB in the Philippines as clear as a bell but could not raise anyone in the States. Usually on the crossing I would call Ascension Island, a small speck of land in the South Atlantic between Africa and South America, which for some reason could always read me well and provide weather for my destination in Germany. The nearest station, Croughton, England, never seemed to answer, but Ascension always did.

Once the commander was gone and the first position report was complete, I would tilt my seat back, sip my coffee, and settle in for the crossing. Although the on-duty flight engineer seated behind me was (usually) awake, I felt alone as I stood deck watch over my space ship and its performance while most of the crew slept.

On clear nights my view would be dictated by the rise and size of the moon. If it was already above the horizon and full or near full, its brightness would obscure most of the stars as the moon hung like a large night light in front of me. There were instances where the moonlight was so bright I put my sun visor down to block it. While only the brightest stars were visible, the cloud formations or strata would be illuminated, often providing a dreamscape of tiered cloud islands that we sailed through.

If the moon was new, or not yet risen, the stars put on a galactic spectacle with the Milky Way passing overhead and all easily identifiable constellations evident. I felt comfortable with either panorama outside the windows of my space ship transiting a large ocean, if not solar systems or galaxies, a star traveler seeking new worlds, or at least one where the inhabitants spoke German.

Night crossing in the winter would remain dark until near, or after, landing in Germany. In the summer, however, with shorter nights, the sun would rise approaching Ireland. This could happen in interesting ways.

Once on a somewhat cloudy morning, the sun rose into view appearing as if a glowing ember from a fire, more square than round as it rose above the horizon while heavily filtered by the atmosphere and thin clouds.

On many clear summer mornings, I could see the sunrise coming, as colors on the horizon slowly shifted from black, to dark blue, to progressively lighter blue, to red as the sun approached rising, to yellow and gold as it broke the horizon. This progression, in reverse, happens on sunsets. The colors appear elegantly, reminding me of the pure, soft visual tones seen in well-dyed Easter eggs in graded shades of blue, yellow, orange and red.

Sunrise brought aggravation on clear days, however, as the horizon became blindingly bright and required a route map to be placed behind the sun visor to block the sun itself.

Approaching Ireland I would revert to VHF radio where normal-sounding conversation could occur. Shanwick would give me my clearance to Germany and I would read it back. I'd then tell the engineer to wake up the pilot for coast in.

Traversing England one night we flew just north of London. Peering down on the city, its lighted roadways appeared as gold and silver strands lain on the black velvet of the landscape. Roads ran from the center toward the outskirts, twisted spokes apparently formed from donkey tracks developed from Roman Empire days, but now as well-lit thoroughfares.

As copilot I would call Mildenhall AB, England, about sixty miles northeast of London, on the UHF (military) radio for a phone patch to the Ramstein command post for arrival weather and to pass our maintenance status.

Crossing the English Channel on clear nights, the stark outlines of England and France became evident, but as we approached Holland and Belgium, they seemed indistinguishable from France or Germany in the maze of lights on the coast.

On the descent into Ramstein we could see Frankfurt in the distance to the east and Kaiserslautern (K-town) just to the east of the base. The Ramstein controllers would usually vector us to an ILS final for Runway 27 or 09 and the mission for the night would be complete. A frothy German beer could be awaiting, even if it was now morning.

CIRCADIAN MADNESS

Long haul air transport takes a significant toll on the body, especially on the circadian rhythm that controls bodily functions. Sleep cycle disruption becomes the most obvious injury.

Scientists tell us it can take a day to adjust to every time zone change. A standard C-5 mission to Europe and the Middle East can cover six times zones a day. By this metric, my circadian rhythm moving eastward would meet my body returning westward somewhere over Europe. This often resulted in bizarre circumstances.

The airlift system thinks it is doing us a favor after landing in Germany by providing us with an 0600 local alert call the next morning. This supposedly starts us off at our standard wakeup time. Except my body thinks it is midnight, the worst possible time to start a long day of flying.

This helped create my insane motto: I can't sleep when I get off the airplane, and I can't stay awake once I get back on. Another standard anomaly is receiving the crew alert call from the command post shortly after finally falling asleep.

Sleep deprivation can also require difficult decisions. After landing and going into 12 hours of crew rest, two imperatives compete: sleep, or eat. If you go to sleep, all eating opportunities may be closed when you awake at 0200 local time. If you eat first, the crew may find you face down in your soup, sound asleep. Further, if you deny your body its first attempt at sleep, it may not award you another one before alert.

1980s C-5 Ports of Call

Frankfurt

Rhein-Main airport lies on the outskirts of Frankfurt, the major city of central Germany. Generally, we arrived from the west, crossing over the field and flying a loop to reverse course to land on Runway 27L. With a large number of aircraft landing, arrival instructions dictated flying 220 knots until approaching the final approach fix, the VORTAC, to slow and configure at the last minute. This unusually late configuration resulted in rapidly changing control forces as the gear and flaps came down and the airspeed dropped rapidly just prior to landing.

On final we often found another aircraft, almost always a B-747 (a nice little airplane) flying alongside us headed for the other, parallel, runway. Rhein-Main seemed the home of the B-747 since the civilian side seemed inhabited by no other type of aircraft, the most 747s I've ever seen in one place.

On one occasion, the tower changed runways from 27 to 9 as we approached from the west at 10,000 feet. This meant I didn't have the 20-mile loop to descend to the 2500-foot final approach altitude. Frankfurt Fritz (my nickname for all German controllers) asked if I could make it down and I guessed yes, although I wasn't sure. We went to idle, threw out the gear and flaps, came down nearly auto-rotating out of the sky and just made it down in time to land on runway 9. After that I always listened closely to ATIS and the controllers to see if they were going to pull another last-minute runway switch on me.

Frankfurt had a stringent procedure for takeoff clearance. When you said you were ready, you'd better damn sure be completely ready. Fritz would clear you for takeoff with another huge jet halfway down final and you had to start rolling immediately upon lineup, no time for checklists once on the runway. If you needed run-up time for a max performance takeoff (rare on this 12,000-foot runway), you had to advise Fritz prior to reaching the hold line.

Takeoff had a wrinkle to it no one informed me of for my first departure. Due to heavy aircraft and radio traffic in the terminal area, I was supposed to silently switch to departure control without asking permission or being directed by tower. So, alas, I asked tower if he wanted me to switch to departure. Fritz took great glee in this. "*Oh, Maauuuck, YOU may switch to departure controoool!*" Ouch!

Some times on departure or arrival Fritz would ask if we could do something impossible, like gain 10,000 feet in five miles with a heavy airplane (no way), or could we lose 10,000 feet in ten miles (no way). When we said no, he'd vector us off-course as punishment. Although these days, the C-5M may be able to comply.

Usually we stayed at the Rhein-Main hotel on the military side of the field, a large three-story structure with two long wings on each side of the main lobby. The rug was an Oriental design of a rich red color. The ground floor had a ski shop on one end and concessions on the other. The cafeteria was up a central staircase across from the entrance.

Later, while the hotel was under renovation, we'd stay in the "round houses," circular buildings a quarter mile or so away.

Near the roundhouses there was a back gate pedestrian entrance to the airport that led to a path through the woods to the Zeppelinheim train station and farther on to "The Log" restaurant, a favorite eatery.

When we got to stay downtown it was usually at the high-rise Holiday Inn on the top of a hill. One of my final stays there in 2003 provided me a two-level room with a spiral metal staircase to the bedroom upstairs. The TV also had X-rated movies. Ah…one of the enlisted guys told me about that. Those enlisted guys!

The university district had an Indian restaurant with the best curry I've ever had. Also, if you had a day or two off, you could take a three or four-hour Rhine River cruise with wine tasting at the conclusion.

The most frequented restaurant was the Baseler Eck in downtown Frankfurt that specialized in a crusty-on-the-outside, tender-on-the-inside pork loin on the bone that is one of the tastiest dishes I have ever enjoyed. The accompaniment of a dark German beer made it even better.

Baseler Eck clientele was usually American military and international air crews. I was there with a Dover crew in the mid-1990s with fellow pilot Bill Spence. Reviewing the international flight attendants at another table, I exclaimed that I had never seen any Japanese women that really turned me on, but those sure did.

Bill shook his head slowly and covered his eyes in exasperation. *"The reason they do that, Jay, is because they are Thai Airways flight attendants, not Japanese,"* he said. As usual, my imagined savoir-faire of women of the world suffered a severe hit!

I had always heard about the fabled "naked man" walking through downtown Frankfurt but didn't think it was true…until. On my last Frankfurt trip we stayed downtown at the Holiday Inn. As we loaded the bus and began to pull out, there he was, walking by the bus on the sidewalk about twenty yards away! The three enlisted females leapt to the windows and started cheering and whooping. He wore a scarf and shoes and socks, but nothing else. Quite a sight strolling down the street with the other pedestrians.

One mandatory stop for new crew members was "The Stairs" hotel in the red light district. Customers start on the ground floor observing women in brightly lit rooms lounging on a bed. If interested in the product, you would inquire of the price and, if satisfied, close the door and proceed.

If you wanted to view other rooms, you would progress up the stairway to rooms on higher floors. Usually the most desirable women were on the lower floors, with the cheaper, less desirable ones on the upper floors.

I noticed something disturbing as I progressed up the stairs. In the shadows on the landings, dark forms of large, bulky men could be seen, the bouncers and enforcers who would spring into action to "manage" any uncooperative or belligerent customers.

I only visited the site once, just to fill the square, and without partaking of the offerings, but some made the trip there a routine indulgence.

MADRID

The Spanish capital of Madrid provided a second marvelous city to explore in the 1980s. The USAFE fighter base, Torrejon AB, located on the outskirts of the city, also served as a major transport aircraft stop enroute to Mediterranean stops or the desert. The base closed after Desert Shield/Storm, but it was a primary stop for the C-5 in the 1980s.

We would take taxis to the outskirts of the city and then ride the subway system to our desired destination, usually the Plaza Mayor. The plaza was as large as four football fields surrounded by four-story buildings that ran continuously around the perimeter. Few venues are finer than drinking wine at an outdoor restaurant on the plaza on a sunny afternoon watching the Spaniards walk by. Under the building surrounding the plaza there was a series of underground grotto restaurants, each specializing in a particular delicacy such as mushrooms or calamari (squid) accompanied, of course, with wine. I skipped the calamari, thank you.

All this would be a warm-up for a meal nearby at Botín's Restaurant, which didn't start serving until 8 PM, and you'd better be in line at that time. This was the restaurant that served the same delicious ham hock as Baseler Eck in Frankfurt, and it resembled a medieval dungeon with brick walls and several floors of tables.

The other imperative Madrid stop was the Prado Museum that housed paintings by many Spanish artists such as Goya, Dali and, my favorite, Velazquez.

SIGONELLA

The next stop on the way to Bahrain on the Navy cargo run was Sigonella NAS, Italy. It is located on the southeast coast of Sicily near the ancient city of Syracuse and on the lower slopes of Mt. Etna, an active volcano whose caldera often glowed red at night. Sig had a marvelous Mediterranean climate and rustic countryside replete with Roman ruins and structures. In the 1980s we usually stayed at a smaller auxiliary military base farther up the slope of Etna in a hotel that had artistic tile floors and a pool with a swim-up bar. Dinner would be pizza or other Italian dishes in a basement restaurant.

Often, as we took the runway for takeoff, a sheepherder would be moving his flock across a field next to the runway. Sometimes I'd yank the chain of one of the crew and quaver my voice as if replicating a sheep's "baaa" and say, *"Henry, I love you."* Sometimes we got caught behind a flock walking up one of the ancient roads near the base enroute to the auxiliary base and remark that the sheep looked like the fighter pilot's dates we had seen in Torrejon.

INCIRLIK

The other notable Mediterranean base is Incirlik near the southern city of Adana on the eastern corner of the Mediterranean. It is strategically located just northwest of Syria and Iraq and just east of the Taurus mountain chain. About five miles north of the base sat a hilltop castle ruin that spoke of some Medieval, or older, army, but I never knew which—Saracen, Crusader, or Persian.

Incirlik was a prime shopping stop for brass lamps, Oriental rugs, and pistachio nuts. The base water tower had an interesting story. Apparently the Americans hired Turkish painters to paint the tower. They told them to paint the surface with standard red and white checkerboard squares for easy visual sighting by pilots. Not fully understanding their instructions, the Turks poured the red and white paint together and painted the tower pink.

Often we would purchase steaks from Ramstein and grill them on outdoor grills built among the billeting huts used at that time. The O'Club was small and usually crowded with MAC crews and fighter pilots from the fighter wing based there.

Smoke House, Mildenhall AB, England

Only a handful of hotels I visited during my Air Force transport career are memorable. The Smoke House at Mildenhall was one.

This hotel was not the most comfortable or glamorous I stayed in, but it was the most quintessentially British that recalled the pre-World War II era. I often imagined I was crew-resting there to fly my B-17 on a bombing mission the next day.

The rooms were small and heated by steam radiators that clanked noisily as they worked. The water spigots in the sink were either hot or cold, but not blended. The only temperature control came from mixing the two streams in the sink to a comfortable temperature. I found this cumbersome and marvelous at the same time. This is how my grandfather and his father must have shaved in the morning.

My favorite spot in the hotel was in the small foyer by the check-in desk. When we arrived I would immediately plop down in a large overstuffed easy chair in front of the fireplace. I had to move quickly or some tanker guy might get there first!

The fireplace was large and ancient but served only as a repository for a lyre-shaped grate about the size of a small suitcase, standing on end, in the center of the opening. The fire would almost always be going on our arrival in all but the few summer months. There would be a large copper tub on the right side of the fireplace with small pieces of firewood about as thick as your wrist and five or six inches long. When needed, I would feed a piece or two into the top of the grate, which was about half the width of the bottom that held the coals of previous pieces. In a separate container, billiard ball sized lumps of coal were available to mix with the wood to keep the fire hot and stoked.

After adjusting the fire to my liking, I would have one of my cohorts bring me a pint of ale. I couldn't go get it myself or some interloper might steal my seat. Over the next hour I would stare dreamily into the fire and sink lower and lower into the chair while imagining conversing with Charles Dickens seated nearby.

My standard meal had to be fish and chips in the bar a few feet down the hallway past the check-in counter. Upon entry, to the right was the bar proper where pints were drawn constantly for the crowd in a space not really large enough for the clientele, about the size of a family room. Most of the customers were local British men. It was "their" pub, but they seemed to tolerate American air crew members mixing in.

To the left a somewhat larger bar dining area held half a dozen tables and booths around another large fireplace in the middle of the right-side wall. The favored table was the one immediately next to the fireplace. The dark wood walls and smoky ambiance made me think Henry the VIII and his entourage might arrive for a meal.

For me the Smoke House was Britain in all its ancient charm and antique features that no modern hotel could possibly match.

BAHRAIN

A small island nation just east of Dhahran, Saudi Arabia and just northwest of Qatar (pronounced "Cutter"), the Bahrain international airport serves as a support base for American naval forces in the Persian Gulf. The Air Force had a small parking area on the north end of the field.

In the 1980s we occasionally crew rested in the city of Manama about a mile away across a bridge on the main island. While the terrain was an ancient dusty desert, the hotels we stayed in provided a near tropical respite from the dust and heat. One in particular had a long escalator just inside the front door that took you to an upper level lobby. On the ascent you passed water fountains, waterfalls and tropical gardens cultivated in the large arboretum surrounding the escalator, a complete reversal of the environment you had just left.

The desert heat had a strange effect on the aircraft also during preflight. The air conditioning system, working hard, would pump clouds of misty fog into the crew compartment at times leading to only a few feet of visibility.

We more often quick-turned Bahrain and needed a somewhere to eat. I finally discovered a local snack bar reached by walking through the large Gulf Air hanger across the ramp to a small alleyway behind it. This cantina served up scrumptious chicken curry accompanied by large, nearly pizza sized, portions of unleavened bread you tore into pieces to devour.

In the later 1980s the Saudis built the 16-mile long King Fahd causeway across the shallow water from Dhahran to Manama. We suspected this allowed devout Saudis to cross to more secular Bahrain to kick up their heels, similar to Americans heading to Las Vegas.

CAIRO WEST: BUZZING THE PYRAMIDS

In 1983 I flew an Egypt mission with Warren, a reserve pilot who flew well but couldn't pass the S&W .38 marksmanship test.

I don't know what he didn't get about lining up the gun, but he repeatedly failed the test. Since this was unacceptable, I told him, on the next firing test, I'd line up next to him and put a few of my shots into his target. I had already attained an expert rating on past tests, so loaning him a few bullets wouldn't matter.

The line instructor shouted out the commands as we stood in our firing position on the range for the open fire phase.

"*Ready on the left, ready on the right, ready on the firing line? Fire!*" he shouted.

Since it was a six-shot revolver, I shot: blam, blam, blam, at my target, then shifted left to Warren's target, blam, blam, blam. Then I reloaded and finished on my target. I had guessed just right, Warren passed by one shot and all was well.

On the mission to Cairo West airport, we managed to land satisfactorily at this field in the desert about twenty miles west of the pyramids located on the western outskirts of Cairo, Egypt. Since this was a quick turn, we were soon off again, headed to Europe. Cairo West did not provide facilities to file a flight plan, so we had to take off VFR and orbit at 5,000 feet while filing a flight plan with Cairo Center on VHF radio.

As we arrived at 5,000 feet, Cairo was busy giving someone else a clearance, so we started to orbit. That is when Warren suggested: *"Why don't we go buzz the pyramids?"* Since he was in command, this seemed within his prerogative, so I sat silently as the copilot, and away we went, aimed at the Cheops Pyramid.

We had gotten about halfway there when the Egyptian military came up on Guard frequency that all aircraft monitor.

"Aircraft approaching pyramids, identify yourself and reverse course! Contact Cairo Center on 124.7 immediately!" It seemed obvious he must mean us. Oh, shit!

"Cairo, this is MAC 2067 on Cairo, were you calling us?" I said, cringing.

"MAC, you cause very big problem for me. You have set off the radar defense network for unidentified aircraft arriving from the west! Return to your orbit over Cairo West immediately!"

Egypt and Libya were in the middle of a tense border standoff and Cairo had rigged its radar defenses to detect low-flying inbound aircraft from the west. By heading for the pyramids, we qualified as such and the entire system went into alarm on our behalf.

I guess the military controller wasn't too mad, because we didn't hear any more about it. We dreaded standing at attention in our commander's office to explain what the hell we were doing trying to buzz the pyramids. Fortunately, we escaped this or any other type of punishment for our lapse.

Chapter Three: Aircraft Commander

Aircraft Commander (A/C) Line Check

After about nine months as a C-5 copilot, the squadron put me up for my line check. Since I had been an evaluator in another weapon system, the B-52, I did not have to attend Altus for A/C upgrade, instead doing it locally in the spring of 1983. Then, after a series of a few missions playing A/C under supervision of an instructor pilot, I would get the line check on a westward trip to the Pacific.

As a C-5 aircraft commander, you are the mayor of small village inhabited by a random selection of citizens. The B-52 had "hard" crews, where the same crew participants usually flew as a team and knew each other well. In the C-5, however, every mission had a different personality hodgepodge, some of whom you might know well, and others you did not know at all. Crews might be as small as six or as many as 12 to 15. Even in the pilot ranks there were twenty or more aircraft commanders a squadron copilot might fly with and the same number of copilots an aircraft commander might encounter. Compared to smaller cargo aircraft, this required a quantum leap in management capability. Each crew would have a primary flight engineer and primary loadmaster who would manage those in their respective crew position, but the A/C had responsibility for the entire group and for the safe completion of the mission.

By comparison, fighter pilots on the wing fly attached to their lead aircraft like a puppy dog on a leash until the action starts and have no one to manage but themselves. They are individual "entrepreneurs" while C-5 aircraft commanders are air crew CEOs with responsibility for a huge span of control. Of course, C-5s rarely have anyone shooting at them and have no fear of blacking out from G-lock, so we all have our crosses to bear.

I cringed at my draw of evaluators, Russ, a senior evaluator and future squadron commander. Russ, at times, had a prickly personality. He could fly into a rant about something he disagreed with, critiqued check rides with occasional arm-flapping tirades and often expressed disbelief that a student could have done something as stupid as he did. Except, he did all these things half–good-naturedly by inviting the victim to laugh about the criticism at the end. It was wise to acquiesce and laugh with him. As long as he eventually laughed, you were probably going to pass.

Russ conducted his interrogations gradually as we progressed westward to Travis AFB, CA, and then Hickam AFB, HI. These consisted of numerous "what if" questions probing for procedural knowledge. He caught me on a few, to his great delight, but most went well.

Preparing to depart Hawaii eastbound to California, Russ debriefed me on a few details as we waited for the crew bus, but then smiled and said the check ride was over, I'd passed. We got on the bus and, standing in the aisle, he shook my hand, turned around and sat down. He now blended in with the rest of the crew and no longer eyed me as a check pilot as he had for the first half of the trip. He elbowed the "noink" (NCOIC, or designated enlisted trip supervisor) seated next to him about some long-standing joke between them and left me on my own.

"OK, listen up," I said. "Takeoff time is 2030Z, that's 1030 local for those of you in civilian status. Checklists thirty minutes prior. Who's doing lunches? OK, Massey is doing lunches. Any questions? Anyone get arrested last night? Driver, let's go to tail number 167 on A-3."

I had been given the car keys to my second large aircraft, and quite a ride it would be.

CREW ETIQUETTE

There are unspoken rules for crew conduct on the road. The imperative one for aircraft commanders and other pilots is to participate fully in the bag drag up and down the crew stairs. Although pilots are officers, they are not crown princes above manual labor. Yes, for us this often meant hauling heavy crates of German or British beer bought by enlisted members up and down the stairs, but it had to be done.

One of my enlisted chiefs, Snake Tilton, starkly outlined an exception to crew efforts on baggage hauling by declaring: "*He who buy Hibachi pot, carry Hibachi pot!*" But, otherwise, everyone bag dragged.

The lead flight engineer and loadmaster helped the aircraft commander manage the crew by keeping other members of his crew position informed of alert times and managing any problems their subordinates might have.

Each crew position had its responsibilities. The flight engineers and loadmasters had to be at the plane early to preflight and load the aircraft while the pilots had a leisurely breakfast and filed the flight plan. However, once airborne, the loadmaster mantra was "wheels up, feet up" and they were off duty until landing, perhaps eight hours away. For an oceanic night crossing, or a stressful landing in bad weather, the pilots had their turn to be front and center.

The loadmasters did occasionally cook scrumptious meals in the galley on long mission legs. Once, as I sat in the pilot seat as we flew back to Germany from Bahrain, I had long since eaten all the food I possessed and was starving. I had been told in my early days on the C-5 that you will someday not have enough food on a long mission and, once you experience this, you will never let it happen again. This was my one time. That is when I smelled German brats being cooked in the back. I thought about how badly I wanted one. I decided, if necessary, I would crawl back to the galley and hug the loadmaster's ankles if he would give me one. Fortunately, he came forward and asked if anyone wanted one. I ate the first one in three bites and then asked for another. Bless you, loadmasters!

While the "crew effort" statute applied to routine bag drags, the aircraft commander would find himself alone when a full colonel or general was displeased with some crewmember's actions, a prime example of which I will cover shortly. No matter who transgressed, the aircraft commander would have to answer for it personally with no one at his side. The standard joke demanded that this is why he got aircraft commander pay (there is no aircraft commander pay, of course).

There were instances where I brought the wrath on myself. A few times when I got off the crew bus at the BX, I would reach for my uniform hat I kept stowed in the calf pocket of my flight suit and make a distressing discovery. While I had slept in the bunk on the inbound leg, the hat had worked its way out of the pocket and was still there under the blanket on the aircraft. This meant I had to make the run from the bus to the BX door, hatless, while hoping to dear God I didn't run into someone who outranked me. Usually I made it, but once I got scolded by a local chief master sergeant who knew he had me dead to rights. Argh.

If an aircraft commander decided to request a crew duty day extension for some exigency, it was proper to ask the crew if anyone had a problem with his doing so. It is one thing for an A/C to volunteer his own time, but everyone else had to pay the extra time premium with him, so it was proper to ask. He might take the extension anyway, but only after explaining why he felt he had to do so.

Failing to observe crew etiquette rules could sour working relationships on long missions and develop negative attitudes toward you as a crewmember on a long-term basis in the crew force.

THE TRIP FROM HELL, 1983

One of my first missions as a C-5 aircraft commander spun into Alice's Wonderland on several levels at once, as if the gods were toying with me for their amusement.

At our first stop in Madrid, Spain, we lucked out and got one of the fanciest hotels downtown for crew rest. I didn't really care about the hotel because the mission from the States had been delayed and we landed just within our 24-hour crew duty day. As a new aircraft commander, I had found it more stressful than I would later, after I had more experience, and I wanted nothing but sleep.

The loadmasters, however, having slept most of the way over, were raring to head for the hotel bar, which they did without bothering to change out of their flight suits.

I had just gently sunk into a drugged-like sleep when the phone by my bed rang. Unaware of where I was, or even who I was at the moment, I answered.

"Sir! They won't listen to me!" shouted one of the loadmasters, a 55-year-old semi-alcoholic whose reputation was not yet known to me, but was about to be.

After a pause to gain my senses, I asked, *"Who won't listen to you? And who is this?"*

"Sergeant "Jones," sir. The hotel manager won't listen! I told him I didn't invite the girl to my room!" he again shouted, slurring his words as he did.

Now I woke up. This had red flags popping out all over it, and I dreaded, with good reason, hearing the details.

It seems Sgt. Jones had become pleasantly inebriated in the bar when a beautiful twenty-something Spanish woman approached him and began chit chatting.

I later asked Jones if he didn't see something wrong with this picture: you, a drunken, smelly, gray-haired 55-year-old being accosted by the most beautiful woman in the bar. Did you not find something amiss here, sergeant?

Eventually, the woman asked if she could accompany the loadmaster to his room. (Again I asked, later, "*Any alarm bells going off here?*") The loadmaster, apparently thinking he still "had it" with the ladies, finally asked her a question.

"*How much?*" he said.

Her answer, to be written in the hallowed annals of the Crew Debacle Hall of Fame, was "*Oh, for free!*" (I should have recalled my utter naiveté with nav wife in book one where I performed with similar cluelessness).

Once in his room, Sgt. Jones told the young lady to have a seat while he jumped into the shower to prepare for festivities. A few minutes later, with shampoo in his hair, he heard the outer room door slam. Now, belatedly, all became clear. Hopping around dripping with a towel around his waist, he discovered he had been relieved of all his valuables except his line badge: wallet, ID card, money, rings, almost everything gone.

Giving chase was out of the question. Oh, wait, no it wasn't! The hotel soon had a drunken, almost naked old man screaming up and down the hallway trying to recover his property from a woman already long gone from the premises.

This spectacle brought on the manager, and the phone call to me.

The next morning, to cover his shame and to attempt to blame the hotel for his utter stupidity, Sgt. Jones kicked in the ornate, beautifully carved wooden door of his room in retaliation for the injury the gods had inflicted upon him. Somehow we got out of the hotel without discovery of the damage.

But this rolling debacle was not over; it was only beginning. At the main gate to Torrejon AB outside Madrid, the Spanish gendarmes in their black triangular hats yanked Sgt. Jones off the bus for improper identification evidence, demanding an Air Force ID card instead of a line badge.

While this seemed richly deserved, it deprived me of a loadmaster, which took us down to "basic" crew status instead of "augmented." This meant we would have to spend the night in the desert instead of quick-turning and returning to Spain on a 24-hour augmented day as scheduled. Further, this meant I had to call home to my ops commander to explain why I had devolved into a basic crew. I had hoped to avoid explaining any of this to anyone to avoid mortification, but now I had to. I imagined the call.

"Hello, sir, I know as a new aircraft commander we haven't interacted much, but I have a problem here at Torrejon. It seems I lost total control of one of my crew and, ah…"

Eventually, with high-level phone calls from the States, we sprang Sgt. Jones from the Spanish police and proceeded on our way to Manama, Bahrain. However, this Magical Mystery Tour was still not over, not by half.

I had been to Bahrain a few times as a copilot, but as such I didn't really deal much with Mr. Bawa, the civilian station chief. Now, however, I had to coordinate with him directly for fuel and upload information. I think he was Pakistani and he spoke in the clipped British accent I'd find prevalent decades later, as most U.S. call centers had moved to the Indian subcontinent.

As I approached his counter, however, I found him in a contentious argument with an American in civilian clothes waving letter sized pages in one hand and protesting to Mr. Bawa about something. Mr. Bawa saw me in my flight suit and asked, speaking past the other man, if I was the A/C off the C-5. I said I was.

With that the man turned to me. He seemed about 50 years old and spoke with a familiar American accent. He read my name tag and said, *"Jay, this man won't let me on your plane. I am a retired Air Force colonel and flew F-4s in Vietnam; why can't I ride with you?"*

I looked to Mr. Bawa and asked what the problem might be. Mr. Bawa said the man did not have the correct papers to depart since he had been working as a contractor and did not have the proper departure documents. The colonel held up his letters he claimed were from a high government official that released him to exit the country.

Had I known then what I came to know later, I'd have told the colonel, *"Sorry, sir, but if Mr. Bawa says you don't have clearance to get on my plane, you can't get on my plane."* The fact that Mr. Bawa had a problem with this guy should have raised a big red flag with me, but it did not.

Instead, I told Mr. Bawa if the colonel had a valid retiree ID card, I didn't see a problem letting him on the plane. Mr. Bawa looked exasperated, but cleared the colonel to board. My faulty logic asked why a retired Vietnam veteran could not get on my C-5. I'd soon find out why.

After a four-hour turn time, the large aircraft tow vehicle slowly backed us out of the parking spot and on to the taxiway. When we parked they always brought us so far into the parking spot that it seemed our nose was almost against the window of the terminal building. This made it impossible to leave without a $5,000 tow job from the massive tow tug.

Having forgotten about the confrontation in front of Mr. Bawa, I advanced the throttles for takeoff as we rolled down the 12,000-foot desert runway. I always marveled that I could unleash a rumbling earthquake within the aircraft as the engines reached full power. I also found the song "Kyrie" by Mr. Mister captured the feeling of gaining the speed to lift three-quarters of a million pounds of aircraft and cargo into the sky. Once in the air I called for "gear up," and then at 1,000 feet called for "flaps up." That is when mayhem ensued.

The troop loadmaster, Sgt. "Jones" of "for free!" fame, piped up on interphone and said *"Pilot, troop!"* I thought to myself I was going to chew out Jones for interrupting during crucial departure procedures, but I told him to go ahead.

"Sir, you need to come back to troop immediately! A retired Air Force colonel and a Navy 0-5 are about to have a fistfight in the aisle!"

Oh, damn, I thought, the mystery colonel Mr. Bawa warned me about! What the hell is he doing back there? *"I'll be there shortly,"* I told troop. Once we had established our climb and were on autopilot, I moved the first pilot from the jump seat to my seat and headed for the troop compartment.

When I reached the top of the troop compartment stairs, Sgt. Jones told me the colonel called a seated Navy 0-5 a fat slob and a disgrace to the uniform. This brought the 0-5 out of his seat. Words were exchanged and a shoving match ensued. The colonel was now seated near the back of the compartment.

When I reached him, the colonel wasn't talking much and insisted nothing had happened, but his eyes were darting back and forth nervously. I thought, "*Oh…my…God, what have I done? I've let a lunatic on to my airplane!*" Sgt. Jones joined me and recited the incident for the colonel, who still was not defending himself or correcting the narrative. He knew the summoning of an aircraft commander shortly after takeoff meant real trouble.

It just so happened that sitting directly behind the colonel were three security policemen sent as augmentees to guard the airplane in Bahrain. These would later be termed "Raven Teams" and would often accompany us to the Middle East and Africa.

I called the lead sky cop forward to us. "*Sergeant,*" I directed him, "*I want you to sit next to this passenger. He is to go nowhere except the head, and is not to interact with any other passengers. Do you understand?*" He nodded that he did. I then looked at the colonel. "*Do you understand?*" He grudgingly nodded yes.

On the way back to the cockpit I told the Navy 0-5 that there should be no further trouble and to have the troop loadmaster notify me if there were.

That seemed to be the end of it, and the rest of the trip to Ramstein saw no further disruptions. I rejoiced that the episode was over…but it wasn't.

The next day after crew rest, we were nearly done with preflight chores on the Ramstein ramp. But a maintenance problem had put us behind our timeline and it would be dicey to achieve an on-time takeoff. As maintenance worked on the problem, I called the command post and told them to send the pax (passengers) in the hope the maintenance estimated-time-in-commission would be valid. If it was, we'd already have the pax on board and be ready to roll.

Shortly after the blue pax buses pulled up, the fiasco reignited. *"Pilot, troop!"* Sergeant Jones said, *"I'm not letting him on my plane, sir!"* The colonel had returned for the flight to the States. During crew rest, Jones had related further details that the colonel had been abusive to other passengers and had then tried to bribe Sgt. Jones to buy his silence about the issue. Jones did not want him back on board. Neither did I.

I called the command post and told them I was probably going to remove a retired colonel from the flight and I'd like 0-6 back up on scene. They said, *"You're going to do what?"* But they said they would send one.

I got out of the seat and headed down to the pax buses. Sgt. Jones was standing outside the first one so I knew where the colonel would be. I went up the first two entry steps and found him about two seats back. *"Colonel, could I have a word with you outside, please?"* He nodded and we went about ten feet from the door on the ramp.

Time was tight, now. I had to load the pax almost immediately to have a chance for an on-time takeoff and there was no sign of backup from the command post. I decided I'd reason with the colonel.

"Sir," I began, *"we had a big problem on the trip up here from Bahrain and I can't allow a repeat of that. If you will assure me that you will be on good behavior, I'll let you board, although Sgt. Jones wants me to deny you access. Do we have a deal?"*

The colonel's eyes narrowed and a sneer came across his face. *"Are you a reservist, captain?"* he asked.

"Yes, sir, I am." I said.

"I could tell," he said, *"because it is obvious your patriotism and dedication to this country are much less than the active duty."*

Total silence ensued. As I have said previously, I only lost my temper a handful of times in 33 years in the Air Force and, prior to this moment, only once. This would be the second.

I don't know what look came across my face, something akin to *"I think I'm going to deck you, you son of a bitch!"* Whatever it looked like, the colonel immediately snapped into a brace, as if a first-year "Doolie" at the Academy, looking straight ahead.

I stepped up to his side, speaking directly into his ear. *"If I hear one peep out of you on this trip, or Sgt. Jones has one ounce of trouble with you, I'll have you arrested on landing. Do you understand?"*

He understood, but he said nothing and kept staring straight ahead. I wheeled and headed for the troop compartment where the sky cops were already seated. I gave them their marching orders of zero tolerance for the colonel and that they had my order to place him under arrest if he transgressed.

Thankfully, for all concerned, the colonel behaved like a choir boy the rest of the way.

Mr. Bawa informed me, on a subsequent trip, that the colonel had skipped the country without paying a $3,000 hotel bill and that proof of payment is what he lacked in the initial confrontation, resolved, stupidly and cluelessly, by me.

For the next twenty years I would joke with Mr. Bawa on the inbound call that I had that colonel on board. He would joke, in return, that the colonel would be on my aircraft for departure.

The colonel did come back to Bahrain, according to Bawa, and got promptly arrested for his past arrears. I never saw him again.

Crew Drunk at Alert

It is aggravating enough to take heat for your mistakes, but also aggravating to pay for mistakes falsely attributed to you. For crews on the road, this often meant actions falsely stuck on you by command post controllers when you were not around to defend yourself.

Rhein-Main AB (Frankfurt, Germany) delivered my favorite example, one I have provided to generations of pilot trainees.

A Dover reserve C-5 aircraft commander, Billy D., got what he thought was his 1000L alert call to proceed on a mission to the desert. The command post controller had a different message, however. He said the plane was A-3 (un-flyable) for a part they didn't have. This would require that the part be driven over from Ramstein. He put the crew back in to 12 hours' crew rest for a 2200L alert.

Billy D. turned to his crew and gave them the news. Abruptly, three enlisted crew members popped beers and began drinking despite the early hour. Billy found this bizarre and asked why these enlisted were drinking at 1000 hours? They said it was just a policy of theirs.

Thirty minutes later, Frankfurt maintenance miraculously found the part to fix the plane. The command post controller called Billy D. back to see if he would take the alert and move the mission. Billy apologized and said he would take the alert except three of his crew had already had a beer. Infuriated, the command post controller put the crew back into crew rest.

Shortly thereafter, someone of high rank saw Billy's A-1 aircraft inexplicably in delay and demanded to know why this important mission was not moving. Who was responsible for this unacceptable lapse? Cracking under the pressure, the command post controller blurted out that the crew had been drunk at alert, so he had to put them back to bed. This was mildly plausible for the second alert call, but not for the first.

The general, of course, went ballistic at this news and torched the phone lines, in all likelihood, through MAC headquarters and down to the Dover reserve wing commander, who owned this crew.

Such situations are a valuable "press-to-test" moment for local commanders to see if they have the integrity to take the heat for their crews as, initially, they must. Most find this difficult, however, under scathing verbal assault from flag rank.

The general probably assumed the drunk-at-alert charge to be true and, also, probably demanded at a high decibel level to know what the wing commander was going to do about it.

Unworthy commanders fold like a tent under this pressure and go to great lengths about the torture and punishment they will inflict on the crew: boiled in oil, castrated, heads on pikes! These weak leaders throw the crew into the volcano to avoid a similar fate from a bellowing three-star.

Worthy commanders, however, do not immediately sacrifice their crew. They might say they will take stern action if the charge is true, but they insist on doing nothing until they have talked to their crew. For Billy this proved impossible because he was back in 12 hours of crew rest and could not be disturbed, lest the mission be delayed again.

An unworthy three-star might then demand to know if the wing commander thought it permissible to be drunk at alert; is that what he was saying? (This inflicts a faulty dilemma on the wing commander. Either you vow punishment or you therefore, theoretically, approve of being drunk at alert).

And again, at risk of his command, the worthy wing commander would hold his ground and inform the general that he never judges a crew until he has their side of the story. *"We do want to provide due process, don't we, sir?"* he might say.

If Billy had any inkling he had been knifed by the command post, he could easily have called home to explain, but such a possibility was beyond credulity, so for 12 hours his crew was, incredibly, "the crew drunk at alert."

COPILOT FRED

One of the 709th pilots I encountered as a new aircraft commander presented me with a perplexing challenge. In my nine months or so as a C-5 copilot, "Fred" was just another copilot with one peculiarity; he was a lieutenant colonel. Ordinarily one must be an aircraft commander to reach the rank of lieutenant colonel in the reserves, and yet here he was, an anomaly.

I did not get an explanation for this unusual combination of rank and crew position until I had been an A/C for a few months in 1983. On a stateside mission that would transit several southeast bases, Fred wound up on the schedule as my copilot.

The day before the mission, the scheduler pulled me aside and gave me a briefing he had given other relatively new A/Cs who did not know Fred's history. After two lengthy attempts at upgrade to A/C, Fred had finally upgraded. This proved short-lived, however, and he was soon demoted back to copilot. It did allow him to get promoted, but when downgraded, he was told he would not be upgraded again. He was copilot for life until he got his twenty "good" years for retirement.

After explaining this to me, the scheduler gave me a warning: do not let Fred into the left seat. Usually, for an experienced copilot, I would alternate seat positions with him on mission segments to provide him experience in the left seat, mainly to practice taxiing the aircraft with the steering wheel on the pilot's horizontal panel by his left knee. But now I had been warned not to use this procedure with Fred.

Fred performed superbly on the first three days of this four-day mission. He was easily the best copilot I had flown with. He was thorough, precise, and way ahead of his duties without needing direction. I thought perhaps the scheduler had been overly alarmist; Fred was fantastic! I told him he could fly left seat for the next segment to Beaufort MCAS, SC.

Why didn't I listen to the scheduler!

When we landed at Beaufort we had to navigate a dicey taxi route to our parking location. As we approached the parking pad, we had to taxi up a fairly steep grade and maneuver between two obstacles, a hangar construction project off our right wing, and a row of F-4 fighters parked off our left wing.

Maintenance had provided a spotter on each wing to advise us of our clearance as we slowly taxied by the obstacles.

I told Fred to keep an eye on the F-4s and I'd watch our wing tip clearance on the construction project. That meant I had my eyes on the right wing tip and the steel girders of the hangar project.

Fred advanced the power slightly to start up the hill on the taxiway. I started assuring him we had room on the right if he needed it. Then, suddenly, and without warning, Fred shoved the throttles up about 300% of the power needed and the plane shot forward through the narrow passage between the two obstacles we had to thread. By the time I gasped and looked to the left to see if we had clearance on the nearest F-4, it was too late; we had already shot the gap and arrived on the parking pad. I had no idea if we had cleared the F-4s or caught one with our left wing tip. Whatever had happened, there was nothing I could do about it now.

We shut down and I scrambled down the crew ladder to see if I had to survey damage to the aircraft and my flying career if we had hit the F-4. I ran toward the left wing tip and saw the left wing spotter staggering toward me with his hands on his temples in disbelief. I asked him how close a call it had been on the tail of the nearest F-4. He raised his hands, one over the other, showing the wing tip had missed the F-4 tail by about two feet passing directly over it. I almost walked to the grass next to the ramp to throw up at what a close call this had been.

I waited until dinner to confront Fred. I asked him how close he thought we had come to hitting the nearest F-4 during taxi. He waved away with his hand the possibility, as he estimated we easily had the twenty-foot minimum clearance. We had good clearance, he insisted.

"*Fred,*" I said, "*our wing tip cleared the F-4 tail by two feet according to the scanner you obviously were not looking at when you shoved the power up. What were you thinking? Do you know what the repercussions of hitting that plane would have been?"* He refused to believe it could have been that close despite me assuring him that is what the spotter had said.

Never again did I let Fred into the left seat when he flew on my crew, but other Fred idiosyncrasies revealed themselves over the years even as I consigned him to the right seat.

About a year later we alerted at Ramstein for a downrange mission. Everyone showed up for the bus except Fred. I asked if anyone had any idea where he might be. One of the loads offered that Fred had said he wanted to visit the commissary to stock up for the mission, something he was famous for doing. He would carry enough food in his helmet bag to feed a small town, all to ensure he would never be hungry.

I dropped the loads and engineers at the plane and copilot at base operations to begin mission planning while I took the bus to find Fred. Sure enough, I found him leisurely walking the commissary aisles with a half-full shopping cart.

"Ah, Fred, what are you doing?" I asked. *"We alerted twenty minutes ago and you weren't there."*

He said he must have misunderstood the alert time, but he was almost done. I corrected him and told him he *was* done and to check out immediately, get on the bus, drop me off at base ops and take the bus to get his things. I marveled that I had become a babysitter for a lieutenant colonel. Very strange.

DOUBLE DOSE DISASTER

In late 1983 I upgraded to Instructor Pilot and got to do so locally at Dover rather than returning to Altus, again because I had already been a B-52 IP. A few months later, near disaster visited.

In Air Force safety school, we learned that many accidents progress through a series of steps, perhaps as many as seven individual events, which culminate in a disaster. However, if any one of those events does not occur, the disaster may be avoided.

As I listened to this I decided that when I saw the event chain forming, I would simply not commit the next error and that would save me. Chain broken, disaster averted.

Except I discovered that is not how it works. In some cases, all events except the last catastrophic one have already occurred before you recognize a sequence has been built. You are already on the brink of disaster when you become aware of danger.

In other cases, the events progress without your input; the chain is built as a chess opponent may slowly force a checkmate on you.

This disaster would be the second type, a slowly building set of circumstances beyond my control that put me in dire aircraft emergency, and political trouble. Unknown at the time, this event would take fifteen years to come full circle and conclude.

The first event in the chain arrived on a bright sunny day in 1984 about halfway across the Atlantic, at 30 degrees west longitude, enroute to Dover from Ramstein, Germany. The flight engineer announced engine #1 was slowly losing oil pressure. If the current rate continued, he said, we'd have to shut it down in about five minutes.

Well, good, I had five minutes to parse this, I thought. Once we shut down the engine, we would not be able to maintain our four-engine cruise altitude, so I'd have to get a clearance to a three-engine altitude. I asked the engineer to figure it. He came back with FL 270 from our current altitude of FL 330.

I then asked him to figure our fuel burn at FL 270 and our range; could we make Dover at that flight level, which would burn fuel at a higher rate than FL 330? A few minutes later he said we could just make Dover but with no extra.

OK, good, now what was the weather forecast for Dover? If it were bad, I'd have to land short somewhere since I didn't have the fuel for an extended instrument approach or possible missed approach and divert. Although I checked again, I knew Dover's forecast was clear and million visibility, so I decided we could proceed to this, our scheduled destination.

There was a wild-card complicating factor, however. We had the new Dover active duty, vice wing commander traveling back to Dover with us. Col. "Bossman," as I will call him, had flown the jump seat for takeoff and would again for landing. There is always a potential problem mixing active duty and reserve on the same crew. If something goes wrong, each faction will retreat to its corner and attempt to cast blame on the other. I had not anticipated any friction but I got it, in spades, after the coming events unfolded, some of the criticism fair, some not.

The oil pressure kept falling. We shut down #1 and began a slow descent to FL 270 that we coordinated with oceanic clearance prior to the shutdown. I thought this would be the end of it. We'd arrive, I'd fly a visual three-engine approach, and that would be it.

Several hours later we checked in with Dover approach control with 22,000 pounds of gas, which sounds like a lot, but is not. A rule of thumb says your gear should come down at 20,000 pounds because you will shortly be landing, somewhere. At 16,000 pounds the fuel gauges become unreliable and flameouts may occur. Approach control vectored us to a visual base leg for Runway 01. Once there I called for "Flaps 40, gear down."

The C-5 gear extension sequence is somewhat convoluted. The main gear must extend and rotate after it comes out of the fuselage. The cockpit gear indicators go: barber pole (gear extending), red wheels (gear is down), green wheels (gear has rotated to forward rolling) when they are fully down and aligned. The nose gear, similarly, shows barber pole when the gear doors open, red wheels as it extends, and green wheels when it is down. The nose wheel does not rotate as the mains do.

For this extension, our nose gear progressively showed: barber pole, red wheels, green wheels, barber pole. By this indication the gear was stuck in some intermediate position, not down and locked.

This was most unwelcome. I was already down to minimum fuel on three engines and this stuck yet another item on the chain of events building toward a possible calamity. I called the tower and asked if they could see our nose gear clearly enough to confirm if it was down. They could not. I told them I would go around and could they send the Supervisor of Flying to the runway to report the position of the nose gear on our next approach.

I began mentally reviewing similar, infamous past air disasters, two in particular. The first was a United Airlines crash on approach to Portland, Oregon, where the crew briefed and rebriefed the possible crash landing and, as a result of the briefing delay, ran out of fuel before they reached the runway. The second was the Eastern Airlines Everglades crash in Miami where all three cockpit crew members tried to fix a possibly malfunctioning gear-down indicator light while the plane was on autopilot. One of the crew inadvertently disconnected the autopilot without anyone realizing it and the plane slowly descended and crashed into the Everglades. No one was flying the plane.

Considering the Everglades crash, I told the copilot I would fly the aircraft because we were on three engines, while he ran the checklist with the engineers. As a previous C-5 instructor pilot, he seemed well suited to do this.

On the radar downwind, as per the checklist for an unreliable nose gear, we sent the scanner down to view the gear through the visual viewing scope in the cargo compartment. This consisted of a long tube attached to a video port that is aimed at a crucial component of the nose gear. As we prepared to turn base leg, the scanner came back with the startling report that the nose gear was sideways in the wheel well! Yet another event in the chain. *"Sideways?"* I said. *"It can't be sideways; the nose gear doesn't rotate!"* The scanner insisted that it was sideways. The fight engineer suggested we send the crew chief down to have a look, so he went.

On base, the tower said they could not find the Supervisor of Flying. He had apparently gone to get his burger at the bowling alley, or gone home to let his dogs out, or something, but he could not be located. I told tower we would do yet another go-around while we completed checklists.

Col. Bossman observed all this silently from the jump seat, except to remind us to bring the flaps up on the second go-around since we had begun arguing about the proper course of action and had forgotten to do so. Score one for Bossman.

On this third downwind we had now gone below 16,000 pounds of gas and voices on interphone were becoming tense. The scanner came back up on interphone and said the crew chief agreed that the nose gear was sideways. The copilot asked if maybe the viewing scope was twisted instead of the gear? (This proved to be the problem; the nose gear was properly down the entire time. The twisted scope made the gear appear sideways.) The scanner insisted that was not the problem. He was wrong, the crucial error. I had to proceed on the assumption he might be correct. If I'd had time, I'd have sent the flight engineer, the more experienced of the two, to perform as the scanner, but I had no time.

Although I had already declared an emergency for a three-engine landing, I told the tower we now might have to land with an unreliable nose gear in addition. I told him we would proceed to the final approach fix for Runway 01, Pesky intersection, and hold while we ran further checklists.

"*Wheels up, Crash Landing Checklist,*" I said while proceeding five miles to Pesky. I shuddered as I called for that. While I had some familiarity with the checklist, it was a dozen items long with several decision trees to be navigated and I had never delved deeply into it; I presumed I would have time to make those decisions. Now I would get to delve quickly…with three engines, no gas, and no time.

As the checklist proceeded, with the troop compartment briefing the 73 passengers on crash landing procedures, I got to shoot from the hip on several checklist issues until, finally, we got to "Hatches—removed." For a true crash landing, impact could twist the fuselage, jamming the hatches shut. "*Should we pull the hatches?*" the troop compartment asked in a voice an octave higher than normal. Pulling the hatches would make communication difficult, as the open hatches would howl in the slipstream.

"*How much gas do we have, engineer?*" I asked. He responded with 12,000 pounds.

Recalling the Portland crash, I decided that was it—we had to land, as is, before we started flaming out engines. "*No, don't pull the hatches. Stop the checklist, we are going to land, now,*" I said.

As we approached the runway I mentally reviewed the landing technique for such a situation. You hold the nose gear off the runway, but not until it stalls, since that would cause it to drop heavily to the concrete. As you slow after touchdown, and before the nose stalls, you fly the nose gear down to the runway for a gentle touchdown. If the gear really was sideways, that is where direction problems would become evident.

That is what I did after touchdown, I flew the nose gear to the runway; it touched down and seemed normal. Thinking we were fully down on the nose gear, I released back pressure on the yoke. However, I had been flying the nose gear up to that point, and when I released the yoke, the nose fell rapidly and banged hard against the shock strut. This made it seem the nose gear might have collapsed, and I reported that to the command post. Soon, however, the smooth rollout indicated the nose gear was normal, so I canceled the collapsed gear judgment.

We taxied to parking and ran through our checklists. When we deplaned, the colonel had a staff car waiting. He shook my hand, told me "*good job,*" and said all he could think of that I might have done was try to steer the nose gear with the steering wheel. That might have helped, but he didn't mention it while we were in the air. With that, he disappeared into his staff car and left.

This was a Friday. By Monday, hell had broken loose. My ops officer called to ask what the hell we had done to Col. Bossman, that he told the combined staff standup that he wanted the entire crew busted for their emergency performance on our flight.

It seems he huddled with his stan/eval crews over the weekend to "Monday morning quarterback" our actions on the nose gear. While I anticipated the novice scanner would get Q-3ed (Qual Level 3, or busted), I didn't see any justification for hanging the rest of the crew, and I never did hear directly what the charges might have been. Also, Bossman conveniently excluded himself as part of the crew.

I got some idea of the standup discussion when my ops officer began grilling me for information.

"*Why were you flying the plane instead of running the emergency checklist as aircraft commander?*" he asked.

"*Because I was on three engines and I wanted to fly it,*" I responded. "*Besides, Lloyd, the copilot, was an ex-instructor and I was listening while flying.*"

"*Why didn't you send the more experienced engineer down to view the gear?*" he continued.

"*Because I didn't have time,*" I replied, "*I was out of gas and I had already sent the crew chief down for a second opinion.*"

The issue between the reserve and active duty wings continued to broil over the next few days. During that time, one of the active duty colonels, not Col. Bossman, committed a sacrilege, in my view. He told the combined standup that he would not let his family fly on any aircraft I commanded. Ah, internecine warfare at its most ugly. At this point, apparently, my wing staff raised the bullshit flag and called the active duty wing on its overboard reaction. Cooler heads prevailed and the compromise solution would be for a numbered Air Force active duty evaluator to give me Instructor Pilot check on a local training ride. A week later that happened. The check pilot debriefed me, saying: you did fine, no problems, Q-1.

In a small modicum of integrity, the colonel who slammed me at standup after the incident stood and retracted the charge six months later, saying he had been mistaken in his judgment. Or, at least, that is what my wing staff told me.

Reflecting on the airborne incident, I did have a critique of myself. As I began making decisions, I ill-advisedly conjured up a review board in my mind second-guessing my decisions after the fact. Why didn't you run this or that checklist, why didn't you consider this, or that? Why didn't you finish all the checklists before landing?

In retrospect, I should have done what I thought would safely recover the aircraft regardless of crossing all T's and dotting all I's. Had I insisted on finishing the crash landing checklist I might have flamed out the engines. Then the phantom review board would demand to know why I flamed out the engines!

Another planning error on my part was assuming I'd have lots of time to parse the crash landing checklist and discuss all options with the crew if it ever became necessary. I never thought I'd call for the checklist with only 16,000 pounds, and 10 minutes, of fuel remaining.

I also generated ire toward the Monday morning quarterbacks who would sit in judgment of my actions. Often they would be staff officers who rarely exposed themselves to adversity on the line. They, who rarely ventured onto the field, would sit in haughty judgment of those of us who, as Teddy Roosevelt said, came off the field, bloodied. From the safety of their staff positions, they would judge me with their well-honed twenty-twenty hindsight. They would evaluate, after hours of group deliberation and consultation with manuals, decisions I had to make in minutes or seconds while flying a three-engine airplane.

This does not excuse me from errors I might have made. I'm still responsible for my actions, but the yardstick to judge me should consider the stress and time constraints I had to work under. I bristle when the staffers roll their eyes to ask why I didn't perform the perfect actions they arrived at after hours of discussion.

Col. Bossman soon became wing commander for a significant stint at Dover before moving onward and upward in rank. Two episodes typify his tenure.

In 1985 we had a major higher headquarters inspection scheduled. In standard preparation for it, the base warned everyone to tighten up their uniform standards to impress the inspectors. I had seen this prep in several different forms. Usually it demanded a mandatory commander's call where the wing commander would cajole and threaten his troops to shape up. He would then drive around base finding slackers to pillory as examples along with their commanders.

Col. Bossman had a different method, however. One day in the BX he stood in line behind a senior reserve technician dressed in his blue pants and blue short-sleeved uniform shirt. After a few moments he asked the technician, Butch Sanders, if he could have a word with him.

"*Are you aware you are out of uniform, major?*" he asked.

Sanders glanced his uniform over, saw nothing improper, and responded, "*No, sir, I don't know what I might have overlooked.*"

"*Your back pants pocket is unbuttoned,*" the colonel said.

Sanders froze to avoid laughing at the ridiculousness of the complaint. "*Sorry, sir, I'll try not to overlook that in the future.*"

When he got back to the squadron, Sanders erupted in the scheduling office. "*I cannot believe what that asshole Bossman did to me at the BX!*" He then recounted the episode to anyone and everyone who would listen. The incident spread rapidly and widely throughout both reserve squadrons, at all levels, the outrage growing with each telling.

I heard the second or third telling and I found it confirmed my previous opinion of Bossman as a prime asshole. Yes, he was! This confirmed it. But, then…I glanced down and noticed my flight suit's left breast pocket zipper was open. I quickly closed it. After I did, I further noticed that the zipper handle dangled loosely, so I tucked it into the fabric channel over the zipper.

As I did this, I froze with my fingers stuck on the zipper. Bossman might be a prime asshole, but a brilliant one, I realized. With this one, tacitly ridiculous, BX episode he had far more effectively shaped up the troops than if he had driven around base yelling at everyone. The pettiness of his complaint ensured the story would be repeated in every office, and the result would be just as it was with me, a subconscious, stringent review of my uniform standards even as I was cursing Bossman. *"You magnificent bastard,"* I thought, paraphrasing Gen. Patton's WWII comment on German Gen. Rommel.

The second episode spawned a tragic episode that may or may not have resulted from a signature Bossman policy.

That policy had become a wing motto advertised on banners and base publications: "Aggressively safe in all we do." This struck me as having our cake and aggressively eating it too, with the emphasis on "aggressive," not on safe.

The incident I'm about to relate came to me second-hand, and I cannot certify the veracity of each component, but it will be close to actual events as related by a reserve ramp worker who witnessed it. (As reported to me by Gary Grimes, aero port reservist working the ramp that night.)

Col. Bossman was aboard this mission aircraft parked on the Dover ramp. The crew was pressing for an on-time takeoff, but had endured maintenance problems, and making that takeoff looked improbable. However, they had gotten the plane fixed and the passenger agents had loaded the passengers up the tall stairs into the troop compartment.

The ground crew now had to get the stairs and crew buses off the parking area so the crew could start the engines and taxi for takeoff. The stair truck retracted the stairs into the stowed position as the ground crew stowed the large hydraulic legs that raised the stair truck off the ground and stabilized it for stair extension. The ramp observer reported they were frantic to clear the ramp to allow for an on-time takeoff with Col. Bossman on board.

The stair truck driver waited impatiently for the legs to be stowed, and finally, it seemed they had been. He backed from the plane in a turn, stopped, and put the transmission into "drive." As he did this, one of the legs had not been properly secured and swung away from the truck. A female truck team member, newly out of tech school, saw this and leapt to the side of the truck to reseat the latch. As she did so, the truck lurched into motion, knocking her under the rear wheels and running over her midsection.

There was a flight surgeon on the plane, apparently, and he soon arrived at her side, as did Col. Bossman from the cockpit. Although still alive, the female had been mortally injured and there was nothing the flight surgeon could do for her. Col. Bossman reportedly walked over to the nose gear tires and vomited. Apparently MAC generals did not connect his "aggressively safe" policy with this incident and it did not impede his promotion potential.

Fifteen years later Col. Bossman and I would encounter each other again, indirectly. That would lead to my first appearance opposite the Air Force on the CBS News program *60 Minutes* with Lesley Stahl. Book three will outline this Dover story, coming full circle, where I would be the Monday morning quarterback who had previously made the correct call as a safety officer. Failure to follow my admonition to the command to procure a specific type of equipment to avoid midair collisions resulted in a midair collision off of Africa between a German cargo plane and an Air Force C-141. Colonel, now Four-Star General, Bossman would stonewall *60 Minutes* on the issue I had raised. He would default to others to explain his judgment for failing to procure the equipment I warned we needed. I had outlined this imperative in multiple letters to the command.

This time, Bossman's rear pocket was unbuttoned.

WING DINING OUT

In 1985 we had a wing Dining Out, where wives could attend, as opposed to a Dining In, where it was wing members only. These formal dinners have rules and formalities, and I warned Bea that she must be on her best behavior and protocol because all commanders would be judging me and her. She said she understood.

We sat at a table with my current squadron commander and two of my future squadron commanders and their wives. After many rounds of drinks, two of the other wives decided to crawl around under our table in their formal dresses, giggling and laughing, while the guest speaker was at the podium. Bea elbowed me and asked if this was the type of transgression she was supposed to avoid, the actions my superiors' wives were taking under the table? I frowned and said, "*Ahhh, well, yes, that is what I was talking about. I guess you were not the one who needed counseling, dear.*"

THE FORSYTHE SAGA

Two missions, separated by about three weeks in 1986, provide a marvelous glimpse of how MAC missions interlocked over time in curious ways. This would not be as momentous as the 1984 nose gear episode proved to be, but would be fascinating nonetheless.

The first crucial mission segment started in Aviano AB, Italy at the base of the Alps. When I walked out of the billeting (now lodging) office, a sheer rock wall a thousand feet high rose before me, the result of the Italian peninsula of the African plate slamming into the European plate over the previous million years or so.

This segment did not start well. We showed up at base ops at 0430 to find it closed. Closed? We scouted around for a phone to call the command post to suggest perhaps they could find someone to open up for us? You know, for the mission? I realized the local fighter boys generally worked banker's hours, but we flew for the "Midnight Air Command" (MAC), so we needed service before 0600.

And this was not an ordinary mission. This scheduled leg sent us to a classified destination (XXXX) in Africa, which turned out to be a secret airfield in the Egyptian desert west of Cairo, for joint exercise with the Egyptians. Someone would not be happy if we showed up late because base ops was not open for us to file our flight plan.

We hustled the preflight, missed breakfast, and took off an hour late. This lack of support put me in a grumpy mood, a mood that would get grumpier.

I can't remember just how we filed to a secret destination; I think we just put four X's for a landing base, which, of course, had air traffic control demanding to know where we were going. Rubbing my forehead, I explained that I could not tell him where we were going and that I would cancel my clearance and go VFR at a specific reporting point, El Daba, once we got into Egyptian airspace. The controller wasn't happy, but accepted the plan.

The grand secret exercise seemed a routine landing and equipment download on an austere desert airstrip in the middle of a large barren valley. I suppose we didn't want to advertise our training with the Egyptians, but I wasn't sure who would be mad, or which of us they would be mad at. If it was Israel, they'd be mad at both of us.

After four hours we took off and headed northwest for a six-hour flight to Mildenhall AB, England for crew rest. My grump meter spiked again when the Mildenhall command post said available local area billeting was nonexistent. We'd have to bus thirty minutes to Ely and suffer minimum crew rest with no credit for the trip to and from Ely.

I called 21st Air Force at McGuire and requested an extra hour of crew rest to make up for the round-trip time for Ely. I added we'd had a long frustrating day and I really needed that extra hour for the crew.

The controller, probably a colonel's favorite major, sounded as if he didn't want to grant the hour. I told him if the hour were refused, I wanted to know who said no, and I would call back after we got to Ely. When I called from Ely, he said the hour extension was not approved. I said, "*Who denied it?*"

He said, "*Col. Forsythe, because you will be carrying high priority cargo on the leg back to the States.*"

I feel sure Col. Forsythe had not been informed of my request, and Maj. Hot Shot merely invoked the colonel's authority to deny it so he wouldn't have to coordinate anything to make it happen. Once he invoked Forsythe, however, it was game over. I walked into the hotel dining room in Ely and broke the bad news to the crew, no extension, go to bed.

The next morning at the command post window, my curiosity demanded I ask just what this high priority cargo might be. The controller looked at his sheet and said, "PCS household goods." That prick, I thought of Maj. Hot Shot at 21st. This is not priority cargo. I've been had.

But there was nothing I could do about it, so pressed on with the flight back to the States and chalked it up to getting screwed by the system once again with no recourse. I could not know that fate would allow me to get even just three weeks later.

This follow-on mission had me flying from Europe, empty, to the island of Grenada in the Caribbean. President Reagan was giving a morning speech at the airport there commemorating our "heroic" victory three years earlier. I wouldn't get there until well after the speech, but that didn't matter because my mission was to retrieve all the port-o-johns used for the ceremony and to return them to Charleston AFB, SC. We would then quick-turn Charleston and proceed to Andrews AFB, MD to drop off the Air Force band that had performed for the Grenada ceremony.

We arrived on the island in the afternoon to find a load team from the 89th MAS, presidential support out of Andrews, ready to start loading the potties. A crusty, curt, impatient Senior Master Sergeant (SMS) was in charge and he immediately began issuing orders to my loadmasters as if this were his airplane. I found that out later.

The estimated load time was three hours, so I asked if there was a restaurant in the area. One of the Andrews loaders said yes, right on that hill over there outside the airport. I told him the pilot team would be there and we'd be back before the load was complete.

Arriving at the restaurant, a quaint Caribbean bistro with bead curtains for doors located halfway up the side of a large hill, I could see the aircraft on the airport ramp about a mile away with its nose section raised for loading. We enjoyed a leisurely meal and headed back to the plane, whose nose was still raised when we arrived. It seemed the loading was not going well, and the Andrews SMS was not happy. We were going to suffer a late takeoff due to excess loading time and he would have to explain that.

Finally, we did launch at sunset for Charleston for a quick turn to download the potties and then on to Andrews to return the band and the Andrews 89th loading team. Enroute to Charleston, however, it became clear our crew duty day would run out before we could reach Andrews. Also, a horrendous ice storm had hit DC, which meant we couldn't get in there anyway. I called 21st and said we'd like to crew rest in Charleston because our crew duty day was up and Washington was iced in.

For some imperative reason, the band had to get back to DC that night and 21st had its hair on fire to make this happen. They requested that we ask for a crew duty day extension, that they would gladly approve, and said the ice storm would have left the city by the time we got there.

I recalled getting needlessly stiffed by 21st three weeks earlier when I wanted a favor from them, and now they wanted a favor from me. I began to sense the stars aligning for me.

"*Who wants me to extend my crew duty day?*" I asked.

"*Colonel Forsythe,*" the controller said.

Well, ho, ho, ho, I thought. I now got to turn the cannon around on 21st. After discussing the extension with the crew, I answered.

"21st," I said on the radio, *"I'm going to request that extension for you and complete the mission, but I want you to realize three weeks ago, when I asked for a crew rest extension at Mildenhall that I really needed, you disapproved it unnecessarily. I'm going to work with you on this, but you have to recognize you must play ball with the crews when they need it if you want them to play ball with you when you need it."*

A long pause ensued on the radio.

When the controller returned on the HF frequency, he fawned all over me and said Col. Forsythe really appreciated my effort and understood my position and was sure they could work well with crews in the future and thank you for bringing this to his attention.

I hoped Forsythe might ream Maj. Hot Shot for stiffing me at Mildenhall, but that probably didn't happen. At least Forsythe knew I was saving his bacon for the late takeoff that would have prevented the band from returning to Andrews for whatever the imperative situation was. I saw it as a small victory, but did not know how crucial it would be.

We arrived at Andrews around midnight and less than an hour after the ice storm had left the area. As we descended below the 10,000-foot cloud deck, the entire world seemed made of crystal with ice coating everything. The lights of the capitol caused everything surrounding them to shimmer and sparkle. It would be a power line disaster for much of the East Coast, but from our vantage point provided a spectacularly beautiful sight.

The next day we returned to Dover to find the entire state of Delaware shut down, power out and roads nearly impassable. It would be several days before I could return to the squadron, but when I did I had an unwelcome surprise waiting for me.

The ops officer said the command headquarters at Scott AFB, IL had received a letter of complaint from the 89th SMS on the load team at Grenada.

It assigned blame for the late takeoff on the C-5 pilots who left on an island sight-seeing tour and returned too late to make an on-time takeoff.

As I started to rise out of my chair in a volcanic eruption, the ops officer held up his hand to caution me to wait a moment. He then said he had another, personal letter of appreciation from Col. Forsythe, 21st ops commander, thanking me for extending my day to complete an important mission. The colonel trumped the SMS and I was off the hook.

I told the ops officer to relay to Scott AFB that I could see the raised nose of the C-5 at all times from the restaurant, which meant loading was still in progress and could have returned immediately had I seen it lowered. We had returned to the plane before the nose came down, so the SMS story was bogus. I don't know if the SMS had to pay for the fabrication or not, but my gambit to shame 21st had paid off and saved me.

ENCOUNTERING THE 89TH MAS, PRESIDENTIAL SUPPORT, AGAIN

I interacted again with the 89th out of Andrews a few months later while they were providing presidential support, separately from our mission, in Spain. This encounter also ended badly. The 89th squadron seemed to think they could invoke special privilege due to their White House connection.

The episode occurred at Torrejon AB, Spain in 1987 in the large billeting complex. My C-5 crew and I had endured a long day and had another long day coming up. We arrived late in the afternoon and were due for alert at 0400 the next morning. Most of our rooms were located on one wing of the large billeting complex.

About 2300, and an hour after I had tried to go to sleep, a party had started two doors down, right in the middle of my crewmembers' rooms on the hallway. I waited about twenty minutes for the partiers to self-police themselves since they were violating quiet hours—and also testing my patience with their revelry. Someone in that room should know better, I thought.

Finally, I'd had enough. As the aircraft commander, it was my responsibility to put an end to this for the good of the rest of the crew.

I put on my flight suit and walked down the hall. I knocked politely on the door. A smooth-talking, probable American embassy political operative answered the door. There were about twenty people crowded into the room, a few in flight suits and several civilian women in party dresses, probably embassy staff.

"I'm sorry," I began, *"but my crew and I are in all the rooms surrounding this one and we have to get up in five hours for a long crew day. Could you take the party somewhere else? We'd appreciate a little consideration on this."*

Mr. Smoothie told me he understood and they would curtail the noise, and thanked me for telling him. I was unsure if he was reassuring me, or patronizing me as a mere crew dog.

I got back to my room and waited for the noise to abate. Fifteen minutes later the noise had not dropped one decibel. At the twenty-minute point, my fuse blew.

I donned my flight suit once again, stalked down the hall, swung square to the door, and pounded it three times. The party noise stopped.

Mr. Smoothie opened the door and I stepped in.

I obviously did not have my happy face on. One of the women in a party dress seated on a couch facing the door took one look at me, got very wide eyes, pulled her overcoat over her head in terror and cowered against the armrest. While that was the effect I wanted, I had to fight off the urge to roll on the floor laughing.

Mr. Smoothie started to speak, but I cut him off and pointed at two young enlisted crewmembers in flight suits against the back wall, the only two identifiable as part of a crew, that I did not yet know belonged to the 89th.

"*You two, you know the crew rest rules, why are you participating in this?*" They looked at each other with stricken visages and said nothing.

"*Who is your aircraft commander?*" I demanded. Again they said nothing, but the anticipation of what was coming seemed to terrify them.

"*You don't have an aircraft commander? I think you do and I'll let him deal with you in the morning.*"

I turned to Mr. Smoothie. "*I want all of you out of here or we can discuss it with the base commander right now.*" He nodded his head and said nothing. I left, and shortly thereafter, so did the party-goers.

At 0445, just before I took my bags out front for our bus, I asked the billeting clerk several questions: who was in room 204, which crew were they on, and what room was their aircraft commander in. That's when I discovered a lieutenant colonel commanded this 89th aircrew.

Their commander outranked me, so I felt some trepidation for what I was about to do, but if positions were reversed, this is what I would want "me" to do. I walked down the hall, around the corner, and knocked gently on the 89th aircrew's aircraft commander's door. It took about 30 seconds, but he cracked the door open and said, "*Yes?*"

I said I really apologized for doing this, but members of his crew had kept my crew awake partying on our hallway until close to midnight.

He frowned and looked like he was grinding his teeth. I awaited his reaction, realizing it was possible he'd unload on me for violating *his* crew rest.

"*What…room…was…it?*" he asked. Room 204, I answered. He said slowly and deliberately, "*I will handle this. Thank you, and I apologize for what my crew may have done.*"

I apologized again, thanked him, and left. There seemed an equality between aircraft commanders apart from relative military rank. I'm sure he took care of business at his crew alert.

LEFT MY BOGIE IN MUSKOGEE (FOG DISASTERS)

In the late 1980s an ORI launch into Muskogee, OK, went progressively wrong and provided an expensive but revelatory lesson or two.

Three C-5s were scheduled to arrive with about thirty minutes spacing at Davis field, a 7,200-foot long runway. All three were heavily laden with cargo, which meant they did not have much extra runway for landing and had to get in on the ground quickly to deploy spoilers and thrust reversers to stop the plane on the short runway.

The additional, crucial factor in the incident was ground fog, which would create illusions during landing that would progress into a major accident. This type of fog is insidious, since looking down directly over the field the visibility was good and the runway could be clearly seen. Arriving on final, however, the slant range visibility would drop drastically during the final few hundred feet of descent to the runway.

The first aircraft, with the wing commander on board, flew into the fog bank and into the illusion. The crew knew they must touch down in the first 1,000 feet of runway to ensure they could stop before running off the far end. As they approached the overrun, the runway approach lights began streaming beneath them. It appears all three crews thought these to possibly be runway lights, which would indicate they were landing dangerously long for this airport. Actually, the approach light began 1,400 feet prior to the overrun. If they had held their glideslope angle as they started to lose visibility, they would have touched down normally, but the lights streaming below them through the fog triggered their fear of landing long. All three ducked under their visual glide path and touched down progressively shorter in each case.

The first aircraft touched down just on the runway, the second in the middle of the approach overrun, and the third short of the overrun. This final aircraft caught its two rear gear bogies on a small hill. (The landing gear consists of four main struts, two forward, two aft, with six tires aligned on a bogie on each structure) This collision broke both off the two aft bogies causing the plane to skid down the runway on the front bogies and tail section. This resulted in extensive damage.

The first lesson: hold your established glide path as you lose much of your visual capability, or go around. This was followed by a second lesson. Neither of the first two planes warned the next arrival of this fog illusion on final. Maybe they didn't know what had happened to them, maybe they thought they'd be criticized for poor flying, but their failure to warn the third aircraft contributed significantly to the crash.

My Fog Fiascos

Ramstein

I had two fog fiascos during these Dover years.

The first occurred on a standard channel mission from Dover to Ramstein with former Navy pilot John Tigart.

Tigart practiced law in Washington, DC, and would spend hours on the pay phone in the squadron hallway conducting business with his DC office. He was famous for once punching out a mugger who threatened him and his wife with a knife on a Washington sidewalk. John, who stood about six-foot-three, was so enraged by the attempt he grabbed the mugger's knife wrist with his left hand and punched the culprit's face with his right. The bandit staggered away and fled, his hand to his damaged head. Sadly, John died young, in his forties, of natural causes.

We coasted in over Land's End at the western tip of England an hour before sunrise and flew across England over scattered cloud decks. I called Mildenhall command post for a phone patch to Ramstein for their weather. The Ramstein observer told me the skies were clear and visibility unlimited. He gave the various pertinent numbers after that, but unfortunately I tuned him out after he said visibility unlimited. What I missed was the temperature and dew point, only two degrees different. If the two numbers converge, it means high moisture content in the air can produce a thick ground fog, and it did about the time we arrived overhead Ramstein. Second, I did not climb to FL 370 to conserve fuel for the last hour of flight since, again, I didn't need to with unlimited visibility. I was about to pay for my lack of diligence.

When we checked in with the Ramstein arrival controller, he sent us to a holding pattern. I asked him why he was doing that. He said the field was currently reporting one-quarter mile visibility and dropping. I asked how this could be since I had received a clear and a million miles visibility from their weather shop. He said severe ground fog had just appeared at sunrise and he had no forecast for when it would lift.

Oh, great, I thought. I checked my fuel and I had just about enough to return to Mildenhall if required, but I couldn't hold very long. Just as we reached the holding fix, the controller told us the visibility had come up to one-half mile and did we want to give it a shot. Ill-advisedly, I said yes. The controller descended us to pattern altitude and vectored us to an ILS final.

We switched to Ramstein tower on final and they were waffling on the visibility, claiming it to be between one-half and one-quarter mile. We needed one-half to land legally. Apparently it was bobbing up and down between the two numbers, so we continued.

The air was smooth and the wind near zero as I approached Decision Height 200 feet above the runway. Tigert called, "*100 above*," the airplane was gliding down the approach smoothly and on airspeed. Tigert called, "Decision Height, go around." I glanced outside and could not see the first glimmer of any ground light, no approach lights, no runway lights, nothing. I then did my first-ever, for real go-around at Decision Height.

We got the gear and flaps up and broke out of the fog about 1,000 feet above the field. I switched to departure control and asked for the nearest suitable alternate. I couldn't believe the answer the controller provided. "*The only open field in Europe right now is Brussels; everyone else has the same fog. Mildenhall is wide open, which do you want?"*

I told the controller we'd take Mildenhall since I had no idea where, or how far, Brussels, Belgium was, or if they, too, would succumb to the fog before we got there. The problem now was I only had 31,000 pounds of gas remaining and had almost an hour's flight to Mildenhall located sixty miles northeast of London. There is a chart in the approach book I had Tigert look up for the optimum divert altitude to use for this several hundred-mile long segment and that is what we requested, FL 270. We would fly up to that altitude and maintain it briefly, then begin a long, slow descent into Mildenhall.

I was pissed. I switched to the METRO weather frequency to have a piece of the forecaster who had claimed unlimited visibility when I talked to him from over England.

"Oh, sir, I'm so sorry, I didn't expect the fog to form, but it did!" he said. He was probably the junior-most forecaster on the midnight shift, but I didn't care.

"You told me clear and a million, and now you say you made a mistake?" I growled. *"Fine for you down there on the ground while I'm up here with no gas and a long divert to Mildenhall. Thanks for nothing!"*

The forecaster again began a long litany of apology, but I switched the frequency and didn't listen to it. He and I both learned a valuable lesson from this.

We landed in England with our proper minimum of 20,000 pounds of fuel, and all was well.

DOVER FOG

I flew a Dover local at McGuire for some reason (I never went to McGuire for transition unless forced to do so due to its screwy holding pattern and initial approach). I was in command as the instructor pilot and occupied the copilot seat.

We had been warned by the weather briefer that the dew point and temperature were converging and Dover would probably get a bad case of ground fog before midnight. I told him to have the Dover command post call the McGuire command post to advise us if fog had begun to roll off Delaware Bay a few miles to the east.

This was the late local that took off at 1800 and landed at 2200. I planned on departing the McGuire pattern about 2130 to return to Dover.

Just before 2100, however, we got a frantic message from Dover that the fog had formed quickly and was moving toward the base from the Bay, and to return quickly if we wanted to get in that night.

I canceled my approach and activated my fight plan back to Dover while pushing up the speed to 250 knots. We were one of two Dover C-5s in the McGuire pattern and we got out first with the other C-5 local about five minutes behind us.

As we checked in with Dover approach control, he said the ceiling and visibility were falling fast and were already nearing minimums for landing, a 200-foot ceiling and one-half mile visibility. I requested a short pattern to final for the ILS to Runway 01.

I now had another, regulatory, problem. A recent incident somewhere in the system resulted from the aircraft commander not being in the correct seat for landing. So a current FCIF (Flight Crew Information File) demanded the aircraft commander be in the left seat for final landing.

Unfortunately, since we had asked for a short pattern, I didn't have enough time to do a double seat-swap to switch to the left seat. I didn't really care, but I'd be hanging by my thumbs if something went wrong. I didn't actually worry about it.

This approach did give me an opportunity to try out a new landing technique, however. On most approaches with weather near minimums, the pilot flying stays on the gauges until the other pilot calls "Go around" or "Land," depending upon whether or not he sees the runway environment at minimums.

This technique can go awry, unfortunately. The pilot monitoring the gauges cannot be looking outside and at the gauges simultaneously; he must shift his vision back and forth, inside and outside, as minimums approach. If he tarries too long on one feature, he can miss the crucial aspect of the other. He may look outside for the runway 50 feet above minimums and continue straining to see runway lights too long and bust minimums. If he concentrates on the altimeter to exactly minimums, he leaves only a split second to recognize the runway environment as he shifts his eyes back outside.

Meanwhile, the pilot flying generally starts taking peeks outside the plane as minimums approach, anxious to go visual as soon as possible. He, too, may keep his vision outside too long trying to catch some glimmer of runway or approach lights and also bust minimums. Both pilots are trying to look both at their gauges and outside at minimums.

The new technique I wanted to try strictly divided responsibilities. The pilot flying the plane would never look outside; he would fly to minimums on his altimeter and commence a go-around when he reached the crucial altitude. His attention would be riveted inside the plane on the flight instruments with no peeking outside.

The pilot not flying, however, after making his mandatory call at 100 feet above Decision Height, would look nowhere but outside. He would no longer be responsible for calling "Go Around" or "Land," he would only look outside for the runway environment. If he discerned the runway lights and runway environment, he would call "Copilot's airplane!" and make the landing. If he never saw the runway, the pilot would automatically go around at Decision Height.

In the old method, with each pilot trying to cover both inside and outside responsibilities, they sometimes missed one, or both, of the crucial parameters they were trying to cover. With the new method, they each had but one parameter to cover and stood a better chance of making a successful decision.

And that is exactly what we did. I instructed the pilot in the left seat to fly to minimums and, if he heard nothing, to automatically commence the go-around. However, if I said "Copilot's airplane," he was to immediately relinquish the controls to me. Right at minimums I saw the runway, called for airplane control, and landed successfully. The second C-5 not two minutes behind us had to go around and divert to Andrews AFB, MD outside Washington, DC.

GUARDIAN ANGEL DOUBLE SAVE

My guardian angel saved me many times over 33 years of flying. I don't know why I deserved to be saved, but I was. On this winter C-5 mission to Bodo, Norway, he (she?) saved me twice.

I flew with George Talley, a contemporary and fellow evaluator pilot in the 709th MAS. Trouble seemed more prevalent with evaluators on board since we all thought someone else was minding the store and let our guard down.

To digress, I have decided to award Talley my "best pilot" award in 33 years of Air Force flying. He was not flashy or aggressive but excelled nonetheless with no major incidents or blunders (that I know of) in over 10,000 flying hours. George is why I consider myself almost the best air refueling pilot ever, since he was better, the bastard.

Sitting around the squadron scheduling desk, George would lean back in his chair and begin: "*I remember once...*" and proceed with a long, involved war story that everyone around the table had already heard numerous times. Eyes would roll and we would settle down to hear the particular story yet again. When someone would finish one of George's sentences for him during the recitation, he would look surprised and ask if he'd already told that one. We only crossed swords once, in 2003, over the anthrax shot, an issue I will leave for book three.

The Bodo mission took us first to Cherry Point MCAS, NC, to pick up Marine equipment for the Nordic exercise. At the base operations desk, I was handed a communication package with exercise information and, most importantly, the approach plates for Bodo, not a regular stop for us. Since I was in command, I got the package.

The unique Cherry Point runway had four individual runways aligned almost as a giant "X" except at the intersection each split in two and offset a few hundred yards. This offset caused the need for the first guardian save.

By habit I would run the "Line up" checklist when cleared for takeoff and when crossing the runway hold line. Except, for the Cherry Point takeoff, we had to taxi down most of the lower runway on this alignment to take off on the upper runway, so we did not run the checklist passing the first hold line, waiting for the second.

Unfortunately, as we got to the second runway, we apparently thought we had already run the checklist, but had not. George was flying, but I was in command, so I own it. We started takeoff roll without having run the checklist, the major oversight being not having turned on the antiskid switch. This might have been a problem if we had aborted the takeoff at high speed, but probably would not have been catastrophic. If I remember correctly, the gear would not have retracted after takeoff until we moved the switch to "on," whereupon we would have realized our error.

The angel intervened at the 80-knot check since my airspeed indicator, for the only time in 9,500 hours of C-5 flying, failed. We did a low speed abort and taxied down to the next taxiway to clear the runway. We then ran the "After landing" checklist and discovered our error that flabbergasted us both. How had we let that happen?

After a maintenance fix, we took off for Bodo. A few hours later, deep into the night, and about halfway across the Atlantic, I decided I'd better review the Bodo arrival procedures. The weather briefing had warned about snow showers in the area of this destination I had never seen before.

I began searching my copilot cockpit position for the package and soon realized…I had left it on the counter at Cherry Point base ops. Damn! We were screwed! I couldn't fly to Bodo in a snowstorm without approach plates! Ooooh, this would be bad! We'd have to divert and I'd get to explain to 21st Air Force why this was necessary.

I swear what happened next is true. I thought for a moment how I would explain this to the crew, especially to George. I'd made an error worthy of a rookie copilot by forgetting the package. How to explain? I grimaced, shaking my lowered head slowly, and reached for the interphone toggle on my yoke to perform a humbling mea culpa.

Just as my finger arrived on the switch, my instrument altimeter began spinning madly from 33,000 feet to zero, again, for the first and only time in 23 years flying the C-5. "*Hahahahahahaha! I thought, "I'm saved! Now we have to divert for maintenance!"*

"*Crew, copilot, I've just lost my altimeter, we'll have to ask 21st for a divert base,*" I said. And, no, I didn't fess up to my error. The divert, to Frankfurt, Germany, knocked us out of the exercise and we never did get to Bodo, so the missing package became irrelevant.

Thank you, angel.

PANAMA

With the Nixon/Reagan drug war in full progress along with a communist insurgency by the Sandinista guerillas in Nicaragua, we flew many missions to Howard AFB in Panama, situated at the southern end of the Panama Canal on the Pacific Ocean. The regular run featured a stop at Charleston AFB, SC, or Hunter AAF outside Savannah, GA, to pick up supplies, and then on to Howard. Flying across the Caribbean, we'd have to skirt west around the tip of communist Cuba, then south-southeast past Cancun and down the coast of

Central America under air traffic control from Merida Center located on the Mexican Yucatan peninsula.

I only had one incident flying this route. After we had made the turn around the western tip of Cuba, we got a "Door Unlocked" warning light. These were almost always an unnecessary pain in the ass, as one of the main door or visor locks would shake loose from its seated position and illuminate the warning light. Emergency procedures demanded we presume the door would blow and this required depressurizing the aircraft. That, in turn, required going on oxygen masks and descending to 10,000 feet, where pressurization is not required. A scanner would have to check the door locks, and it would be most unfortunate for him if the door blew open as he tried to inspect it; thus the need to depressurize.

I got permission from Merida to descend from 31,000 feet to 10,000 and the pilot in the left seat started his descent. I was in command but was flying this leg in the right seat. Once at 10,000 feet, the scanner quickly determined a malfunctioning door lock indicator had set off the light. He bypassed the warning mechanism and our warning light went out.

I asked Merida for a return to FL 310 and he cleared us to climb. This had put us in a situational performance trap. The Military Rated Thrust throttle position bar had been set for 31,000 feet, not for 10,000. Pushing the throttles forward to that much higher setting might severely overboost the engines and cause damage. I had seen this before as a copilot where the pilot saved me from overboosting. I now returned the favor and blocked the throttles with my arm as the pilot pushed them toward the FL 310 setting. I was reading back the climb clearance to ATC with my right hand at the time so I couldn't verbally warn him. "*We need a new setting*," I explained and asked the flight engineer to give us one. Once I blocked the throttles, the pilot, an engineer, recognized the warning.

The canal always interested me as we flew over it, a series of narrow, sharply defined channels through the jungle connecting open lakes. I had read the David McCullough book *Path Between the Seas* and appreciated what a stupendous engineering achievement the canal represented, as well as the efforts to combat yellow fever during construction in the early 1900s by Army doctor Walter Reed.

Approach control usually flew us down the western side of the airfield and turned us on a base leg inside Taboga Island that lay south of the field in the Pacific. I was always visual; I never flew an instrument approach into Howard.

The Howard ramp represented a taxiing challenge in the C-5 since the base's multiple missions required many aircraft types crammed into too little ramp space. The tight turns into parking went slowly and carefully, with wing walkers and scanners on full alert to avoid catching a wing tip.

The Howard runway had an unusual feature in that its elevation rose rapidly from the south to north, so you usually landed uphill and took off downhill, a natural advantage for each event. Again, I always landed to the north and took off to the south.

I found this rising runway feature at one other field half a world away in Fujairah next to the Straits of Hormuz in the United Arab Emirates. This one runs east-west and the runway rises rapidly moving east to west. As with Howard, I always took advantage of the slope and landed uphill to the west and took off downhill to the east. The striking difference in the two runways is their surroundings. Howard lies nestled in a dense, vibrant jungle while Fujairah lies at the base of a barren mountain in a desert moonscape in the Middle East, all rocks and sand with no vegetation.

Howard's base architecture resembled late 19th century colonial style with colonnaded porticos, whitewashed walls and red tile roofs, even though it was built in 1942 at the behest of AAF Gen. Hap Arnold. Interestingly, the base included horse stables and riding venues. That must have been from the army cavalry influence prior to the Air Force splitting off on its own after WWII.

We usually stayed in Panama City across the huge Bridge of the Americas. Our bus trip to the hotel often took us through the barrio slums of the city famous for producing boxing legend Roberto Duran, who fought all the welterweight contenders of the 1980s to include Thomas Hearns and Sugar Ray Leonard. One of the most impressive title fights I've seen had a youthful and neatly short-haired Duran dismantling lightweight champion Ken Buchanan of Britain in 1972.

One of the most used hotels had an open-air lobby with no doors, no walls (just support posts), and no windows. There was no need for these because the temperature was always between the 70s and 90s, year-round. The Panamanians did not usually wear suits and ties. Instead they favored a white shirt pleated down the front that proved much more comfortable in the ever-present heat and humidity. The downtown of the 1980s was far older than the skyscraper skyline of today. It held a rustic, early 1900s quaintness where I would not have been surprised to see a donkey cart on one of the back streets.

The notable restaurant downtown, La Cascada (waterfall), had an owner who went totally overboard with nautical statues of whales, dolphins, King Neptune and other symbols of the sea. He also provided sumptuous and plentiful platters of food, usually fish, for an astoundingly low price. We ate in an open-air plaza, surrounded by the statues, weather permitting. The restaurant has been torn down and replaced by a high-rise condominium.

Panama also gave me my longed-for jungle fix. The verdant fauna seemed to threaten to retake structures of civilization if not constantly contested. I most enjoyed deep jungle excursions where the jungle seemed to be winning and I reveled in such trips.

On departure we often asked the controller for a "canal tour" vector so could show the structure to crewmembers who had not seen it before.

In 1977, President Jimmy Carter negotiated giving the canal to the Panamanians in 1999. This became a hot political issue with American conservative shouts of "*We built it, we paid for it, it's ours!*" I never really cared one way or the other. However, I now think it a small, token amount of reparations and restitution we owe for what the abominable American drug war has done to Central and South America with no discernable effect on American drug usage. We owe them far more than just the canal.

HARV THE HAMMER

One of the stalwarts of the 709th technician pilot corps at Dover in the 1980s was my cohort, Harv (the Hammer), the mildest-mannered, nicest guy I have ever known. The "hammer" moniker was an opposite indicator of his personality; Harv never hammered anyone. Nothing perturbed him, no reservist ever got him angry; quite a feat. I wondered during this period if anything, or anyone, could ever get a rise out of Harv. Finally, one day I thought it was going to happen; Harv would snap for the first time in his life.

The provocateur in this rising argument was "the Dodger," who, himself, was usually a great guy, until he wasn't. On this day the Dodger was irate, angry, and off-his-rocker irrational about some task he felt he had been unfairly stuck with. I can't remember what it was, but he was so far off the charts in his position I almost laughed from the sideline as I watched him plead his case indignantly with Harv.

After the Dodger's initial, ludicrous salvo in Harv's face, Harv came back in his best Harv the Hammer manner, calm, friendly, and reasonable, explaining that the Dodger had been stuck with far less than all his contemporaries in the matter, and he was sorry he was upset about this.

The Dodger, rather than being mollified by Harv's conciliatory response, instead went nuclear in Harv's face, eyes bulging, spittle flying, arms flapping, rationality gone, self-serving, dumb-ass self-righteousness exploding from every pore of his body.

Yes! I thought. No one could keep his cool after such an onslaught. Jesus H. Christ would have slapped the Dodger silly for a complete loss of sanity and decorum, in addition to being a total dumb shit.

Harv looked down at the floor. My eyebrows rose and I smiled because I was finally going to see it! Harv the Hammer finally hammers a blithering idiot who is asking for it in spades! *"Do it, Harv!"* my mind screamed. *"Blow his ass away, Harv!"*

Then Harv looked up and said: *"Well, Dodger, I'm sure we can work something out for you on this."*

My jaw dropped. *"Nooooooo, Harv!"* I thought, *"You can't let him off on this!"*

Since Harv didn't snap, I did. I leapt between them, nose-to-nose with the Dodger. He was taking appalling advantage of Harv's good-natured personality and he was going to pay for it.

"You frigging moron!" I shouted, blowing the ears off everyone in the room. *"You are the dumbest shit I have ever seen, you fucking, whining jerk. I ought to throw you out of the unit right now after kicking your ass and throwing you out of the building. And if you don't get out of my sight RIGHT NOW, I might do it!"*

(Of course, I had no authority to do any of these things, and the Dodger may well have kicked my ass, but why let factoids get in the way of an irrational tirade?).

The Dodger's jaw dropped and he went pale. *"But, I'm getting screwed and…"* He stopped in mid-sentence, turned and left the building.

Things calmed down after this little explosion and we all got along afterward, but I again lost my bet with myself about what it would take to blow Harv's cork. His threshold remains far above mine, so I guess I'll never see it, since my cork would always blow first.

TRAVERSE CITY AIR SHOW

There are moments from all careers where you think back and cringe at some of the things you have done over the years. *"How could I have done that?"* you ask yourself.

My prime example happened at the Traverse City, MI, air show in July 1987, held in conjunction with the National Cherry Festival. As stated previously, air shows are second in danger only to combat. The crews' guard is down, and thousands of people are watching, a sure mix for disaster. Although this fiasco would be almost entirely self-inflicted.

Air show planners wanted us to arrive early in our C-5 out of Dover. We could wind up blowing little airplanes away if we tried to maneuver into parking by the passenger terminal after other show aircraft had arrived.

We arrived in bright sunlight Friday morning. The "Follow Me" led us to the side of the terminal, where the final marshaller guided us in close to the structure. As the pilot in command in the left seat, I had concentrated on the marshaller so I could follow his instructions precisely. I had no idea where he was taking me; he was in control.

Finally, he raised his arms above his head in an "X" with his wands, and I set the parking brake. As I looked around after running the shutdown checklists, I grew concerned over how close we were to the terminal. The marshaller's responsibility was to get me into the spot, not out of it. That was on me, but I had let them park me without surveying the spot first.

As I deplaned I walked to the right wing and saw trouble. Although we were well clear of the main terminal building, a covered concrete passenger walkway descended down a small hill by the terminal to the ramp about a hundred feet from the cockpit. I saw immediately we could not clear it horizontally with our right wing. I could taxi over it and probably make it, but that would be highly illegal and I might learn why they attach pilot wings with Velcro patches; so they can rip them off if you screw up.

This was the era of "rope-a-dope," where we had lengths of rope to gauge if we had enough room to clear obstacles by our dictated minimum of 25 feet. (The rope-a-dope term came from the 1974 Ali vs. Foreman fight where Ali lay on the ropes and let Foreman punch himself into exhaustion). I didn't need the rope to know the score, however. At least 10 feet of wing would pass over the tunnel with about 10 feet of clearance, if I was crazy enough to try it.

I decided I'd just have them back us up with a tug at the end of the air show and that would be that. On Sunday when I contacted ground control, however, they said they didn't have a tug big enough to move us. I was on my own.

In my right mind, which I usually am, I would have called Dover and explained my plight, and asked for them to fly up a tug. This would be excruciatingly expensive and the air wing would squawk mightily about how I had let myself get cornered like this. However, I had no choice; that is where they parked me! In addition, however, there were several reservists on this large air show crew who had to be back at work on Monday morning, and that wasn't going to happen if I had Dover fly in a tug. Then, the final wrinkle appeared that pushed me into insanity.

In talking to the air show manager trying to obtain a tug, he told me CINCMAC was flying in Monday to address the Traverse City Chamber of Commerce. What? You've got to be shitting me! The four-star? Here tomorrow? I could just see him spotting my C-5 pinned to the terminal and strolling over to ask me how I had been so stupid to get myself boxed in like this. And, by the way, who is my wing commander?

Now, in retrospect, I should not have cared. I followed the marshaller's instructions, I parked where they put me, and that was that. You wouldn't want me to do something truly stupid, would you, sir?

All these factors percolated in my mind Sunday during the air show, the heat I would take from Dover commanders, the heat I was already taking from the reservists who had to get home, and the theoretical heat of possibly getting reamed by a four-star.

I found myself so distracted I failed to partake of standard crew shenanigans, such as holding a contest for female superlatives in the air show crowd, best breasts, best ass and best overall (the breast award could not go to an obvious silicone job). I also failed to warn the loadmasters not to take any babes in short shorts up the crew stairs to show them the cockpit. Once they were spotted ascending the stairs, a hundred-person line would form at the bottom of the stairs awaiting their turn to be escorted to the cockpit.

I kept contemplating doing the unthinkable…and then I decided I'd do it, taxi that wingtip over the tunnel and escape all heat, unless, of course, I hit the tunnel, and then the heat would be unbearable. Fuck it, I thought, I have ten feet of clearance, no way will I hit it. I let the improbable vision of Gen. Cassidy pinning me to the wall overcome my common sense. I would, however, have to convince the other two pilots, who were also evaluators, to go along with this.

As this ill-advised plan unfolded, it got worse than I anticipated. So I took one more shot to avoid doing the unthinkable; I went for a final legal option. The C-5 can be backed up with reverse thrust if you are lightweight, which we were. It needed a higher headquarters waiver, however, because if you hit the brakes too hard, the plane would sit on its tail. I decided to ask because if I, as an evaluator, wasn't qualified to do the maneuver, who was?

I called 21st command post and got connected, via the command post controller, with Zark the Shark, a long-time headquarters evaluator who would occasionally give no-notice evaluations on local training missions at Dover. If you showed up at base ops and saw Zark's helmet bag, you knew you were "it" for a no-notice that day. Zark was actually pretty mild-mannered and easy to work with, but I was about to test him.

I told him that I had been taxied into an untenable parking spot at an air show, but I could extricate myself if he would waive me to back up the plane about fifty feet. His answer was swift: not only no, but hell, no, get yourself tugged out. I explained the airport didn't have a tug. He told me to have one flown in. There went my last legal option to leave that day.

I had discovered during my career that if I got a sick feeling in the pit of my stomach as I contemplated doing something dicey in an aircraft, I should heed that warning and NOT DO IT! Too often, alas, I did it anyway and usually got away with it. I would be playing Russian roulette with my career; I had five chances out of six of getting away with it to avoid a relatively minor sanction. I cannot fathom why I took that chance.

So, the unthinkable would become the plan. The other pilot evaluators shot glances at each other as I explained what I wanted to do. One was senior to me, one junior. After a few moments of silence, they said OK, they would join the conspiracy. They, too, thought the wing would clear the tunnel easily and we would be "outta here."

Surveying what I would have to do, I saw another problem. I had to make a very hard left turn to escape the spot. That would mean I'd have to use high power on engines three and four to overcome the drag of the nose wheels turned hard left. That meant hurricane-force winds would be unleashed behind the right wing, and in the direct path of that blast was a lot full of rental cars. Great! I walked into the rental office and told the manager he had to move all the cars because a hurricane was coming when we started to taxi. He soon had the cars moved.

The show ended and the small planes took their own sweet time clearing a path for us, but finally, it was show time at the air show.

The senior evaluator climbed atop the tunnel to wing-walk me over it. The scanner would clear from the ground. That scanner was a female sergeant nicknamed "Big Bird," and she positioned herself well in front and left of the aircraft nose.

We started engines and asked for taxi clearance to the runway. Ground cleared us to taxi and I started the power up. The turmoil in the pit of my stomach went into overdrive. I pushed up engines three and four, leaving one and two at idle for maximum differential power. The engines rose and fairly screamed before the friction of the cocked nose wheel finally broke loose and we started to slowly taxi out of the spot in a hard left turn.

The wing approached the tunnel and my "tunnel scanner" said it looked good. Just as the wing started over the tunnel, however, Big Bird suddenly screamed *"Holy shit!!!"* on interphone. My heart lodged firmly in my throat and I slammed on the brakes. The right wing shuddered and began flexing up and down over the tunnel.

"What is it, scanner?" I shouted.

"You should see the spectators running for their lives, pilot!" she said. Apparently a few hundred show-goers wanted to watch the C-5 taxi out and had gathered on the far side of the rental car parking lot I had insisted be cleared. As the engine blast swung toward them, the crowd caught the hurricane torrent sweeping across the lot as it picked up trash, debris and dirt and scoured them with it. Some turned and staggered away in the torrent of air, others dropped their belongings and fled. I'm sure it was quite a sight, but it came at exactly the wrong time. I wanted to kill Big Bird on the spot.

"You've got it made, pilot," said the tunnel scanner. *"I'm coming back aboard."* I finished the turn and I had escaped; it had worked.

As Big Bird came back on board I upbraided her for shouting at just the wrong time for something irrelevant to our desperate task. I was wrong to do that. It was my fault. I did this to us and if anything happened, it was on me, as this was. I wanted to lambast her as a surrogate for blasting myself, instead, for doing this. There was only one guilty bastard here, and it was me.

So the reservists got home to go to work, I got to miss Gen. Cassidy arriving in Traverse City, and Zark the Shark apparently never checked to see how I got out of town. I had been ill-advisedly playing on my proverbial train tracks again, and the train had missed me yet again.

KUNSAN, KOREA

In 1987 I flew an eventful trip to Kunsan AB, Korea. These west trips to the Pacific were always a treat, but this one provided a few more thrills than anticipated.

I was matched on the pilot team with Mike Kelly and Jim Rubeor. I was an evaluator, Mike an experienced aircraft commander, but Rubeor had just upgraded to aircraft commander. He flew in command to help build his 150 hours so he could fly without supervision by another A/C or IP. (As an aside, it seemed a pilot's first major emergency usually occurred immediately after he got his 150 hours and did not have an experienced pilot with him.)

The schedule had us crew resting at Kadena AB, Okinawa, then flying out to Kunsan and back to Kadena. At Kunsan we would drop off a large weather trailer the size of a single-wide house trailer, mounted on a flatbed wheeled trailer for transportation.

We landed at Kunsan, an air base adjacent to a Navy base on the west coast, in the early evening. We went in to file our flight plan at base ops, grabbed some food at the snack bar, and returned to the plane.

The download was not going well. The loadmasters were having trouble locating the 5-ton truck required to pull the weather trailer off the plane and onto the tarmac. In order to move the load forward, the cockpit stairs had to be raised because they would block the weather trailer if extended. We got back on time to get into the cockpit before they raised the stairs. We would be "trapped" in the cockpit, but we didn't mind because we were going to take naps in the bunk room anyway.

About an hour later I floated blissfully in dream-filled sleep when something crashed into the aircraft. I jumped up, still wrapped in my blanket, and stumbled out of the bunk, tripped on the blanket encasing my legs and blundered into the far passageway wall. I wondered if a radar guided missile had somehow struck us. I got to the crew stairway door that had the stairs folded up against it and looked through the opening to the cargo compartment below.

On the cargo side ramp I saw Fred Massey, one of the loadmasters, with his hands pressed to his temples and a horrified look on his face. It took a while to discover what had horrified Fred. Our only semi-graceful method of escape from the cockpit was the rope ladder at the back of the crew compartment which none of us had ever used. Among the three of us we finally figured out how to work it and climbed down the ladder to the cargo compartment.

It seems the download had gone horribly wrong. Kunsan maintenance had decided to attempt to remove the weather trailer with less than a 5-ton truck since they didn't have one. As the trailer started off the cargo deck and onto the slanted ramp, its weight overcame the connection to the too-light truck and snapped it loose. This shot the truck down the ramp and onto the tarmac and left the front of the trailer momentarily suspended over the ramp. After that brief moment, the trailer dropped, stanchions first, into the ramp, punching two large holes in it and remaining embedded. That collision with the ramp is what had awakened us. Now the entire load was hung up under the cockpit on the ramp with no graceful way to move it. It would take the Navy two days using industrial cranes to clear the load from the aircraft.

Someone had to call MAC Headquarters to inform them of our fiasco. Mike and I both chuckled, slapped Rubeor on the back, and told him to enjoy the phone call since he was in command. And, by the way, don't wake us when you finally get to the hotel.

Rubeor, whom I nicknamed "the Rube," would, years later, have two stars, command Travis AFB, and also, I believe, one of the reserve Numbered Air Forces.

Billeting sent us to a downtown Kunsan hotel and I slept well. The next morning I awoke early and decided to explore the local area alone. Just down the street was an open-air market partially under tents with paths or streets underneath, perhaps an acre square, full of vendors of all sorts of goods.

At one of the main intersections under the tents, a butcher, who resembled a sumo wrestler, scowled proudly over his butcher shop offerings at this prime corner location. Other vendors up and down the alleyways carried a wide variety of goods, and this Saturday morning crowd of customers eagerly flowed among the shops.

I thought this operation seemed very similar to the souks and markets I had seen in the Middle East in Cairo and Dhahran, very different cultures, but very similar markets.

As I pondered this unexpected similarity while walking down one of the tented streets, an elderly Korean woman fell in step with me and began jabbering at me in Korean. She was short, squat and ugly and I immediately dubbed her "toad woman." She seemed to want me to follow her for some reason, although I had no idea what she could have that I would want.

At the end of this path we emerged from the tent covering where, about ten yards away, permanent structures ran perpendicular to our path. She walked to a narrow alleyway between two buildings and motioned me to follow. Curious, I complied.

I had taken a few steps down the alley when toad woman stopped, stepped beside me, and pushed gently on my chest. I stepped backward toward the side of the alley, passed through a bead curtain, and then felt some object catch me at about knee height. I found myself sitting on a bed. This was starting to make sense, but surely toad woman was not the proffered offering!

And, she was not. Her job was to procure; others would carry out the transaction. Almost immediately an attractive Korean woman about my age (40) knelt between my legs and began rubbing my thigh with one hand and grabbed my crotch with the other. "*You want girl, GI?*" she asked. (How did she know I was a GI? Oh, never mind). My brain had not quite caught up with events and I said nothing.

The woman, dressed in a white blouse with hair pulled back in a ponytail, and strikingly beautiful even without makeup, looked into my eyes almost with longing. She then gently squeezed with the hand on my crotch and a visible shudder ran through her. A shudder then ran through me as well. If her job was to close the deal, she was almost there.

Our little mutual infatuation was interrupted by a male voice in a room somewhere behind us berating someone followed by a loud slap. A few moments later a groggy girl about 18 lurched around the corner, obviously having been woken from a deep sleep. Apparently she was the proffered morsel for my attention. To heck with her, I thought, I want mama san. I found the older woman far more attractive than the younger. The man, toad woman, the girl, and mama san between my knees looked at me for an indication of assent.

My libido wanted me to pull mama san into the bed and get down to business, but other thoughts intruded. First, I had never broken my marital vows, and being married, I couldn't afford to carry venereal disease problems home. Second, I realized a goon squad could step in here, carve me to pieces, and no one would ever find me. I was ten feet from the street, but was totally invisible to anyone who would search for me. Unfortunately, I hadn't even told anyone where I was going when I left the hotel. No, I had to leave...now.

I jumped up, apologizing, and moved toward the door. Mama san hung on my arm, beseeching me to stay as I moved through the bead curtain. I again apologized and stepped back into the sunlight.

KELLY AFB CREW TRAINING

Also in the mid-1980s, the C-5B model began to come on line and the number of C-5 bases would expand significantly to include Kelly AFB, TX, Martinsburg ANGB, WV, and Westover AFB, MA, among others.

Since Kelly would be the first expansion base, their crews had to train first. I flew many missions with a Kelly crew as an instructor to get them mission qualified. We would depart from Dover on regular channel missions.

One mission stands out in my mind. First, I got to train my first female aircraft commander. This went well except she thought I was picking on her for exceeding the 250 knot airspeed limit below 10,000 by ten knots. I told her I didn't care, but some prick HHQ evaluator might, so slow it down to 250. (When I was such an evaluator, I was just such a prick!)

This mission went downrange to Bahrain IAP with a four-hour quick-turn there. About half a dozen Kelly crew members wanted to take cabs down to the local souk to shop. I told them that was fine and to be back an hour before takeoff.

While they were gone, however, Bahrain ground control called us and told us we had to push back from our parking spot onto the taxiway an hour and a half prior to takeoff. Apparently the heavy-duty aircraft tug was needed on the other end of the field around our push back time. I asked if there would be a problem with us blocking the taxiway and they said there would not be. So an hour and a half before takeoff, the tug showed up and began slowly pushing us back a hundred yards onto the taxiway.

Just after we started moving back, the shopping cadre arrived in their cabs about a quarter of a mile away at the perimeter gate on my side of the plane. The sight of us apparently departing without them sent them into a panic. They began sprinting, as well as they could, with tightly held packages flying around and smacking against them as they ran.

I tried to figure out some way to notify them that we were not actually leaving, but there was none. I just sat back and laughed as the encumbered steeplechase sprint continued with occasional dropped packages slowing them as they frantically ran back to retrieve them. They finally arrived, sweating profusely in the 110 degree heat after the needless sprint. I couldn't blame them. Were positions reversed, I'd have been in a panic too.

The final moment of note occurred on the leg back to Europe. The Kelly loadmaster instructors were debriefing their students in Spanish, every one of them. I suppose I should not have been surprised, given their location in San Antonio, but it seemed curious to me to hear fluent Spanish on the flight deck.

Soto Cano

In the middle 1980s we had regular weekend missions to Soto Cano, Honduras. This was compliments of the Reagan drug war as well as the Contra/Sandinista skirmish in Nicaragua and all those entanglements with the Iran-Contra affair.

I only did one mission to Soto. It was the favored weekend jaunt for full-time reservists to get their minimum-required two overseas sorties within a six-month period, so they flew most of them.

Soto provided a vivid flashback to Vietnam for me. The airstrip we landed on was surrounded by jungle and had jeeps driving along rutted roads next to the field. I felt like I was back at Tonle Cham, Vietnam.

We had a near incident on arrival, however. Center had cleared us to descend to 13,000 feet enroute to the Tegucigalpa VORTAC from the east. The cloud ceiling was about 13,500 feet. We had some confusion over what altitude we should level off and were initially headed to 12,000. As we broke out of the clouds we agreed that 13,000 was the altitude. Good thing.

Coming from the northwest to the same navaid was another C-5 from our squadron with our squadron commander on board at 12,000. Had we mistakenly gone to 12,000 we'd have nailed them right over the navaid. That would have been a spectacular 709th fireball.

Baby B

In late 1986, Bea and I received the happy news our current pregnancy would provide twins, two girls. We became the object of effusive joy from all branches of both families and my work environment. Everyone wanted the latest update and estimate of when the arrival would be.

The girls were labeled Baby A and Baby B because "A" was more prominently placed in the front and somewhat masked "B." All vital signs on both were very good.

I greatly looked forward to the event, although I had endured some angst at the delivery of our first daughter, Jessica, in 1984. As she was halfway into the world, the doctor exclaimed, *"Oh, I've made a mistake, it's a boy!… Hahaha, just kidding!"*

I realize he did this several times a week and could joke about such things, but I was not in a joking mood. I didn't care which gender it was. The whole episode proved too much for me and I fled to an empty hallway, collapsed against a wall and cried my eyes out for five minutes in joy and humility over the event.

Now I tried to prep myself for another birth saga. The date would be late April 1987 and, as it approached, I bought two boxes of cigars, one for each daughter, for the office. I placed the open boxes on the squadron reception desk on my last day in the office prior to the delivery. All the squadron secretaries were giddy over the prospect of the blessed event.

The process began on April 22, but the six-hour labor pushed the birth dates back to the 23rd. After several hours I had had it, and wasn't even the one in labor! I wanted to shout: *"Put this simulator on freeze, I need a break!"* And I took one, going to the hospital cafeteria for a sandwich and coffee. Bea, of course, could not "freeze the simulator"; she could not take a break and there was nothing anyone could do about it. My admiration for her and for what women must endure reached profound levels. Men endure war, women labor, about an even proposition.

Finally, Baby A made her arrival, crying and thrashing her limbs spasmodically as all newborns do. The nurses smiled and worked their process smoothly and efficiently, laughing and joking, this being a routine daily occurrence for them. I kissed Bea's perspiring forehead and headed for a pay phone to advise my mother it was one down, one to go. She was overjoyed.

Returning to the delivery room, I was told Baby B was about to arrive also. I sat on the sidelines and watched as she came into the world with the same cry and movements of Baby A.

I raced back to the phone to notify my mother that her third granddaughter had arrived and I'd call back soon.

On my return to the delivery room, however, something wasn't right; something was off. The nurses were silent and frowning with worried looks on their faces.

They brought Baby A to Bea wrapped in her birth blanket and placed her on one of Bea's arms. After a few minutes, Bea asked when Baby B would be brought to her. The nurses remained silent, glancing back and forth at each other. Bea asked again about Baby B and, again, did not receive an answer.

Then the realization that something was wrong became apparent.

"*WHERE IS MY BABY? I WANT MY BABY, NOW!!!*" Bea screamed.

I watched this primordial sequence unfold, the maternal instinct demanding her child, even if damaged or dying, to hold, protect and comfort from whatever was coming.

The doctor reentered the room with a stricken look on his face and told Bea that they had to run some tests, but that she would have Baby B shortly. Bea and I looked at each other, distraught and bewildered.

Shortly thereafter, the doctor asked me to step into the hallway to talk, a discussion that would be very difficult for both of us. He apparently had not broken his news to Bea yet.

My next call to my mother was somber and I spoke slowly, haltingly, and with overpowering sadness.

"*Mom…there's a…there's a…problem…with Baby B.*" That's as much as I could utter initially. My mother dissolved on the other end of the line. "*What? What is it! Is she still alive? What! What! Tell me!*

"*They think…they think she has Down's syndrome,*" I said. My mother tried to hold it together for me, but had a hard time doing it.

I now sat in an outer room, lost and crushed. All I could recall about Down's syndrome children was visions of them staring vacantly into space with their tongues lolling out of their mouths. I was devastated, for me, for Bea, and for Baby B, and didn't know how to recover.

When they brought Baby B to her mother, I returned to the delivery room to meet my new daughters. After some minutes I asked to hold Baby B. In a moment of humor lost on everyone at the time, the nurse handed me Baby A, thinking it to be Baby B. That was the first indicator that of the wide range of Down's syndrome capabilities, Baby B would be somewhat above average some respects, especially in appearance. Both girls would spend time in the Intensive Care Unit.

I will return to the Baby B saga more fully later.

I wrote two notes to put on the cigar boxes at the squadron. On the left one I wrote: Karen Flynn Lacklen, 3.9 pounds.

On the right one I wrote Kay Flynn Lacklen, 6.2 lbs. Then I continued on the note with the outlook Bea and I had agreed on:

"*Some are born with challenges but can live happy lives,*
and bring joy to all they know,
And they will be loved without reservation regardless."
And thus it would be.

1987 ASEV

In the middle 1980s those of us who had become ARTS since 1983 found ourselves stuck in a frozen promotion sequence. All the top squadron technician positions were inhabited by "homesteaders," or officers who planned on retiring out of their current position as lieutenant colonels, perhaps ten or fifteen years down the road. They would not be promoted due to the unofficial reserve rule that you had to move to another base to attain the 0-6 rank; you could not homestead into it at your current base. That was fine with them because they didn't want to move and didn't care if they were not promoted.

Those of us one rung below the homesteaders on the promotion ladder were out of luck because we arrived after the positions were already taken and were close to the homesteaders' ages ourselves. Our only recourse for promotion would be to transfer to another base.

In 1987 such an opportunity arose. Westover AFB, MA, was converting from C-130s to C-5s in 1988 and they needed C-5 instructors to transfer to Westover to train the crews and accept operations commander positions. An ART in the other squadron, Larry Mercker, previously stationed at Westover, had taken one of the positions and asked if I'd like to follow him to Westover and work with him as his assistant. Initially, I said no, I didn't particularly want to move with a wife and three small kids in tow.

But then the 1987 ASEV (flying evaluation) arrived.

The inspection team checked on flight procedure standardization, both in flight, and on publications. They would test on emergency procedures, check pubs and regulations, and fly local training flights to ensure correct flight procedures were being followed.

SAC had the same type inspection, labeled CEVG, and I explained in book one how I viscerally hated them. The best you could do on such an inspection flight was break even if you passed. However, I also explained that they were absolutely necessary to ensure compliance with regulations that would help ensure the safety of the fleet. Knowing we would have to perform to the command's standards, we taught to them specifically. Also, we could not count on getting a break from command inspectors as we might from our squadron buddies, so we had to toe the command line on all our training flights.

My squadron ops officer had a peculiar view of this inspection, however. As one of the sea gull brothers I mentioned earlier in the book, he flew very little and absolutely would not fly in command with ASEV evaluators even though he was an skilled pilot. His mantra said this was a reservist inspection and they should carry the load, not the technicians.

I strongly disagreed with this position. ASEV wanted to ensure compliance of squadron instructor pilots, and those who flew the most local training sorties were technicians. We should not exclude ourselves from inspection; we should be the first ones in line!

So, appropriately, I volunteered to fly in command for the first local training flight to be evaluated. I gritted my teeth, but I did it, and it went well. I was the only squadron technician instructor pilot to fly in command during the inspection. Others flew on evaluation flights, but not in command, apparently hiding behind the sea gull's example.

A few months later I had to write my OER (professional evaluation), as we all did. They were nearly worthless anyway, so we had to do the work, and the evaluator, your boss, would make any corrections he felt necessary and then sign the form. But I was up for lieutenant colonel and I used a little extra care on this one. I cited that I was the only squadron technician to fly in command with ASEV and handed it in to the ops officer (Lt. Col. Sea Gull) who would sign it.

A few weeks after that I dropped by Base Personnel to review the OER to see what kind, and level, of endorsements I had received. In reading the front of the form, however, I saw the statement citing my flying in command for ASEV had been removed.

The next time I was in the squadron I stepped into the ops officer's office and brought this to his attention. "*I can't find the sentence about me flying in command with ASEV,*" I said.

He frowned and nodded his head to imply he had had to make a difficult decision and said, "*I know, Jay, it was a tough call, but I had to remove that sentence. It would have made all the other ARTS look bad.*" (Especially him.)

Stunned, I couldn't speak, and didn't.

I turned, walked down the hall to another office, and called Larry Mercker at Westover.

"*Larry,*" I said, "*I'm ready to move. Is that position still open?*"

It was, and off I would go to Westover for the next five years as Assistant Deputy Commander for Operations (ADO).

CHAPTER FOUR: WESTOVER AFB, MA

I arrived at Westover in Chicopee Falls, MA, in June 1988. I'd spend the summer in the BOQ just over a hill from the "old" command post inside wing headquarters. I remember that summer as unusual because the temperature set some record for the most days in a row over 90 degrees.

I stayed in the Q while B/G Walker, the wing commander, and I tried to get me set up in one of the manor houses on "General's Row," a series of four colonials on the hill above the headquarters building. These were home to senior officers during the base's B-52 days in the 1960s when Westover served as the 8th AF command base for all eastern SAC bases. Walker had promised me one of those houses when I agreed to take the job, but a complication had arisen.

Before my arrival, Walker had gotten into a squabble with the agency that controlled base housing, the Navy sub base in Groton, CT, of all places. I presume they were the nearest active duty military installation and thus the control rested with them.

However, Walker, in one of his ornery snits, had started charging the Navy for Air Force fire coverage for the base. Playing tit for tat, the Navy officials controlling senior housing took back control of the houses and said they would not allow me to have one of them as retaliation for the fire coverage charge.

This dispute escalated until the chief of the reserves, a two-star general, petitioned the Navy to relent. They took great glee in not doing so. Even more outrageous, they denied me the house again at the start of Desert Storm when I performed as the Deputy Commander for Operations for an active war and had a dire need to be located on the base. Wartime necessity be damned, they preferred sticking it to Walker rather than aiding our war effort. Petty bureaucratic squabbling during a war, incredible.

Next I put down a deposit on new townhouses being built just outside the main gate, but the project went bankrupt, leaving me, again, with no housing. I finally rented a four-bedroom house in east Springfield, right on the township line with Wilbraham, about twenty minutes from the base. This often left me managing aircraft emergencies by phone from home since I had no easy access to the command post unless I had moved in there. Sometimes my family thought I had done that.

In August, our family of five drove up in our Dodge Colt compact car with a torpedo-shaped luggage container on the roof to await the moving truck with our household goods. We traversed unfamiliar roads and highways I would come to know well in the years ahead, the Palisades Parkway, the Tappan Zee Bridge, the Long Island Expressway and the Connecticut Turnpike.

FIRST WESTOVER STANDUP

Shortly after my arrival that summer, I introduced myself to the Westover wing staff at a daily standup briefing in the old WWII headquarters building at the back of the central ellipse near the main gate. The conference room seemed a movie set for a Second World War drama. It featured lots of dark wood molding on white walls and with a long, heavy rectangular wooden table and a large single window behind the wing commander's seat.

There were two groups of personnel arrayed before me. Those were permanent party who had many years of service at Westover and would never leave, and the transients, of which I was one, who came in from other bases and would probably leave in a few years. Almost all of the top operations commanders were transients. The military, rightly, moves top commanders around the system to prevent an old boys' club from forming at any given base.

As previously stated, lieutenant colonels generally could not be promoted to full colonel unless they moved to another base, or to a non-operations position.

This policy had the salutary effect of shaking up base operations structures, but it also resulted in ossification in the reserve ranks, where "homesteader" lieutenant colonels at one base would sit in their O-5 rank position and never leave. As explained, I only jumped the structure from the squadron to wing level by moving from Dover the Westover, since the ops officer would forever block me and the rest of my cohorts.

The Westover wing hierarchy started at the top with B/G Gen. Mike Walker, in his mid-fifties, who would finish his career at Westover. With a leonine head and wavy gray hair, he cut a commanding figure. His personality ran from thoughtful and courteous during most standups to obstreperous and bull-headed if he thought he had encountered his nemesis, a bureaucratic dunderhead who should be shown the door with Big Mike's footprint on the culprit's ass. (Walker's term was somewhat more colorful than dunderhead.)

Photo by Whitey Joslin

B/G Mike Walker

Walker represents my third and final candidate for best commander in my Air Force career. While he could be prickly and overbearing, for some reason he never was with me. I don't attribute that to my stellar management abilities because he rode a better man than I, Larry Mercker, into stepping down as DCO.

During Desert Shield in the early days of the Gulf War in 1990, he had asked at standup, almost rhetorically, why there was a KC-10 on the ramp that morning. I manned the DCO position at the table that morning and I had no clue where the -10 had come from or why he was here, and I said so.

Walker looked down at the table and said, *"He diverted here for fuel and maintenance, and will depart this afternoon."* He knew this because he prowled the ramp from morning to night so nothing would escape his attention. Had he so desired, he could have eviscerated me in front of the wing staff for not doing my job, but he did not. He just let it go. He provided this management lesson for me but did not make me pay for it. He did as a pride lion might: demonstrate a stalking technique to a cub, but not severely penalize him for not getting it the first time.

The Westover commander job had been a difficult one to fill from the AFRES ranks. It was the largest reserve base and had just begun a transition from the C-130 prop cargo aircraft to the largest jet transport in the inventory, the C-5 Galaxy. Reportedly, few senior officers wanted to risk managing this dramatic aircraft conversion. Walker, instead, relished the opportunity and requested it. He would finally be top dog on his own major base. He would have the latitude to do it his way, the better way in his view and mine, without interference from the dunderheads at headquarters. He had made B/G on his last promotion shot after having alienated many in the AFRES command structure. He seemed to have a permanent simmering rage to show the command he could excel at this position. This, despite their view of him as a loose cannon who too often begged for forgiveness instead of asking permission. A year and a half later he would get that chance to prove his mettle after Saddam Hussein invaded Kuwait, and he would succeed, spectacularly, in showing them.

The Vice Commander, Col. Ralph Oates, affectionately known as "RUTA Ralph," (never showed up for regular drill weekends but did alternate, or replacement training days), had commanded my squadron, the 709th, at Dover and moved to Westover just before me. Politically smooth and calculating, Oates provided the perfect complementary presence to Walker's sometimes emotional and hip-shooting decision-making style. Oates would pick up the apples and neatly rearrange them after Walker had turned over the apple cart in a fit of pique. Walker would often ask for Oates to give his pronouncements "a sanity check" before he issued them. I fear neither of them would have succeeded as spectacularly as they did if not for the other. Walker had the brilliance and instincts, Oates the stability, balance and political acumen.

Photo by Whitey Joslin

Col. Ralph Oates

Oates had been propelled up the ranks for his performance during a dire aircraft emergency at Dover in 1983, a performance that earned him a Distinguished Flying Cross.

On a heavyweight morning takeoff, the C-5 Oates commanded had entered a 500-foot overcast cloud ceiling. Shortly thereafter it ran headlong into a V-shaped squadron of Canadian snow geese leaving the nearby bird refuge to fly across the base to the myriad of corn fields beyond. The collision proved catastrophic. The two right-side engines disintegrated and one caught fire. Oates declared an emergency and asked for vectors for a precision radar approach back to the runway he had just left. Copilot Dave Roberts later said his instrument panel was vibrating so violently he could not read his instruments.

As Oates fought to keep the plane airborne on only two engines, he limped around the radar pattern and began the precision final in the clouds. Holding course and glideslope can be challenging with a perfect airplane, something Oates did not have. As he approached minimums, the approach controller commanded: "*Too far right for safe approach, go around.*" Ha! Oates knew he could not go around on two asymmetrical engines; he was going to contact the ground, somewhere, very shortly. As he broke out of the clouds, he was able to yank the plane back to the runway and land safely. This event, plus his political savvy, would propel him upward in rank. He would get the second star Walker never did.

Walker came from the same C-130 background as most of the base pilots had (Westover had flown the slightly smaller C-123, also). Oates, along with Larry Mercker and I, formed the C-5 nucleus necessary for the transition. Within a few months, several of the local instructor pilots would become proficient in the Galaxy, but we three formed the initial cadre.

Walker, for a reason unknown to me, arranged a quirky operations command structure. His reserve DCO would be Col. Whitey Joslin, a longtime Westover pilot who, according to policy, should have had to transfer to another base to become a DCO. Also, Joslin had no experience as an instructor pilot or evaluator, generally a requirement for the position. This left it to Mercker and me to make operational and aircraft emergency situation decisions for wing aircraft. So, officially, Joslin would be the reserve DCO and Mercker the reserve

ADO, while on the civilian side, Mercker would be the DCO and I the ADO. Regardless, either Mercker or I would have the DCO's "brick" (radio) in our hand 24/7.

Larry Mercker had become an ART a few months before me in 1983 at Dover, although he was in the 326th MAS while I was in the 709th MAS down the hall. Mercker had also been previously stationed at Westover as a reservist and had jumped at the chance to transfer for the DCO position when offered. He discussed the ADO position with me, but, as described above, I wasn't inclined to move at that point, a situation that changed as a result of the next ASEV inspection.

I found Mercker fascinating to watch in motion. He attacked problems and situations methodically, logically and enthusiastically. But he did so while maintaining a positive and collaborative demeanor. He would broach his plans by identifying the problem, outlining what he thought needed to be done, and detailing how he, or we, would do it. When he finished presenting his plan of action, he'd look up and ask what we thought and remained open to altering his plan after discussion. Compared to other my-way-or-the-highway commanders, he was a gift from heaven. Knowing his command manner helped make my decision to transfer as his subordinate.

I was next down the line as ADO but with an "additional duty" as chief of the command post. At Dover, with a reserve and an active duty wing, the active duty ran the base with the reserves pretty much along for the ride as augmentees to the active duty base structure. Active duty commanders occasionally reminded us the Dover fleet belonged to them, and if they didn't like one of our aircraft commanders, they could threaten to deny him access to "their" airplanes.

At Westover, of course, we ran the show completely, something new for me. My new position demanded I become proficient in tasks I had never performed before such as command and control and supervising aircraft emergencies. Fortunately, I had about 18 months to become comfortable with these tasks before Desert Shield hit in 1990 and jacked up our aircraft flow several hundred percent from peacetime levels.

The two other major players around the wing standup table were the base commander, Col. Tom Hargis and the Deputy Commander for Maintenance, Col. Hal Lawrence.

Hargis always seemed mellow and congenial; I can't ever remember seeing him angry. Despite few apparent hard-charger genes in his personality makeup, he performed well, and seemed open to the many changes Desert Shield/Storm demanded of us all.

Lawrence, a Louisiana Southerner, presented a laid-back persona similar to Hargis. Hal always seemed to have a Southern quip to explain his positions or to describe situations we faced. He, too, displayed few hard-charger traces in his demeanor but drew incredible maintenance performances during the war that enabled us to excel among the major C-5 stage bases. His subordinates, my counterparts, were Lt. Col. Clune and Maj. Friedhofer. The one hard charger in his organization, Capt. Cam LeBlanc, seemed everywhere at once on the ramp during the war and drove the flight line troops to exceptional performances.

Except for Mercker, I knew none of these personal characteristics of the wing staff at this first meeting, but I did sense a congenial group I could probably work well with, and that is how it turned out.

MEETING THE COMMAND POST STAFF

After this first standup I had but a short stroll down the hall to my new command post home. As I entered I saw a large, cavernous, windowless room at the center of the wing headquarters building. Banks of phones at several consoles were arrayed in a semi-circle beneath a large white board with a checkerboard of lines on it tracking base missions and aircraft.

The command post chief, Ken, a master sergeant, met me upon entry and introduced himself. Friendly and affable, Ken at times seemed to shrink back like a puppy afraid he was about to get spanked, residue from past episodes at other locations, I suspect. Strangely, he lived an hour away in Schenectady, NY, home to the New York Air Guard. There was a story why he worked for us, but no longer for them, but I can't recall it. He often spent the weekdays at a local crash pad, then returned to New York on the weekends. He smoked fairly heavily and, I suspect, drank some too, but he held the reins well on most occasions. In my five years there, we had no command and control fiascos, so Ken kept us straight.

Ken took me into the depths of the cavern to meet his assistant, whom I will call "Susan," also a master sergeant. Dark-haired and attractive, she shook my hand and looked me in the eye just slightly longer than necessary.

Susan quickly recalled a flight warning for me. When planning for an instrument departure in the aircraft, some of the instructions on the plate may have a black upside-down triangle with a white "T" in the middle. This means the pilot must read detailed instructions to avoid some obstacle. Pilots call this the "Trouble T" and must be scrupulous in avoiding the trouble it may cause.

Having immediately smitten me, Susan had "Trouble T" written all over her. We sat at adjoining consoles beneath the great white board and chatted briefly. All became apparent; we were both married, she to a chief master sergeant from the aero port. And, of course, she was enlisted and I was an officer, the standard multiple taboos.

We fell silent smiling at each other, then both seemed to recognize we still had an eye lock going. The smiles faded and we turned toward our respective consoles. I imagined us both then reaching for a metaphorical seat belt, pulling it across our chest and hips and clipping it firmly into the metal latch to keep the gravitational pull between us at bay. This succeeded for the next five years working together closely until my very last day on the base, but there were times…

After about two weeks we had a conversation going among several of us in the outer office. During the conversation someone made repeated use of the term "retard." Later, I asked Susan if she could step next door with me to discuss something.

As we sat in a table in an office down the hall, she had a look of dread on her face, apparently thinking I was going to chew her out for something. I smiled and told her not to worry, I just needed to advise her that I had a Down's syndrome daughter and, while use of the word "retard" did not particularly bother me, she might feel badly when she discovered this, and I wanted to head that off and assure her I was not offended.

Her eyes grew wide and she gasped that she was so sorry they had used that word. She said she would never have allowed it had she known. As she said that, she reached over and placed her hand on top of mine. Ooooooh! I felt myself straining against the mythical seat belt!

As the months passed it seemed we both realized the score, significant mutual attraction that must never be acted upon or suggested in public or private. As far as I know, this worked, except on her husband "Johnny."

After a staff meeting one day he asked if he could talk to me and wondered if maybe we could go have a beer sometime. I said sure, but we never did. Right then I knew that he knew, probably deduced indirectly from Susan's actions and statements. I wanted to assure him nothing would happen, but that would also confirm his fears, so I remained silent.

This exquisite agony recalled the dilemma faced by Dr. Zhivago in the 1960s movie with that name. Zhivago had performed as a doctor for months in a wartime hospital during the Russian Revolution in 1918. He worked closely with his main nurse, Lara, and had grown desperately fond of her despite his strong ties to his wife, Tonya, and their child.

As the hospital staff disbanded, Zhivago began to express his feelings for Lara. Lara held up her hand to stop him and told him they had done nothing he could not tell Tonya, and that is how they must leave it. That barely held

Zhivago off, once, but a second encounter would occur. So it would be with Susan and me.

At a wing social function, Bea met Susan and they hit it off, becoming good friends, aggravatingly for me. Susan visited our house often, sometimes to babysit the girls, although usually when I was on a trip.

After working together for five years, under difficult circumstances during Desert Shield/Storm, I came in to say good-bye to the staff in the summer of 1993 before leaving Westover for Dover. I shook hands all around and shook Susan's last. Tears welled up in both of us, but that is how we needed to leave it.

I turned and departed through the two cypher-locked doors, walked down a short hallway and turned the corner toward the exit door to the parking lot. Then, behind me, I heard the two doors opening and closing rapidly. I turned back and Susan launched herself into my arms. We spun around a time or two moving around the corner and out of sight of the command post doors, squeezing five years of repressed embraces into one long one.

She said, "Good-bye, friend!" and I promised, "I'll be back on a C-5 soon!" And then she was gone, disappearing into the ladies' room to compose herself. Good-bye, Zhivago; good-bye, Lara.

I actually didn't make it back for ten years on that C-5, and then only for a quick-turn enroute to Dover in 2003. I called to see if she could drop by base ops. She had some sort of party going, but she said she would be there. We had not spoken since I left Westover.

About thirty minutes later she appeared at the base ops door at the end of the same short hallway I had last seen her. No words were spoken. We melted into a clinch in about the same spot from a decade earlier, desperate, overjoyed, and frantic. I looked around for some nook to gain privacy, but there was none. The rest of my pilot crew was around the corner in the lounge and there was no other private space.

In a short conversation I learned Johnny was battling terminal cancer while she learned I was sliding toward divorce. We promised to reconnect and, after another desperate clinch, she left.

We spoke several times afterward but that was the last time I saw her. By the time Johnny died, I had divorced and reconnected with a previous high school flame and was no longer on the market. I also learned from Facebook postings that she had remained far right, politically, while I had drifted leftward after no Iraqi weapons of mass destruction were found in 2003. Our compatibility had lessened significantly. Life has strange twists and many potential paths we might have trod are blocked by fate or our choices.

Meeting the 337th Airlift Squadron Personnel

My next stop, across the ellipse at Westover, was the flying squadron located on one side of a large hangar on the flight line. The hangar had two long floors of offices on each side of the large expanse of open hangar floor in between. The squadron had the north-side offices.

I knew, generally, what to expect. All reserve squadrons are somewhat alike, with cliques and histories among their personnel. The Westover group would have similarities to my Dover squadron but with different personalities. I would find many of the same groupings, airline pilots, commercial pilots, technicians, local members, commuters from outside the local area, and pilots from a variety of different aircraft now flying C-5s. Except none of the Westover group had C-5 experience.

There would be senior members, some of whom would think they owned the place, and junior members who sometimes felt abused by the senior members. The cliques would also take umbrage at other cliques and work behind the scenes to prevail in getting their way.

There would be positive and negative personalities, strong and weak pilots, and social intrigues among all the groups, all standard squadron conditions throughout the Air Force.

My job was to remove detrimental aspects of squadron operation and get the wheels spinning as smoothly as possible to complete the mission. I had no history here, had no buddies, held no grudges, and didn't know any of the past infamous episodes that can be long-lived in squadron lore. Most importantly, whoever thought they had my predecessor in their pocket had to start from scratch with me with no guarantee they could schmooze me similarly.

But they all immediately tried! Welcoming smiles and salutations were mixed with slightly narrowed eyes trying to gauge me, to deduce what my preferences might be, and where my red flags might be that would set me off. Would I be a good guy or a prick; would I be a reasonable guy or a screamer; would I be an honest broker or have a favored clique? Also, would I be a lapdog for Gen. Walker, or would I stick up for the crews if necessary and risk Walker's wrath?

I would be gauging them, also, asking many of the same questions. The old regime was gone and we had to build a new, fresh one, the creative destruction necessary to keeping a squadron functioning well.

I had to watch my actions as well. This squadron had a long and storied history in the C-123 and C-130 aircraft, and the crews would not appreciate me coming in as Mr. Know-it-all on the C-5 who dismissed them as knowing nothing because they didn't yet know the C-5. The squadron had many vastly experienced, top-notch pilots who would be temporarily at a disadvantage in a new aircraft but would soon be highly capable.

Almost immediately I got tested on that front. On an air refueling training sortie, I had warned the other pilots of the possibility of them doing a "wing tip check" on their early attempts. This occurs because the pilot over-controls the aircraft and winds up swinging wildly from one tanker wing tip to the other. Maddeningly, the harder the pilot tries to correct it, the worse it gets.

Thus it was for Dave Doyle, the squadron ops officer. The swaying back and forth off centerline started slowly but gradually increased. Doyle began muttering on interphone, disbelieving that he could be having such trouble. Finally, while thrashing the yoke left and right, and closely checking each of the tanker wing tips, he gave up and pulled the throttles back to fall behind the tanker far enough to start over.

Doyle was livid and embarrassed. He was one of the squadron's most experienced and capable pilots and he had just failed miserably on his first air refueling attempt. I told him that happened to me, too, on my first attempt and not to worry about it, just get back in there.

He stabilized in the pre-contact position and approached under much better control and had it pretty well down by the end of his turn.

ROGUE WARRIOR

Shortly after I arrived at Westover I received a call from a Dover active duty instructor pilot who was departing active duty and looking for a reserve position at Westover. Ordinarily we would be eager to hire an experienced C-5 pilot into a squadron without many. But there was a problem.

This pilot, "Victor," had a spotty record with Dover active duty. He had pulled a few stunts in the airplane that put him on the bad-boy list with his active duty commanders. They told the Dover reserve commanders that the active duty would not allow him to fly Dover aircraft if the reserves hired him (the active duty "owned" all the Dover airplanes). Thus his desire to join the 337th AS at Westover, where the reserves owned the planes.

I got a call from my primary nemesis, Lt. Col. Sea Gull, from my Dover squadron (the one who refused to "let me make the other ARTs look bad" on my OER) explaining all this to me. He related that Victor had arranged an unscheduled air refueling off Nantucket on a channel cargo mission against a tanker that had lost his training receiver. Vic heard the tanker cancel his refueling for a receiver no-show on the center frequency and volunteered to accomplish an impromptu refueling with passengers on board. This is a legal maneuver, in itself, but it had not been scheduled, so the active duty chastised him for it. Next, he did a touch-and-go at Barbers Point in Hawaii with passengers on board to complete training on one of his pilots. Touch-and-goes with passengers on board is a no-no, so the active duty effectively admonished and grounded him, forcing him off active duty.

As I listened to the Sea Gull explain all this to me, and to almost forbid me from hiring Victor, I started bristling. *"I'll hire him if I fucking want to, SG!"* I wanted to shout into the phone, but I listened politely, thanked him and hung up. I now held a higher position at Westover than he held at Dover, and I'm sure that galled the hell out of him. I always considered the active duty the best recruiter the reserves had with their sometimes overly punitive and abusive management style.

I talked to Gen. Walker about hiring Victor. Walker had the same reaction I did. He stuck out his lower lip like an unhappy youngster and said we'd interview Victor, but we'd hire him if we damn well pleased and fuck the active duty. And we did (hire him, that is). Walker loved the guy, as did I, a rogue warrior who had gone outside the box but had gotten the job done. Victor promised not to get outside the box again without our permission and that seemed sufficient for us.

Operationally, it would prove a sound call. When the balloon went up for Desert Shield in 1990, Victor volunteered to take the first mission into the system that did not yet know what it was doing. At standup each day we'd query MAC headquarters to find out "where in the world is Victor?" Sometimes he was so lost in Africa or the Middle East even MAC headquarters wasn't sure where he was. He stayed out for two weeks and led the force in creating the new wartime mission. Walker and I both wished we were with him and envied him his opportunity.

Over the three years he flew for us there would be only one incident. Victor landed at Hanscom Field in eastern Massachusetts and allowed his copilot to make the landing even though a NOTAM warned not to land long, since there was temporarily no available taxiway to taxi back for takeoff. The copilot landed long, about 100 yards past the intersecting runway they were not supposed to cross.

However, from that position they would have closed the entire airdrome if they remained on the runway, and the only way to remedy the situation was to back up the airplane with reversers. This required a waiver from Gen. Walker. Somehow, Hanscom could not find any of us to ask for the waiver. After five minutes, Victor told them he would assume a waiver and back the plane up anyway, to clear the runway and reopen the airport, and he accomplished this without incident.

When we found out he had backed up the plane without a waiver, our Chief of Stan/Eval wanted Vic's head on a platter and wanted him busted on the spot when he got home. This got thrashed out the next morning at standup. The stan/eval chief insisted Victor pay for his unauthorized maneuver with a Q-3 disqualification from flying until remedial action had been accomplished. I told the assembled wing staff that had Victor not backed up the plane, Hanscom would still be closed and there would have been hell to pay, that he was an instructor and could plausibly have anticipated a waiver and he did request one. Stan/eval was having none of it, they wanted him busted.

After listening to the discussion, Walker's head started swiveling around on his neck, warning he was about to issue an edict over which he would brook no objection.

"If I had been contacted, I would have issued the waiver, so Victor had a waiver, and you…will…not…bust…him. Any questions?" he asked as he glared at the stan/eval chief. There would be no questions.

Concurrently, the Air Force had gone on a weight control jihad. Everyone had to be within parameters and Victor was not, being about 30 pounds overweight. We discussed it with him, and within six months he had reduced his weight to well below the maximum standard, astounding me and everyone else. He had also quit smoking while doing so. Incredible.

But later, after Gen. Walker had retired and been replaced as wing commander by a bureaucratic climber, "Ski," the rogue warrior went off the tracks while off duty. Since Walker was gone, the only name remaining on the hand receipt for hiring Victor was mine.

The phone rang one night in late 1991 and it was Ski. "*Jay*," he said in his deceptively soft and friendly voice, "*Victor is in jail for attempting to hold up the shoppette on base. You need to get with him tomorrow after he is arraigned. He'll be in the Springfield jail.*"

I sat, stunned. He did *what*? This seemed inconceivable but apparently it happened because the next afternoon I found him in the Springfield jail.

I in-processed as a visitor standing with about 20 others in a waiting room with locked barred doors going in or out. My stomach was already churning in reaction to the facility. Built in 1890 of brick, its dark cavernous interior harkened to the realms of Dante's Inferno; I half expected to see flames licking up the far walls. We entered the visitation area and I sat on a stool fastened to the floor before a long counter divided lengthwise by a metal mesh resembling chicken wire but much thicker, and by dividers that provided minimal privacy between stations. I felt a deep depression settling on me, and I was outside the wire! I could not imagine being inside.

After a few minutes, Victor emerged from the gloom and sat across from me, as dejected and forlorn a person as I have ever seen. "*Hi, Jay, fancy meeting you here,*" he deadpanned, his face slack and gray.

"*Vic, what the fuck happened? I can't believe this!*" I said.

Quickly, the story emerged. Vic had developed a gambling problem after his brother was killed as a long-haul trucker. He had crashed and burned to death in the cab. This profoundly affected Victor and sent him reeling, he said. He had been an occasional gambler, but soon became an addicted one because, as he explained, it was the only time he felt in control of his life after his brother's death.

He was not in control of the cards, however, and he had gambled away his family's savings and their college accounts for their four children now aged 6 to 14. He had also maxed out his government American Express card where payment was due Monday. He had jumped on a weekend C-5 trip to San Juan to try to win at the tables the $3,000 due to American Express and had even tried to borrow money off other crew members to keep playing, but had failed.

When they landed at Westover Sunday night, Vic went to his BOQ room and collapsed into a chair. He reviewed what would soon happen when he would be unable to pay the American Express card bill the next day, on top of having blown his family's finances. He cracked.

He said he felt detached from himself and was watching what happened next from outside his body.

He stood up and put on a military raincoat over his flight suit. (I wanted to stop him to ask why on earth he would prepare in such a clumsy manner, but I just let the story spill out.) He got in his car and removed the .38 revolver he carried for protection while driving through the Bronx to JFK Airport for his job as a TWA pilot. He then drove to the shoppette on base, intent on getting the $3,000 he had to have the next day. This time I couldn't take it; I asked why he didn't go off-base. The shoppette alarm would close the base gates and there would be no escape. He looked down at the table and almost whispered that he wasn't rational by this point.

He pulled his gun on the female clerk and told her to fork over the money. Apparently he used significant verbal pressure on her, because her distraught testimony at trial weighed heavily against him. As soon as the gun appeared, he had earned a minimum five-year sentence, but none of that yet registered on him. The clerk hit the silent alarm button, and soon, sky cops, who had several patrols on duty since they were still activated, screeched to a halt all around the building. (I imagine the cops thought this was another frigging drill, until they realized it was not. Holy shit, they must have thought, some moron is actually trying rob the shoppette!)

Vic now panicked and ran into the back room of the facility. Rationality had now returned somewhat, and he assessed his situation. He knew what the gun would earn him in jail time and tried to find a floorboard to hide it, without success.

Next, as I anticipated, he said he considered suicide but realized he didn't have the guts to do it. He lamely hid the gun on top of the freezer, raised his hands and walked to the cops.

He got 18 years with the possibility of parole after six years for good behavior. He might have gotten far less for being a Desert Storm veteran and for almost 18 years of service and no previous record, but pulling the gun and terrorizing the clerk negated all that.

I tried to be helpful. I said that when he got out, he should go into the service industry, since they didn't really care about past transgressions and he could eventually work for himself and not have to worry about his record. He tried to smile, but couldn't quite pull it off.

As he left he waved good-bye briefly and disappeared into the darkness where shouts and deranged cackles rang down the hallway from other denizens of this hell. It took me a week to mentally recover from this visit.

One of the saddest sights I have ever seen was him saying good-bye to his wife and kids outside the courtroom. What could he say? What could he promise? He had been within 100 points of an active duty retirement from the Air Force (18 "good years" that would put him in the sanctuary zone). He had lost this military pension, his TWA job and pension, and was leaving them high and dry.

I have not seen or talked to him since 1991. From hearsay I understand he did his time in the newly built Ludlow prison facility on the other side of the Westover runway, where he could watch his former compadres shoot touch-and-goes.

I also heard, again from hearsay, that he is now doing well and owns two restaurants in Denver. I don't know if that is true, but I hope it is.

DALLIANCES

Percolating beneath mission activity we had extracurricular affairs going on that could have caused significant problems but, thankfully, did not.

The primary dalliance involved Gen. Walker himself. His wife and family had stayed at his last station in Ohio, so he lived alone in one of the General's Row houses on the hill to the right of the main gate. On many nights he entertained in the rear deck hot tub, sometimes with a group of people, and sometimes with one in particular, a female captain. Their affair seemed an open secret on the base and no one seemed upset with it. But as with all such affairs, my previous ones included, it went against military protocol on two counts, in this case, adultery and fraternization with someone in your chain of command. As always, Walker didn't give a damn about protocol. I don't know if Col. Oates consulted with him on this, and if so, what his advice had been, but the affair continued throughout my tenure there.

Military discipline on this issue fluctuated over the years. As I recounted in book one, I took a squadron enlisted woman to my final squadron picnic at Castle AFB, CA, in 1979. That violated two military taboos, fraternization in the same chain of command, and officer/enlisted dating. And did it right under the squadron commander's nose. Further, I was white and she was black, something that ensured everyone would notice. Yet, I was not sanctioned or even counseled about the action.

Four years after I left Westover, in 1997, CINCMAC Gen. Ron Fogleman issued his *Little Blue Book* outlining his stringent "one strike and you are out" edict. Adultery and fraternization were two of those strikes. Ironically, during the tenure of the *Blue Book,* Air Force Reserve Command (the new name for AFRES) commander was married to an enlisted woman, although the marriage had taken place years before.

I have no idea if Walker's superiors at AFRES headquarters knew of his extracurricular activities, but I must presume they did. However, several of them had been in trouble on similar grounds, so the black kettles at headquarters laid off the black pot at Westover. I, too, was in no position to critique Walker given my past activities of violating the officer/enlisted, and chain of command, taboos. Even with that, I recognize that these things happen. Would we have removed Dwight Eisenhower just prior to the D-Day invasion over his apparent affair with Kay Summersby? The 2012 affair of Gen. Petraeus with Paula Broadwell showed that even America's, at the time, most esteemed general and current Director of the CIA was not immune to extracurricular activities.

So if you are going to participate in such activities, make sure you don't get caught if the military is currently enforcing its strictures.

BABY B, CONTINUED

Photo by Jay Lacklen

Kay (Baby B) and Karen Lacklen

After six months in Massachusetts, the twins, Karen and Kay, were crawling and getting ready to walk. Karen had developed faster, as we expected due to Kay's Down's syndrome, but Kay gamely tried to keep up.

They loved climbing the carpeted stairs from the downstairs to the upstairs, and occasionally I'd have them race for the top, something they loved to do. Karen won the first time, so the second time I tried to help Kay by boosting her diapered butt to help her along. She would have none of it, however. She growled at me angrily when I tried to do so, insistent she wanted to do it on her own. She again lost but beamed at her accomplishment of attaining the top of the stairs.

She looked back at me, perplexed that her dad was rubbing his eyes with his thumb on one eye and his forefinger on the other, tears on his cheeks.

During family arguments, Kay would listen to the shouting for a while, but would then shut down the argument cold by hugging each of the antagonists and conveying that they were making Kay sad.

One of the initial hurdles after Kay's birth was managing the reaction to her. Everyone was heartbroken and didn't know how to react, and I can't blame them. Although Kay's condition was not immediately recognizable as an infant, as they began walking and riding in a stroller in the mall, it became evident. Women would stop to coo over them in their tandem stroller and suddenly stop cooing as they discovered Kay's different appearance. They would then glance at me, unsure of how to react, and I would smile at them knowingly and thank them. That usually defused the situation.

I initially had trouble out in public with the girls as well. Was I being judged as the father of a less than perfect child? Did this reflect on me? Was Kay's condition my fault?

Fortunately, I got over this angst fairly quickly and the lingering glances we received no longer bothered me. I thought I was being judged more on how I handled the situation than the situation itself, so handling it graciously and well became easier.

I had a troubling discussion with our delivery doctor a month or so after the delivery. I demanded to know why we didn't know about Kay's condition well before birth. It seemed I subconsciously, and ludicrously, blamed him for

Kay's condition. He explained that an amniocentesis was too hazardous with twins. And then he asked the question that crushed me.

"*What would you have done, had you known? You can't abort just one twin; you must abort them both,*" he said.

In a sense, twins would have tilted the decision to allowing birth, but the decision would have been agonizing for a single birth. However, that was then; it would not be agonizing now, in retrospect. Kay is one of the most delightful, joyous personalities I have experienced. I often half-joke that if I didn't already have a Down's syndrome child, I'd adopt one to keep me tuned up, to cheer me up from my doldrums, and as an inspiration when I failed to summon sufficient diligence toward some lofty task. Recognizing Kay will never be capable of some achievements, I should demand more of myself since I am capable and should do it for Kay, as she would, if she could. When I begin to slack off on important efforts, I can hear Baby B growling at me to persevere.

Photo by Ann Wyborski

Dad and Kay, Christmas, 2015

In 1988, Bea and I decided to go for a boy after three girls. There was no male heir to carry on the family name and we wanted to give it one more shot.

My mother was apoplectic that we would try another pregnancy after Kay's, but we were undeterred. In June, 1989, perfectly normal, fourth daughter, Amanda arrived. Not a boy, but still a joy. Ironically, after being born in Springfield, MA, our "Yankee" daughter graduated from Ole Miss and lived in Mississippi after graduation.

THE GENERALS' TOUR

In the fall of 1989, Gen. Walker, in his standard style, arranged a C-5 European tour (boondoggle) for a passel of Air Force Reserve generals. The ostensible alibi for the trip was for a NATO conference at Ramstein AB, Germany. But the real reason for the tour was for Walker to show off for the reserve brass, who had often thwarted and maligned him. He wanted to give them a show, Mike Walker style, and it proved a huge success.

Walker hand-picked the team to fly the mission, Sgt. Ronnie Robbins, his primary scrounger and facilitator, and me. The flight to Europe provided an interesting wrinkle. Walker, Robbins and I served as flight attendants for the brass to include offering hors d'oeuvres and nonalcoholic beverages (the booze would come after we landed). The brass seemed flattered to be served very attentively by a general and lieutenant colonel.

The two-day NATO conference went routinely with long nights at the Ramstein O'Club schmoozing with the senior old boys' club of the Air Force Reserve who had bedeviled Walker his entire career.

The second mission imperative took us to Tempelhof AB in Berlin, for a dinner trip into East Germany shortly before the Berlin Wall came down. A blue Air Force bus took us through Checkpoint Charlie and the entire world went dark, figuratively, when we crossed that threshold. East Germany glowered at us menacingly, dark dirty-gray concrete walls with sullen unfriendly pedestrians on the streets. The East German soldiers at the checkpoint and at other locations around the city brought forth the same wariness in me the

Gestapo must have provided to my father's generation during WWII, scowling, menacing, and evil. I felt we were being watched constantly and felt an unease worse than during an upcoming trip to Russia in 1991. East Germany was far worse than Russia, although the entire Soviet edifice had come down by the time I got to Moscow.

The restaurant staff, however, seemed cheerful and pleasant as they served us. I found myself seated with a reserve fighter wing commander and we found common dread at our surrounds, noting that this is what we spent our careers to defeat. The victory we sought proved much closer than we imagined as the wall came down shortly after our visit.

As we drove back through "Charlie" I felt as if I had escaped from a prison dungeon, and the entire world seemed brighter.

GEN. WALKER'S GRAND BEAR HUNT

In 1989 Gen. Walker took a long-planned bear hunting trip to Alaska. Incredibly, while he was gone, a black bear invaded his back yard on base quarters and climbed a tree, where local animal control had to sedate and remove him. Walker came home without having seen a bear on his trip, only to find out we had all seen one in his back yard.

HALIFAX, NOVA SCOTIA

Westover employed a devious method to skirt a command requirement while also having a marvelous crew rest. It was just terrible that we did this, yes it was! And I got on every such mission I could to remind myself how terrible it was!

MAC dictated that pilots must fly two overseas sorties per semi-annual period to ensure proficiency. The intent centered on traversing the NAT Tracks, or highways in the sky, between the U.S. and Europe to maintain familiarity with oceanic procedures. Flying from Westover to Halifax satisfied none of this currency except, technically, we did fly over non-U.S. oceanic waters for an hour or so.

To avoid the appearance of a self-serving boondoggle, we would often arrange for the Halifax airport fire department to "train" on rescue procedures on a C-5 to instruct them on responding to a C-5 ground emergency.

I thought of Halifax as the San Francisco of the Eastern Seaboard, with steeply graded hills overlooking a harbor, much as its American counterpart does. As always, you often forgot you were not in America since Canada is so utterly similar as long as you didn't stray too closely to the French speakers in and around Quebec. The only reminder you might not "be in Kansas anymore" was the Canadians' penchant for putting "hey" at the end of their sentences. ("That's sure a big airplane, hey?")

We walked up and down the San Francisco-esque streets looking for a restaurant and found *The Five Fishermen* on a corner halfway up a hill. I didn't realize it as we walked in, but this would be one of the best restaurants I would encounter in my worldwide travels.

The interior went heavy on wood floors and walls and sported several floors arranged so you could view most of the other floors and balconies around an open atrium. After we were seated on a balcony halfway up the structure, I looked at the menu. We had passed a mussel bar on the way up, and I wondered how much they might be. I almost dropped the menu when I found it; free! A free mussel bar, no way!

I tossed my menu on the table and told my compadres I'd be back with a bowl full of mussels and don't order without me. The mussels were scrumptious and I went back for more, twice. When we finally ordered, I was so full I didn't think I could eat any more, but I managed to down a seafood platter that was also superb.

Fully stuffed, I headed back to the hotel to sleep it off. This was my kind of overseas sortie!

Now, over twenty years later, I plan to visit Halifax again specifically to eat at *The Five Fishermen* restaurant. It will be worth the trip.

TOTAL QUALITY MANAGEMENT

In the late 1980s the Air Force became enamored with Total Quality Management, or TQM. This management system held such allure for the brass that my reserve base held a paid weekend retreat for all top officers to receive instruction in it. In 25 years I had never seen such a push for indoctrination in a management method.

TQM basically identified individual processes within an office's span of control and used methods to continuously improve quality in these processes. It also encouraged input from those with their hands actually on the levers of the process to suggest improvements to their supervisors.

There is more to the total concept, much of which I can't remember, but there were two spectacularly effective methods presented, one of which is similar to a concept presented in management books from the times by author Tom Peters.

INVERTED PYRAMID

During peacetime, the military is run from the top down. Headquarters directs levels and methods of training and sends inspection teams to ensure its directives are being met. This is a sometimes awkward alternative to open market forces a business uses for feedback on its efforts. This displays the standard pyramid formation that narrows at the top and spreads wide at the bottom.

The military's open market is war, and that, obviously, must be simulated by the inspection teams.

In the Strategic Air Command (SAC), this became the Operational Readiness Inspection (ORI). As shown in many movies from the time, such as

Strategic Air Command, *Bombers B-52*, and *A Gathering of Eagles*, an inspection team would arrive unannounced at a given SAC base shortly after an alert had been issued to the base and a klaxon horn sounded.

Once the klaxon went off, all the bases' tankers and bombers must cross the runway hold line, simulating takeoff, within 15 minutes to ensure they could escape a nuclear blast that would surely occur at the base from inbound enemy missiles.

The inspection team would observe how well the base performed on this task, a frantic escapade of crews diving into their alert trucks, or sprinting from their alert shelter, to start engines and taxi within the allotted time.

Then, a few days later, the base crew force would fly a simulated nuclear strike mission to include air refueling and, for the bombers, flying a predesignated low-level route somewhere in the States to simulate dropping bombs on targets in Russia or China.

Once the klaxon went off, crucially, the pyramid inverted, or had better invert. Now the former bottom of the pyramid rotated to the top. The lowest level personnel, to include the individual crews, single-stripe maintenance crewmembers, and shop dispatchers beccame the imperative performers. Whatever they needed, the commanders, now at the bottom of the pyramid, had better provide. The former bottom rung was now running the show at the imperative action points and they, not the brass, called the shots. The peons were calling the tune, and the commanders had better dance as fast as they could to that tune.

WHO IS THE CUSTOMER?

This dovetails with my single most imperative concept from TQM, proper identification of the customer in a specific interaction: "*Who is the customer?*" This is not as simple as it might seem.

In the bureaucratic military hierarchy during peacetime, the person who outranks you is usually the customer who must be pleased. The higher your rank, the more "vendors" you have trying to satisfy your demands.

But when war arrives, and the pyramid inverts, it is often the lower ranking individual, trying to work the levers of the military machine, who becomes the customer. "*Sir,*" he might plead, "*we've run out of imperative widgets!*" The commanding officer, upon hearing this, should take that as an order to him to provide more widgets. The senior member has been subordinated to his former charges and must act accordingly.

Failure to invert the pyramid, thereby leading to misidentifying the proper customer, is a common wartime military failure. Desert Shield would be replete with examples of this failure to adjust. During peacetime training, those of higher rank instruct and train those beneath them. In the war, however, the roles must reverse.

These command features may give America a military advantage over strictly authoritarian militaries (Soviets), who seemed to deny an imperative feedback mechanism in their top-down command structure even during war.

CHAPTER FIVE: DESERT SHIELD

Painting by Charles Edwin Fripp

Battle of Isandhlwana

ISANDHLWANA

The British soldiers awoke to a splendidly bright morning on the South African veldt in the shadow of the Islandhlwana mesa in 1879. They anticipated a leisurely day in this base camp for the task force seeking the fearsome Zulu army. Yet, before the noon meal, almost all 1,500 would lie dead and disemboweled in their crisp, red brocade uniforms.

While the main British force searched in vain for their Zulu prey a day's march away, the main Zulu force fell suddenly upon this British base camp with a ten-to-one numbers advantage. Yet, initially, the Tommies felt little fear. They knew they could overcome their numbers disadvantage with vastly superior technology, including cannon and modern cartridge rifles to contest the Zulu cowhide shields and stabbing spears, called assegais. However, their own internal process contradiction betrayed them, and they fell to their Stone Age opponents almost to a man.

This British massacre, that happened two years after a similar American army debacle at the Little Big Horn, displays an inherent bureaucratic weakness that affects armies as well as corporations. I will discuss this weakness as displayed during the first Gulf War in 1990–1991 at Westover AFB, MA, an Air Force Reserve base flying C-5 cargo aircraft in support of the war.

While the British army of 1879 would seem to have little directly in common with the American Air Force of 1990, both suffered from this endemic contradiction in their structure. This proved fatal for the Brits if only inconvenient for the Americans, but it runs through all corporate structures, military or civilian, and has brought many to ruin.

The simple question these bureaucracies fail to correctly answer: Who is the customer?

At the battle of Isandhlwana, the British armorer demanded the customer role when he should not have, and almost the entire unit died as a result.

During peacetime routine, the armorer was properly the customer. He played the tune, the soldiers danced. His imperative demanded all bullets be accounted for and safely maintained. His report card reflected his diligence in returning every unused bullet to the armory after maneuvers. Troopers were held strictly accountable for every cartridge issued to them. To protect the cartridges during transport, they were securely stored in long crates that loaded and traveled easily. Each crate was tightly bound in metal bands that held the lid secure. To further ensure no case broke open during transport, the lids were also fastened down with multiple screws. No cartridge could possibly escape this tomb, and this led to the Tommies' doom.

The base camp had not anticipated any action. The major column had gone in search of the Zulus and all assumed they would engage the enemy. About ten in the morning, a small British cavalry squad on reconnaissance from the encampment crested a ridge and beheld twenty thousand Zulu warriors crouching in a shallow valley in silence awaiting an order to attack.

The British horsemen, thunderstruck, turned and raced for the base camp. The Zulus, eager for battle and having been discovered, began their attack in their very effective three-pronged (horns and chest of the buffalo) formation, where the horns try to turn the left and right flank, while the main body rams into the middle of the enemy formation.

The horsemen's speed allowed some time for the camp to prepare, but not enough. Although, at first, the Brits seemed confident in their chances. Some could be seen joking in the lines as they fired at the Zulus cowering under their shields a few hundred yards away, afraid to risk a charge.

But then, the cartridges began to run low on the front line. Each squad sent a runner back to the armory position deep in the middle of the formation, shaped in a half moon with the mesa protecting their rear, but most failed to return. What could have happened to them, the troops must have wondered as they pondered the bristling forest of assegais before them.

What happened was a failure to relinquish customer status by the armorer. While properly the customer prior to hostilities, the armorer found himself ill-prepared to now provide service to the new, proper customers, the runners dispatched to bring desperately needed cartridges back to the front line troops. The troops were now playing the tune, but the armorer could not dance. All the armorer's stringent rules and extensive packaging efforts defeated his one imperative task, delivering cartridges to the troops in battle. All his training, all his procedures, all his diligence, were to serve but one purpose, to deliver the cartridges when needed, yet now, he could not.

It seems he had traveled short of screwdrivers to remove the lid screws from the ammo crates. If he had enjoyed the luxury of an hour to prepare, this would not have been a problem, but he did not have that luxury. The Zulu impi formation swarmed the British position with only minutes' notice, and the armorer and his apprentices could not open the crates fast enough to supply the troops.

As the armory squad tried desperately to smash the impenetrable crates with rocks, the armorer insisted the runners line up in proper formation to receive the meager number of cartridges he could provide. He also dismissed some of the runners because they were not the designated runner for their platoon. He, laughably, demanded strict adherence to peacetime rules to cover for his inability to perform the primary task he was paid to perform. While his diligence did successfully get the cartridges to the battle, his lack of preparation and planning to reverse his role from customer to vendor defeated his only required, imperative task, supplying the runners with cartridges when they arrived.

With no ammunition to fend off the enemy, the center of the British formation crumbled and retreated to the supply wagons. The Zulus rose and swarmed through the gap and soon slashed freely inside the camp. While a few horsemen managed to begin a desperate race to the many miles' distant British fort at Rorke's Drift, the remaining clumps of British soldiers began to fall as assegais overwhelmed bayonets. Over the next hours the Zulus looted the camp and methodically disemboweled the soldiers to release their spirits to heaven, a possibly charitable act in their view that horrified the British attack column when it returned.

When the commanding general and the rest of his command did arrive at the camp after nightfall, the horror of the battlefield was too much. He marched his troops off the field before the sun rose to spare them the grisly sight of their mutilated comrades while the burial detail worked.

The British armorer represents a common bureaucratic misalignment. For most, if not all, of an armorer's career, his job is to secure the bullets. Yes, everyone knows his imperative task is to provide the bullets during battle, but that is rarely required. His actual imperative is to secure and hoard the bullets and nothing further. Promotions go to those who tightly grip and control their inventory, so that is the daily imperative during peacetime. Consequently, when the Zulus swarmed, the armorer could not reverse course to flood the runners with cartridges. His alignment as a hoarder and securer could not be overcome, and nearly the entire British camp was slain as a result. Ironically, those who rise bureaucratically during peace often fail abysmally when the Zulus swarm. They excel at peacetime maneuvering and alignment, but are ill-prepared to execute their primary mission, to deliver the goods to their customers on the front line.

GOING TO WAR

Most of what follows would not have happened, of course, had there been no Persian Gulf War in 1990–1991; but there was, so it did.

For a brief moment during this war, a brilliant effort emerged from an unlikely group in an unlikely place—Air Force reservists and local townspeople operating in the cradle of American antiwar liberalism in western Massachusetts. These marvelous achievements sparkled brightly, if briefly, before being firmly squelched by military bureaucratic might that tolerates innovation as a vampire tolerates the sunrise.

Westover AFB, an Air Force Reserve base in Chicopee, MA, would have continued in its Cold War mode as a backwater military installation had Iraqi dictator Saddam Hussein not made the neighboring country of Kuwait a new Iraqi province. Relationships between the Air Force Reserve and the active duty Air Force, and between the base and the local civilian community, would have maintained their long-accustomed staid demeanor, and nothing much would have happened. The war, however, disrupted both these relationships and provided fascinating episodes of genius, triumph, comeuppance, stupidity, tragedy, moral duplicity, and glorious celebration.

This is the Westover story as it happened from base air show on August 4, 1990 to the aftermath of Hurricane Andrew in August 1992, when the military boot came down on Westover's innovative culture. The footprints in the sand from this timeframe have been thoroughly washed away, but they happened, and those who lived them still reflect on the triumphant aura of the time, and the exaltation of the achievement.

CHAOS

Chaos severely hampered the initial American military response to the Iraq invasion of Kuwait, but it also liberated the most effective forces to complete the mission.

During peacetime, the bureaucratic model reigns; when the war starts, the effective wartime leader model arises. Westover is the story of the wartime leader model overcoming the bureaucratic model and providing inspirational leadership and unfettered ability to do the necessary at the expense of the extraneous. Therefore, thank the gods for chaos.

The American Civil War displayed the same phenomenon. President Lincoln suffered a string of bureaucratically talented generals who excelled in all realms but war. The South had the advantage of raising an army in chaos from scratch. Confederate president Davis didn't suffer successful bureaucratic generals because he didn't have any. He fielded the best commanders in his estimation, and allowed ability to rise as the war progressed. Lincoln spent years purging his bureaucratic generals before bureaucratically impossible, hard-drinking, sloppy dressing, back-from-the-civilian-world, U. S. Grant arose in the west to provide Lincoln with his most effective commander. Even then, the bureaucratic headquarters generals almost sank Grant's career for his most brilliant maneuver.

Grant had marched his army south of his objective city of Vicksburg, MS, and cut all contact with the U.S. army as he maneuvered freely across Mississippi. After successfully engaging a series of Confederate forces at Port Gibson, Raymond, Jackson, and Champion's Hill, Grant lay siege to Vicksburg in May 1863 until the city fell on July 4, 1863.

However, the U.S. Chief of Staff, Gen. Winfield Scott, who determined that no success should go unpunished, threatened to reprimand Grant for failing to keep the army informed of his operation. Apparently Scott preferred a well-monitored defeat to an unmonitored victory.

AIR SHOW KICKOFF

The Westover Air Show came off grandly and without many problems on August 4 and 5, 1990. The Sunday weather had been exceptionally hazy and had obscured several of the flying demonstrations put on for the large crowd. As the cleanup began on Sunday evening, base personnel thought their extraordinary efforts were over. Actually, they were just about to begin.

Two days before the air show, on August 2, 1990, Saddam Hussein sent the Iraqi army into neighboring Kuwait. Resistance was limited, and the Iraqis swept quickly down to Kuwait's southern border with Saudi Arabia. Whatever mixed signals the Bush administration might have sent Saddam before the invasion, there were no mixed signals the day after the air show. President Bush declared that this Iraqi action *"will not stand!"*

On Tuesday, August 7, Operation Desert Shield commenced to protect Saudi Arabia from possible invasion. This required massive amounts of men and material to be transported as quickly as possible to Saudi Arabia since the Iraqi army now badly outnumbered the combined force of Saudi and American military units in the theater.

Westover reservists began pitching for action in the operation, not wanting the active duty crews to monopolize the missions. They would soon realize getting missions would not be a problem. A call to Military Airlift Command (MAC) planners at Scott AFB, IL told the story. The planner said: "*I have 256 C-5 loads on the board right now, I don't think you have to worry about getting action.*"

This is when the chaos began. An American military still aligned for Cold War requirements would now try, on the fly, to realign for no-notice regional warfare. The developing picture would not be pretty.

The first designated unit move was the F-15, 1st Fighter Wing at Langley AFB, VA. Since everyone's hair was on fire to get this lead fighter unit to the desert, outrageously optimistic projections were presented. Langley vowed, incredibly, that they could load a C-5 every 30 minutes with their equipment, and would start them coming.

Langley actually meant they *wanted* to be able to load a C-5 every 30 minutes. That might have been mildly plausible if all the loads had been built, and weighed, and inspected, and properly strapped to pallets and lined up next to the taxiways for loading. When Langley turned the airlift fire hose on themselves, however, they had not even identified what cargo would go on which "chalk" (each aircraft load represented a chalk), did not have all the cargo on the base, and absolutely did not have pallets built and ready to load.

Photo by Whitey Joslin

Loading a helo at Westover

The consequence of this utterly overoptimistic plan was an airfield parking area clogged with C-5s waiting for loads that had not even been planned yet, and with C-5s orbiting the base waiting for permission to land. Most of the orbiting C-5s were sent home to wait for Langley to catch up with its plan. (In fairness, some of the congestion resulted from broken C-5s waiting for maintenance support from Dover.)

The Langley fiasco presaged the near total system chaos that rapidly developed. This chaos outlined not only the lack of current planning for this mission, but woefully inadequate preparation for this eventuality by generations of military planners. I'll cover the top several examples.

ROAD WARRIOR CREW CHIEFS

USAF Photo

Road warrior crew chief on modified C-5-C model

One of the primary Desert Shield lessons learned the hard way was the price of failing to shift from bureaucratic peacetime methods to wartime methods. One of the starkest examples was the utter stupidity of putting out C-5 crew chiefs on a base airplane, and leaving them there, to be sure all its airframe time was recorded for the home wing.

The problem was, the base didn't own the planes any more, the system did. Planes kept moving, crews crew-rested at stage bases, the pony express in reverse—the pony kept going and new riders got on at each station.

Since we had tied our crew chiefs to our airframes (figuratively), they never got to crew rest. They had to keep moving with the plane. After a day or two, the maintenance commanders finally figured out they didn't know where their crew chiefs were, or how they were doing. Since they never got to crew rest, the answer was…not worth a damn!

One of our wing crews connected with one of our crew chiefs out in the system and reported he looked like a derelict vagabond, dead tired, very smelly, and very hungry. The A/C, incredulous, interrogated the crew chief about his situation. Hearing he'd been on the road for a week without crew rest, he ordered him off the plane and the mission. He further ordered him to sleep as long as he wished and then to deadhead back to Westover. Finally, he called us to ask if we had lost our minds, sending crew chiefs out indefinitely with no crew rest, and told us he had ordered him off the plane and home.

The maintenance commanders slapped their foreheads at standup the next day and wondered what they had been thinking. From then on they sent the crew chiefs out with the crew, the method everyone in the system finally adopted.

This was but one of many failures to shift to a wartime footing that I will cover. Westover generally outperformed other stage bases, but we started out "stupid" like many others did.

FIRST MISSION

Since the initial Desert Shield missions came with extended FSRTs (Firm Scheduled Return Times) and on short notice, most early crews were made up of "bums" and ARTs. I got one of the first missions to Ramstein, Dhahran and return. Our first stop, as usual, was Dover AFB, DE, to pick up cargo for the desert. This is where the first of several revelations occurred.

When the crew reported in to the Dover command post, we were directed to meet with medical personnel in the base ops publications room, out of public sight. This seemed bizarre, and I had no idea of the purpose of the meeting. Once we had entered the pubs room, a medical officer said we had been directed to take a vaccination to improve our immune response to chemical weapon agents, in case we encountered any. We all looked back and forth at each other, perplexed, as the medical team began preparing the shots for us. I got mine in my left ass cheek through my flight suit and wound up with a small blood stain on the suit. They said the shot was gamma globulin. This is one of several dubious medications we had to take, along with pyridostigmine pills, most of which got thrown away instead of taken. There was later conjecture that something they gave us caused Gulf War illness. But I would not become embroiled in that issue until 2000, after the infliction of the anthrax shot on the troops that I will cover in book three. After the inoculation, we took off for Ramstein.

WAR SYMBOL

After crew rest at Ramstein, we alerted for our downrange mission to Dhahran, Saudi Arabia. As one of the first crews into the system after President Bush had vowed to remove Saddam Hussein from Kuwait, we found the system was not yet geared for war.

We took the crew bus to the armory to draw our weapons, .38 revolvers all around. But while the armory had the weapons and boxed ammo, they did not have any holsters to carry the guns. Since it was August, and hot, we had left our flight jackets on the aircraft. This left us with no graceful method to transport the weapons (this was well before all the guns were carried in a crew gun case). The crew bus dropped us pilots off at the O'Club so we could eat.

This was also before MREs (Meals Ready to Eat) were provided for the crews, so it was imperative we eat in preparation for our 24-hour mission.

I suppose, in retrospect, we should have had the E's take our guns to the plane, but we had signed for our individual weapons and didn't want to let them out of our sight. So we got off the bus, empty guns in hand, and entered the O'Club for Sunday buffet brunch.

It didn't occur to me what was about to happen until I approached an empty table in the middle of the room. I got to my chair, paused, and laid the revolver on the white tablecloth next to my plate and silverware, as did my crewmates.

A ripple of shocked silence flowed away from our table in all directions. I didn't look up. I didn't need to. I knew every eye of the hundred or so diners, many with their families, was on us. This was their notification that war had come to Ramstein and things would be different.

I picked up my plate and headed for the buffet table as conversations resumed around the room. Desert Shield had commenced.

Our upcoming flight from Ramstein to Dhahran is recounted in the book prologue, "Where the Air Force Lives."

GOING WEST

Returning to Westover I got to fly one more mission before stage base operations at Westover demanded I stay home and help manage the stage base mayhem.

This would be a coveted west trip to Hawaii, on to U-Tapao, Thailand and a final leg across India and up the Persian Gulf to Jubail, Saudi Arabia. We'd be carrying a full load of Hawaiian marines and their equipment to be delivered to the front lines in northern Saudi Arabia.

I had a near mental meltdown at Hickam, however. MAC operations were cranking full bore to get the marines to Saudi Arabia to reinforce our badly outmanned forces staring at a large Iraqi army just across the Kuwaiti border. If Saddam decided to send his army south into Saudi Arabia, we did not have the forces to stop him. Thus the imperative nature of our mission to get the Kaneohe marines to the front.

However, walking around the air base, no one besides MAC folks seemed to show concern about these missions. The Pacific Command was business as usual, with no one seeming to appreciate that America was at war. Their soldiers were not at war, but many other soldiers were, on their base, and we needed some consideration. Perhaps we should be allowed to go to the head of the line at the chow hall, or at the BX. In the O'Club on the night we spent there, I wanted to stand up and shout:

"What is wrong with you people? There's a war on and you don't seem to realize it! You know, a war, our reason for being, to get ready for, and to pursue!"

Had I known then, I'd have further shouted:

"I'm getting ready to be within a hair's breadth of dying with a full airplane full of marines tomorrow and you're concerned about the local softball league standings and base-wide yard sale this weekend? I'm not asking you to line up outside base ops to applaud us as we head to the war zone (although I would find that conceivably appropriate), but at least acknowledge something important is occurring on your base and find out what you could do to help." Passing civilians walking on one of the streets near base ops, I wanted to grab their shoulders and shake them and plead, *"Don't you get it? I understand the tourists down on Waikiki not getting it, but not those of you on base!"*

So the next day, to no fanfare or extra consideration, we boarded the crew bus for our airplane to fly into a typhoon and a war.

Typhoon Diane

It seemed, at times, the better a mission began, the worse it eventually became. This 6,000-mile mission segment from Hickam to U-Tapao AB, Thailand would be a prime example. In the middle of this 14-hour mission, we became deathly entangled with developing Typhoon Diane, a storm we had not been told about, that had camped out over our only alternate air base on Guam. From a bright exotic beginning in tropical Hawaii, we progressively flew into the clutches of one of nature's most horrific events. Worse, as we arrived in the depths of the storm, with a full load of marines and their equipment, we were out of gas with nowhere to land except in the roiling ocean beneath the storm.

I pondered how I had wound up in the most dire position I would experience in thirty years of aviation when I had done nothing wrong. Lord knows, I got into enough fixes when it had been my fault, but I had made no mistakes this time. Yet now I was one bad break from near certain catastrophe. I also ruefully remembered a joke I had told my students as a C-5 instructor pilot: *"If you are ditching at night and, when you turn on the landing lights, you see the face of a 60-foot wave coming at you, what do you do?"* This always stumped the students until I gave the wise-ass answer: *"You turn off the landing lights!"* The flippancy of this humor now mocked me horribly as I had to anticipate what my landing lights might reveal if I had to ditch in a developing Pacific typhoon.

Our takeoff roll seemed to last forever on the outside reef runway at Honolulu International Airport. We had a full load of 73 marines from Kaneohe Naval Air Station in the upstairs troop compartment, and a full cargo bay of their equipment down below, all bound for Jubail, Saudi Arabia, about twenty miles below the Kuwaiti border.

Everything about this mission would be on the limits: our gross weight, our takeoff roll, our fuel weight, our climb rate, our fuel burn rate, everything. Since the entire route went east to west on the same tropical latitude, it would be hot the entire way. This meant we could not climb high enough for maximum fuel efficiency and would be burning gas at a high rate at lower altitudes between 25,000 and 29,000 feet. Farther north, in cooler temperatures, we could gain maximum gas mileage between 31,000 and 35,000 feet, but not here in the tropics. We had fueled to our maximum takeoff weight, 769,000 pounds, or about three-quarters of a million pounds, which included 250,000 pounds of fuel. Even at that, we would have to maximize our gas mileage by climbing to a higher altitude as our fuel burned off, our weight declined, and our engines could carry us there.

Eight hours west over the island of Guam we were scheduled to meet three KC-135 air refueling tankers to replenish our fuel load for the further six-hour flight to Thailand. This represented a challenge. Our training flights required us to get ten minutes "on the boom," five with tanker autopilot on, five with tanker autopilot off. (Autopilot off is about three times as demanding as autopilot on, because the tanker is no longer as stable a platform.) This Guam refueling, however, would take almost an hour of boom time, far beyond our normal practice requirement. We felt pretty well prepared for this. I had been air refueling for twenty years, since, as a B-52 pilot in the 1970s, I had refueled on every mission. I had continued to carry air refueling qualification for ten years as a C-5 pilot. My copilot, Maj. Pete Gray, however, was on his first flight after air refueling qualification. He had never done it for real, and now he'd get to perform in catastrophic conditions during a war his first time out of the chute. Luck of the draw for him. It would take every ounce of effort from each of us when the time came.

Mission planning at Hickam Base Operations the morning of the departure, we paid our required visit to the weather forecaster. He did not know the conditions around Guam, eight hours and almost 4,000 miles of ocean away, as intimately as he did the Hawaiian weather. He had to depend on Guam for their forecast and it called for "isolated thunderstorms," almost a standard tropical condition. There were almost never zero thunderstorms, so "isolated" did not ring alarm bells. Several hours after our takeoff, however, the Guam forecaster issued the typhoon development warning for Guam and the surrounding area, and to stop the C-5 aircraft flow of one every two hours. We didn't know this until three hours out of Guam, by which time it was too late to do anything about it.

The early part of the flight was splendidly uneventful, with bright sunshine and a million square miles of deep blue ocean surrounding us. Just after the sun set, the first "isolated" thunderstorms appeared. I remember this one distinctly because it stood alone in its towering beauty, giving no hint, from our distance, of the mayhem that broiled inside it. As we passed by it forty miles to the side, individual lightning bolts would illuminate small parts of the dark purple column that rose 35,000 feet out of the sea. It seemed a large hotel with individual guests turning their room light on and off, first one in the upper right, then one in the lower left, then randomly all over, with about five seconds between flashes. I could idly ponder the awesome spectacle of this isolated thunderstorm, but would soon be frantically dodging and fleeing dozens of such storms around Guam.

The first realization we had trouble came during an HF radio call to the tankers on the ground at Andersen AFB, Guam, about three hours before our air refueling rendezvous. I found the lead aircraft commander (tanker lead) and told him we were on time for the refueling. In a somewhat strained voice he told me he didn't know if they were going to get airborne or not. I looked at Pete as if I had misheard the transmission. Why would that be, I asked? The tanker pilot fairly pleaded that there were so many thunderstorms around the field he didn't know if he could take off. The import of this hit me immediately. I told him: *"If you can't take off, how am I supposed to land? Because if you can't meet me for air refueling, I must land almost immediately on Guam since I'll be out of fuel. I'm barely going to make it as it is."* The tanker pilot assured me they would do everything in their power to get to us. They did.

Twenty-four years later I met the tanker lead pilot who said they ran from the crew bus to their plane in ankle-deep water in a driving monsoon rainstorm.

An hour out of Guam, and well after dark, we encountered what the tanker pilots had complained of. It began as heavy static on our radios, a sign of static electricity in the air that increases in the vicinity of thunderstorms. Soon the storms were evident as well. Our weather radar screen painted progressive lines of intense thunderstorms ahead, the spiraling pinwheel arms of the tropical storm. Had I been anywhere else in the world, I'd have turned around, but I could not turn around. There was nothing to turn around to but empty ocean. As we tried to pick our way around the lines of storms we hit moderate turbulence that shook the plane and made it shudder randomly, occasionally buffeting us off our altitude.

Then, the ghostly apparitions began—St. Elmo's fire. This glowing, clinging, static electric aura usually starts on the windshield wipers, cocooning them in a white, green, or blue halo effect. It can also suddenly appear, as it did for us, as stark white lightning bolt–shaped discharges on the windscreen, jagged multipronged miniature bolts that sizzle momentarily before the eyes before disappearing. St. Elmo's fire is nature's method of warning you to leave the area because severe convective activity is nearby, and it certainly was. Unfortunately, we had no choice but to continue deeper into the developing storm.

Meanwhile, the three tankers floundered in the depths of the storm and suffered mightily for it. On the common interplane radio frequency, we heard their tense, shouted radio calls as they attempted to evade the dozens of individual thunderstorm cells in the darkness and still remain in a loose three-ship formation. I felt a deep affinity for them because they were risking disaster to save us. They could have legitimately stayed on the ground and let us fend for ourselves trying to land on Guam. I take back every "tanker toad" joke I ever told.

They were flying down at the refueling altitude, 17,000 feet, which was near the freezing level, which meant they had all the worst effects of the thunderstorms, from lightning to turbulence. We had finally gotten up to 33,000 and remained mostly above the storms that seemed to top out at 28,000. Even above the storms, however, we were taking a beating.

Regulations forbid flying within twenty miles of a thunderstorm, yet all of us were thrashing around well within ten miles of numerous storms. We had to. I don't know if the tanker squadron commanders gave their pilots a waiver to do so, or if they just looked the other way, but wartime demands dictated we do this. The troops I carried had to reinforce our forces in Saudi Arabia as fast as possible, so all the stops came out to get them there.

Tanker lead decided the scheduled air refueling track near Guam would be impossible to use, so he directed us 200 miles north of Guam, where we hoped the air would be clearer and the storms less intense. This proved a fateful decision. While the storms were slightly less severe, it meant we *had* to get the gas from the tankers; if we could not, we would not have enough gas to return to Guam to land. I realized this later; I did not realize it then. Going north meant the air refueling might be a do-or-ditch event.

The storms were slightly less numerous to the north, but the turbulence continued. Finally, the tanker cell approached us from the west and we relaxed somewhat. As the tankers closed to within 50 miles, however, we discovered a squall line of thunderstorms across the path between the tankers and us. Tanker lead invited me to descend to 17,000 feet to meet them. I told him, incredulously, there was no way I was descending into that line of storms, and that I'd meet him on the other side. We picked a low notch in the cloud tops and flew through.

The tankers apparently miscalculated and made their 180 degree turn to our westerly heading near or within the squall line. Tense voices on the interplane frequency became shouts and near screams as the three aircraft lost sight of each other and were buffeted heavily by the storms. Somewhere in the mayhem they performed a cell formation breakup procedure, because when we all emerged on the west side of the storms, the tankers were arrayed below us with ten miles lateral separation between them, the center tanker 16,000 feet directly below us.

For what seemed like the fourth time in five minutes, the flight engineer reminded me of how little fuel we had. We were below 30,000 pounds, which sounds adequate, but is not. We always try to land with a minimum of 20,000 pounds since, as noted in "Double Dose Disaster," the gauges become unreliable below 16,000 pounds and engine flameout can occur. Most troubling, we were still about 20,000 pounds' worth of fuel away from Guam. This would, indeed, be a you-bet-your-ass refueling.

I called the middle tanker, below me: "*What number are you, in the middle?*"

He responded, "*I'm tanker #2.*"

I said, "*No, you are now tanker #1 and we are on the way down. Also, just to warn you, if we don't get this gas right now, we are going swimming.*"

We swooped down through the ink-black sky to prepare for the refueling contact. As we approached the pre-contact position 50 feet behind the tanker, the last two bits of misfortune arrived. My engineer said, in a voice a half-octave higher than normal, that we were down to 25,000 pounds of gas. Then the tanker dropped the final bit of bad news on me. The boomer said, "*Ah, I hate to tell you this, MAC, but we don't have our autopilot tonight. The other guys do, but we don't, sorry.*"

I will fess up now that all this gave me a perverse glee. There are many things I cannot do well, but there is one I could, and that was air refueling. I had learned the essential secret as a B-52 pilot on active duty and had used this secret to often shame my fellow pilots behind the tanker. I was among the two or three most proficient air refueling pilots in the wing and I showed off and hot-dogged on training flights, demanding to get my turn during weather, or when the tanker was maneuvering and the refueling more difficult.

There were times in my life where I welcomed a stringent test, and there were other times I dreadfully feared them. As a baseball second baseman as a youngster, with the game on the line, I mortally feared a ball hit in my direction because I might flub it and cost us the game. I feared being the last batter in a losing effort, as if my failure to get a hit would overshadow the team's overall failure that had put me in that situation. As a high school wrestler, it seemed I always drew the other teams' captain, which caused great anxiety as I awaited my turn on the mat.

However, as a high school football halfback, I feared nothing and welcomed every opportunity to use skills in which I had superb confidence. In the military I had great confidence in my ability to present written arguments and sought out such assignments.

Of all my flying skills, I was most proud of my air refueling prowess, and now I would get tested as not one in a thousand pilots would ever be, and I welcomed it.

The secret is peripheral vision. It isn't what you are looking at, directly; it is what your eyes and brain encompass over the full field of vision. If you are trying to match another car's speed on a dual-lane highway, it is difficult if you concentrate on only one specific part of the car, such as the bumper. If the bumper is all you see, no matter how well you see it, you will not be able to perfectly match the other car's speed. To precisely lock-in the matching speed, you must use peripheral vision to encompass the entire car. Your eyes might be aimed at the bumper, but you must expand your awareness to take in the full parameters of the car. When you do this, you will not actually see the car begin to move forward or backward in relation to you, you will feel it. Most important, you will not only sense movement, you will sense it precisely and immediately. It is this ability that makes precise air refueling possible. If you depend upon the director lights on the belly of the tanker to direct you, you will be flailing throughout the refueling because you will never be able to see tanker movement precisely or immediately.

Still, even in my confidence, there could be trouble. Occasionally, the tanker or receiver air refueling system suffers a mechanical failure. For some failures, there is no remedy and there will be no air refueling. If this happened now, we were going swimming, no matter how big an air refueling hot-shot I thought I was.

Also, in my confidence, I decide to let Pete try the first contact. It would be an immense confidence booster if he could hang on the boom for a while under these conditions. I told him to give it a go, but if he fell off, I got to take over for as long as I could hold on.

This perplexed the crew. Why was the aircraft commander asking his copilot to get the gas; couldn't he do it? They all realized the dire trouble we'd be in if we didn't get the gas. In retrospect, I don't know what I was doing, but it had seemed like a good idea at the time. I didn't know that when I did that, the troop loadmasters had broken out their ditching checklists.

The rear end of the tanker hovered before us in the utter blackness like some sort of alien space ship, more glowing chimera than airplane. In some ways it appeared to be a large manta ray with two radiant eyes that were the under-wing illumination lights of the tanker. Night refueling is more difficult than daylight because less of the tanker is visible and, therefore, fewer clues are provided about its relative movement. More unfortunate, the tanker made constant quick turns to avoid the storms and this aggravated our job trying to stay with him.

Pete called "*Stabilized pre-contact,*" and the tanker cleared us to the contact (air refueling) position. Pete got into contact, but I saw he was still closing instead of stabilizing. He, apparently, didn't see it and coasted gently through the inner limit, resulting in a disconnect from the tanker. The engineer later related he was sucking his seat cushion up his ass at this point.

As Pete backed away from the tanker, I told him it was my turn. Finally, I could put to use twenty years of practice. After all those scrimmages, it was now game time. The tanker shuddered and bounced in the turbulence in front of us. I aimed my eyes at the tanker's director lights, but took the entire aircraft into my field of view and called "*Stabilized, pre-contact.*"

I don't think I fell off during the next twenty minutes, but I can't really remember. I just remember the flight engineer announcing "*We're taking fuel!*" as if he were announcing childbirth. After twenty minutes we had drained the first tanker and now had enough fuel to orbit Guam until the storms opened up, or even to make the Philippines if we had to. However, I was shot, both mentally and physically. I was already tired just from the flight, and the air refueling finished me. Pete did the next two tankers solo as I sat there as a lifeless puddle, Mr. Air Refueling defaulting most of the action to the total rookie. I don't remember Pete getting any disconnects on the last two tankers.

By the time we had finished with the third tanker we were more than halfway to the Philippines from Guam. The thunderstorms, still numerous, were no longer part of an organized storm system as they had been around Guam. However, we would soon have to choose between dodging storms, or flying, unannounced and uninvited, into Vietnamese airspace, where the storms abated. I told Pete I didn't care what he did, and I didn't want to know. I was going to the bunk room to sleep and he could do anything he wanted. I never asked which choice he made, and I still don't know, but we arrived in Thailand uneventfully.

In retrospect, my ego-driven desire to be air refueling king probably saved our derrieres that night. Twelve days prior to this mission, there was no war, no imperative mission, and no reason for me to anticipate dodging typhoons in the Pacific. However, once the war effort began, there was no time to get good, or to practice, for this horrendous event. We often think that if a war arrives, we can fly concentrated training to hone our skills, but for Desert Shield there was no time. The airlift system immediately took all our planes for missions, and there would be no training flights. It was a come-as-you-are party, and your life and your airplane might be riding on how well you could do selected aspects of your job.

I now stress to students that minimal proficiency is not acceptable. If you cannot refuel with aplomb under favorable training conditions, you will be lost when conditions degrade on missions. Most imperative, there will be no time to sharpen up when a war starts. Pilots will be thrown into the breach with whatever level of ability existed the day before. I use our experience on this mission as a warning for what awaits them in any of many forms.

U-Tapao AB, Thailand

We landed in Thailand and were billeted in Pattaya Beach, about twenty miles up the road from U-Tapao toward Bangkok. I had a history at Pattaya from my B-52 days in the early 1970s, and I greatly looked forward to visiting again.

The resort had grown since the early 1970s. Turning off the Bangkok road toward the beach there was a rice paddy with a water buffalo foraging in 1973. In 1990 there were wall-to-wall concrete buildings from the Bangkok road to the beach with numerous beachfront condo developments along the coast above and below the resort. I hardly recognized the place.

The next morning at our hotel we awoke to a bright tropical morning and sat down to breakfast on an open-air terrace at our hotel. Both the morning and the breakfast were exceptional. The morning provided the tropical version of my Cairo "Eden" experience, bright, clear, and impossibly green foliage making it seem anything might be possible. The only negative aspect of the view was the Gulf of Siam shore that had turned an industrial brown in the fifteen years since I had been there. The breakfast had the usual bacon and eggs selections, but most prominently provided mountainous serving bowls of assorted tropical fruits to include mango, papaya and pineapple. Could it get any better than this, Pete and I joshed with each other?

Well, it could, if we could get an extended crew rest here. I hoped the typhoon might have briefly stopped the C-5 flow and we would get a day or two in Eden. But, no. While the aircraft flow had stopped for about 16 hours, the flow had begun again and our airplane would arrive and provide us only minimal crew rest. Drat. The imperative to get the marines to the front was back in force.

Our final leg into the AOR (Area of Responsibility), in this case, Jubail in northern Saudi Arabia, took us down the coast of Siam and unnecessarily south for some diplomatic clearance reason. We then turned northwest across the Indian Ocean and Bay of Bengal, over the heart of India (Hyderabad was one of our waypoints) up the Persian Gulf and in the "back door" to Saudi Arabia. I had flown in many times from the west; this would be my only time from the east.

I had never flown over India and I looked forward to it. As we approached it after dark, however, I was winding down fast and slept all the way across the subcontinent, never seeing any of it.

I awoke as dawn arrived over the Gulf. Pete assured me India was actually there and he saw it, even if I did not. When we landed in the heat of Jubail, we parked among several other C-5s that had flown in from Europe and mixed with the crews on the ramp, some of whom we knew from Westover and Dover. They all volunteered to fly our plane home across the Pacific and let us fly home westward as we always had. I declined with a laugh.

Photo by Whitey Joslin

Marines on the ramp at Jubail, Saudi Arabia

We had delivered our marines, who deplaned, lined up and marched off to war. After the download we took off for Diego Garcia, the small island speck in the Chagos Archipelago straight south of the tip of India, for crew rest. The rest of the return trip would be Kadena AB in Okinawa, Travis AFB, CA, and back to Dover where our aircraft would reenter the continuous circular world-wide flow.

That would be my last Desert Shield/Storm mission. I would be ensnared in running the Westover command post nonstop for the next five months. I would soon add *de facto* Deputy Commander Operations responsibilities once Larry Mercker stepped down from that position in November. I'll cover that shortly.

In a final bureaucratic abomination, the Navy at Groton denied me one of the senior officer houses at Westover that had come open in December. Rather than finally allowing me, as a senior operations officer, the imperative of living on base for the upcoming war, they again took revenge on Walker by placing an army major, with no connection to the war effort, into the house.

SHIFTING GEARS FROM PEACE TO WAR

I initially thought: "Where were their minds?" What were Air Force planners thinking when they matched major upload locations with short runways? In three instances: Ramstein AB, Germany; Pope AFB, NC; and Norfolk NAS, VA, C-5 air crews had to endure repeated white-knuckle takeoffs with maximum cargo loads of highly explosive ammo on runways barely long enough (and sometimes *not* long enough) for a legal takeoff. All three runways were under 9,000 feet in length, when 10,000 to 11,000 feet was the minimum sufficient length. Suddenly, the jokes about roasting hot dogs at the crash scene off the far end of the runway were not so funny. For a crash with 220,000 pounds of aviation fuel and 120,000 pounds of highly explosive ammo, you could probably roast the dogs from the other end of the runway.

During peacetime it rarely mattered that the runways were too short. Planners merely reduced the payload, if necessary. Besides, most of the missions were stateside exercises, so a large, and therefore heavy, fuel load was not required. Also, the smaller planes stationed at these bases did not require long runways, so there was no daily imperative to extend them.

This runway shortfall often put C-5 crews in an untenable position. The war effort demanded that as much cargo as possible be moved to the war zone, but the cargo loads were predicated on perfect forecast takeoff conditions. If any of these conditions degraded, the crews had to delay the mission to download cargo—or takeoff, anyway, knowing their theoretical safety factor had been removed. The crews almost always pressed on, eating the safety factor and crossing their fingers that they would not lose an engine at a critical point during takeoff.

An aircraft requires a certain length of runway for a given payload of cargo and fuel. Appropriately, this is termed the "critical field length," where the plane can accelerate to liftoff speed, lose an engine, and either continue the takeoff or abort the takeoff successfully in the remaining runway. A second factor then comes into play, the climb rate. Some runways have obstacles that intrude into the takeoff corridor. The plane must be able to clear these obstacles on three engines. In some instances, these obstacles preclude takeoff, rather than the runway length.

The best example of solving the climb rate problem occurred at Torrejon AB, Spain. An offending obstacle badly crippled the amount of cargo C-5s could carry on a hot day (heat lengthened the takeoff roll and significantly degraded the climb rate after takeoff).

Somehow, someone, somewhere, declared that MAC had waived the climb rate restriction at Torrejon during Desert Shield. This allowed crews to ignore the restriction and carry maximum loads off of this exceptionally long runway. Months later, no one could determine just who had issued this waiver, but this restriction removal greatly increased the cargo loads out of Torrejon at a crucial time. If MAC managers knew this and kept silent, or did not know, no one will ever know. I'd like to think Gen. Johnson, CINCMAC, knew but said nothing.

CHAPTER FIVE: DESERT SHIELD

My experience with the short-runway issue began at my first Desert Shield mission upload base of Pope AFB, NC. I needed at least 9,000 feet of runway for takeoff with my 120,000 pounds of highly explosive cargo and required fuel to fly to Ramstein. Pope had only 7,500 feet. I asked the flight engineer (who computes the takeoff data) how much fuel I could put on. His answer disturbed me. The pilot calculates the required fuel load, and I knew the flight engineer's maximum takeoff weight would not allow the amount of fuel I felt I needed. Technically, with the reduced fuel load, we could just make it to Germany if everything, and I mean everything, went right. The temperature over the Atlantic Ocean had to be as advertised, or colder, and oceanic air traffic control would have to let us climb to higher altitudes (that require a lower fuel burn) immediately when we were capable of doing so (due to reduced weight from declining fuel weight). If anything: winds, temperature, or air traffic control, presented unforeseen problems, we would have to declare a fuel emergency and land short of our destination in, perhaps, England.

I told the engineer to put on the maximum fuel load allowed by his takeoff data, and then to put another 10,000 pounds on (which represents about 5% extra). I explained that there was a one-in-a-thousand probability that I would lose an engine at go/no-go speed, but a nine-in-ten probability that I would not have enough fuel to reach Ramstein. I said I was going to cure the 90% problem at the expense of the .01% problem. He agreed.

My ire rose against the military planners who had put me in this predicament. If I crashed, they'd cluck that I should not have sacrificed my safety factor, forgetting the tremendous pressure on the crews to move the mission regardless of such problems. I got to cover for their maximum load planning with my ass, and I didn't appreciate it. The load planners would get to crow about how much cargo "they" moved by overloading my airplane and forcing me to fork over my safety margin to cover them.

I observed another crew who had sacrificed their safety factor the next day at Ramstein. As I sat on the hot cargo pad on the far side of the runway at midfield, I watched from my cockpit as a C-5 flown by a Kelly AFB, TX, crew started their takeoff roll. I recognized the C-5's optical illusion that makes it appear to be moving too slowly to fly, but as I watched this Kelly crew lumber down the runway, I believed they would not attain liftoff speed before the end of the runway. I'm about to watch a C-5 crash, I thought. Finally, in the 1,000-foot overrun on the departure end of the runway, the C-5 struggled into the air, blowing a huge cloud of dust and dirt off the overrun. I'm sure the pilots thought they might die right there. I certainly thought they were going to. Had they lost an engine after the go/no-go point, I don't see how they could have gotten airborne, even using the overrun.

A second chaos producing factor would be the system traffic flow to and from the desert. The major stage bases: Ramstein and Frankfurt, Germany; Torrejon and Rota, Spain; and Dover, DE, initially all had traffic flowing in both directions, causing monumental traffic snarls and SNAFUs at each. Crews would be alerted to empty parking spots for planes that were supposed to have arrived, but had not. Tracking planes departing and arriving in different directions from a long list of various bases resulted in chronic traffic information problems throughout the system. MAC asked managers from throughout the system for suggestions on how to smooth out the flow. Finally, someone figured it out.

That solution created a circular flow from the States, to Germany, to the desert, then a return flow from the desert to Spain, to Dover. But one component for the C-5 flow was missing from this equation: an outbound stage base from the States. The ideal location for such a stage base would be on the northeast coast closest to Europe. This would cure two problems. First, it would allow heavy loads to be picked up at a myriad of stateside locations without having to carry a heavy fuel load to fly directly to Germany. The stage base would be an imperative refueling stop to allow maximum cargo loads. Second, it would provide an outbound stage base to relieve the pressure on Dover.

So the solution was a C-5 base in the northeastern United States with a long runway to allow for maximum takeoff weights. The obvious choice was Westover. The problem with that choice: Westover was a reserve base without the manning or equipment to operate a full-blown C-5 stage operation. Further, Westover personnel had no experience running a stage base servicing dozens of transient crews and aircraft arriving and departing each day, seven days a week.

But it had to be Westover. MAC had two choices: allow the reserves to attempt to manage the stage operation, or ship in active duty teams to run the show. When MAC headquarters broached the two options to Gen. Walker, he demanded, with a gleam in his eye, that Westover would run this stage without the active duty, thank you very much! The gleam in his eye warned he would make the Westover stage the best in the system despite having no experience at the task, far less equipment and far fewer personnel than the established stage bases—and he did.

Things did not start smoothly, however. Walker's initial marching orders from 21st Air Force, the east coast active duty headquarters location, said: do the best you can with what you have and don't worry about reliability rates. Walker did worry about them, but it took several weeks, starting in September 1990, to build the stage structure. After a few weeks, MAC Headquarters complained that Westover's reliability was lower than the other stage bases. Walker complained that he was told reliability was secondary for the time being, but if they wanted reliability, they would soon get it.

Walker did not micromanage the building of the stage processes, but he closely monitored key action points for results. Our orders from Walker for setting up the crew stage? *"You've seen how not to do it in the system, so set it up as it should be done."* Period. He would check none of the specifics of our plan, but he would review the results like a hawk.

Since we and our crews had been out in the system for a few weeks, we knew what the complaints were. First, crews had to drag not only their professional gear to their hotel rooms off base, they also had to cart their chemical warfare bags in addition to personal suitcases. Our solution, concocted by the flying squadron, was to build sets of cages six feet wide by eight feet long and six feet high for each crew to store their professional gear and chemical warfare bags during their crew rest, utilizing their own locks for security. Soon this idea (by crew demand) was replicated at all the other stage bases.

We had to scrounge equipment from other non-stage bases to provide capabilities we did not have prior to the war. One imperative item was a heavy-duty "K-loader," a rolling, motorized platform that could be hydraulically elevated to aircraft cargo compartment height to allow palletized cargo to be rolled off onto the loader, and then lowered for transport to storage or, most often, to another aircraft. This proved essential in transferring cargo from a broken aircraft to an operational one to minimize delays in moving that load.

I flew the mission to Pope AFB, NC, to pick up a "spare" K-loader from the C-130 operation there. When we arrived to load it, however, I got suspicious. The loader looked decrepit, with oil stains and peeling paint. I asked if this junk heap actually worked. The Pope loaders claimed it did. OK, I challenged them, let me see it extend to maximum height and retract back to its lower limit. As I guessed, they could not make the loader deck move at all. We spent four hours on the ramp while they worked feverishly to repair what was, in all likelihood, the hangar queen of their K-loader fleet. They were not going to give us their good stuff; they were going to foist their dog on us and keep the good equipment for themselves. Finally, the loader creaked up to full height, and back down, once.

When we got it back to Westover, our maintenance shop had to essentially rebuild the motors to raise and lower the platform deck to make the unit operational. This was my first experience of other units fiercely holding onto assets they were not using. We were in dire need of the equipment, but they wanted to retain the items just in case they did eventually need them.

My second frustration came when I petitioned AFRES headquarters for new computers for the ops staff since the stage operation had commandeered ours. The new Air Force units were called "PC-IIIs," and I asked headquarters for half a dozen because the regular supply chain said it would take months to get them to us.

I tried to get a special requisition from a lieutenant colonel at Headquarters in Georgia, where there was absolutely no "war going on," as there was at Westover. He told me, in amazement, *"I don't know why you can't get the new computers, we all got them here at headquarters last week!"*

The third outrage actually resulted in a response from the civilian community that choked me up and brought tears to my eyes.

Our command post badly needed a hotline telephone connection to 21st Air Force to coordinate the stage aircraft flow. I petitioned the Air Force communication system, requesting an expedited contract to establish the hotline. After several appeals, the best I got was a six-week estimated wait for the service. The problem, they claimed, was with AT&T.

Just out of curiosity, I decided to call AT&T. After a few phone calls I found the woman who controlled emergency installations and repairs for Ma Bell in New England, Sharon Beckett in Bellville, IL. I explained my problem, that we needed a hotline to headquarters to manage our stage operation for Desert Shield. Is there anything she might be able to do for me?

There was a short pause as she checked emergency orders on her computer. Then she said, *"This is required for Operation Desert Shield, is that correct?"*

I said it was.

"It will take me a few minutes to cancel scheduled emergency repairs in your area," she said. *"I can have an emergency crew to you in an hour. Would that be satisfactory? ...Sir...sir...will that be satisfactory...sir?"*

"Yes," I finally said, softly. *"I'm sorry, it is just so much more than I expected. Thank you. Thank you very much. The troops salute you."*

The first diligent, correct response I received from any agency in a long while and it was some civilian lady working for a civilian company who FUCKING GOT IT! This, while all the military bureaucrats and headquarters did not! We should have booted out the HQ bureaucrats and put AT&T's Sharon Beckett in charge. What a commentary. AT&T later hooked up a full wall of phones in the main hangar for returning troops passing though Westover to call home for free. Again, bravo for AT&T.

In order to crank the Westover stage up to, and beyond, current state standards, Walker knew he needed additional personnel and equipment. A 21st Air Force team and an AFRES team came to Westover to see what could be done. The bigwigs sat around the conference table while we relative peons sat behind them around the wall. There were probably sixty people in the room.

We made a specific request for equipment, I can't remember exactly what, from a base that had the piece but no active role in the war effort. Their representative, sitting opposite me on the far wall, objected to letting go of the equipment; it was theirs and they *might* need it. But we *did* need it.

I raised my hand and asked, "*What are you saving for, a war?*"

We got the equipment.

One imperative support measure provided for us was four GDSS computer specialists with their machines that were essential in tracking aircraft movement throughout the system. But there would be a catch. As soon as the war started, and Desert Shield turned into Desert Storm, the specialist's home base recalled them for their own use, leaving us without this important capability, even though no one needed it more than we did. When the balloon went up, everyone clung to their equipment and personnel even though they likely would not need it...just in case. No one at the top of the command structure would overrule individual bases to get equipment to the locations that had the greatest need.

But then, someone at the top did start kicking butt to realign thinking to wartime necessity.

GEN. H. T. JOHNSON REALIGNS TORREJON, AB, SPAIN

Lest you think the war revealed only reserve wartime leaders, the active duty produced a doozie and a rarity. Four-Star Gen. Hansford T. Johnson commanded the Military Airlift Command (MAC, now renamed the Air Mobility Command, or AMC) that ran the airlift for the Iraq mission. Gen. Johnson proved adept at both bureaucratic and wartime leadership functions, a rare and fortuitous combination.

I had worked for Gen. Johnson when he was a colonel over ten years before at Castle AFB, CA. He commanded this SAC training wing and I flew under his command as a B-52 bomber instructor pilot. My only direct contact with him had come when I presented my separation papers to leave active duty service. As detailed in book one, he invited me in to his office to discuss my resignation. While I stood stiffly at attention, he threw his leg over the arm of his chair, smiled, and said if I wanted to get out, that was fine, but he thought I should stay.

Photo by Whitey Joslin

Gen. Johnson presenting the Air Force Outstanding Unit Award to Westover AFB in 1991.

His display of utter nonchalance did not convey sloppiness or carelessness, it told me he knew to a certainty that he would eventually be a general and could afford to be casual. He had been entirely correct in his promotion estimation.

But now, in 1990, Johnson had a problem—his airlift network was in chaos and not performing the job it must do to help win the war. A primary problem area seemed to be Torrejon AB outside of Madrid, Spain, a major stage base where aircraft landed as a halfway point going to and from the Middle East. Crews would be held in reserve at the stage to take over the mission from the incoming crew, who would enter the stage to be recycled back into the system a day or so later after crew rest. For some reason, Johnson was hearing ominous noises from Torrejon, so he did just what he should have; he went to see for himself.

As a former SAC commander, Johnson knew how to disguise himself to avoid alerting his target base that he was coming. SAC used stealth maneuvers to send its ORI teams to their destination base. The team would take off from Headquarters in a KC-135 tanker for a bogus destination. While enroute, the plane would divert from the original destination to the target base in an attempt to surprise the installation. Of course, every one of the dozen target bases would be tracking the plane and would also be notified of the divert, so they would have a thirty-minute or so warning that they were the target. Torrejon, however, was unaware Johnson might be inbound.

Johnson used similar stealth to approach Torrejon; he arrived unannounced as a C-5 crew member. This ensured he would see raw, unarranged conditions, just as he must see them to analyze the situation. He succeeded spectacularly.

As he walked off the flight line, several crewmembers dropped all protocol and gave him both barrels about operational complaints at the base. The easy rapport seemed mutually agreed upon without explanation or discussion. If the general was mixing with crews unattended by staff, the crews realized what he was looking for, and gave it to him "with the bark off," a favorite Walker expression for necessarily unadorned and straight. The essential, imperative information flowed freely, as it must to correct the problem. In thirty minutes, Johnson knew more than a month of staff reports could have told him.

In his travels around base, Johnson learned even more.

In a large maintenance hangar adjoining the flight line, he found the football field size hangar floor covered with cots and crewmembers. Incredibly, this is where his crews were being billeted. This outrage would later be compounded when Johnson discovered space-available military "tourists" housed in the Bachelor Officer's Quarters (BOQ) and Visiting Airman's Quarters. This also included teams for a USAFE volleyball tournament. At least some of the crews should have been billeted in these rooms. Some enlisted crew members bunked in the base morgue for several days with two fortunate features: there were no "regular" inhabitants and it was air conditioned.

Valid crew rest proved impossible under these conditions, as crews with vastly different alert times were intermixed on the floor. When one crew was notified to report for duty, all those crews around them were inadvertently awakened too. After suffering these ridiculous, illegal, and unnecessary crew rest conditions, Johnson's crews were then launched on 24-hour missions under very strenuous conditions, only to return to the same mayhem after the mission.

Next, he discovered that the Torrejon Officers' Club, in an attempt to keep the hordes of MAC pilots out of their main building, had set up a crude tent in the side yard so the crews could drink beer elsewhere and not interrupt the normal club function. When allowed in the club, the crews were charged double the going rate for many services.

MAC, it seemed, was at war, while Torrejon was not. This would soon change.

Since I was unable to follow Gen. Johnson around the base as he realigned it, I will take poetic license to imagine how it might have occurred, and how I wish it could have occurred. All these changes were made as cited; only the method is fanciful.

The Johnson confrontation with the Torrejon wing commander left no doubt about how Torrejon would change. Apparently the fighter pilot, colonel, who reported to the Tactical Airlift Command, not to Johnson, explained that he must keep his fighter wing in total preparation mode in anticipation of the Soviets sending their tank columns to attack NATO. He must be stand ready for this "real" war, and didn't seem to have the resources, or inclination, to hamper his primary mission to help the MAC airlift mission for this relatively minor theater war in Kuwait.

In all likelihood, he misinterpreted Johnson, as many had. With his bald pate, folksy grin, and easygoing manner, it was easy to be disarmed and put off guard when Johnson approached. If presented in bib overalls and a straw hat, you might think him a farmer who had come to town for seed. His eyes provided the only warning of stern underlying scrutiny approaching. Their hawk-like intensity showed he saw and analyzed everything before him. Johnson concluded his analysis on the Torrejon operation and took action, quickly.

The next morning (reminder, my fantasy vision here), the club officer found his desk under the crew beer tent outside the club and the crews drinking from a beer keg in his office. Sputtering with rage, he called the wing commander's direct line to report this outrage. Gen. Johnson answered the phone. He explained that if that tent was sufficient for wartime crews to use, surely it was acceptable for a peacetime club officer, didn't he think? Also, he would be able to speak to the wing commander, but Johnson had spoken to the TAC four-star commander (his roommate from the Air Force Academy) and had the fighter wing commander fired for failure to adequately support the Iraq war effort. So, did the club officer have any more questions? Johnson asked. If not, Johnson had one for him: how long will it take to put the club on full 24-hours-a-day operation to support the aircrews with no price gouging?

If the answer is immediately, Johnson drawled, the club officer could have his office back and keep his job. The club went immediately to 24-hour operation with the help of the Officers' Wives Club, who gamely and diligently served as chefs, waitresses, and dishwashers, now that "war" had finally been declared at Torrejon.

This is the first example of a marvelous phenomenon the war created. Only part of the military was at war, such as the MAC aircrews, but those most directly affected, the aircrews' stateside families, could not "be there" for their soldiers at overseas bases, where they would have gladly performed heroic deeds for their crewmembers. Since the stateside families could not perform, it fell to overseas families to support the crews, even though their own soldiers still lived at home. They would have to serve other families' soldiers as if they were their own, and trust others would "pass it forward" to their men when the time came. While the latent desire to perform such service has always been with the families, it took actions such as Johnson's and Walker's to unleash it. Torrejon fighter pilot wives flipping burgers and jerking beers for AMC aircrews at 2 AM was the first example of such pitching in for the cause when needed. The motto seemed to be: you are an American soldier at war, and I am here for you, even if you are not my soldier.

Johnson's next stop was the billeting office. He strode directly to the desk, requested to see the manager, and gave him a proposition. If the manager had every space-available guest, to include all the volleyball teams, out of the hotel by the next morning, he could keep his job. If he could not do this, Johnson would personally throw them out, and then fire the manager. The space availables were gone the next morning, and crews were put in the rooms.

In less than 24 hours, Johnson had realigned this crucial and problem plagued wing to the war effort. He left the base as he had arrived, in a C-5 commanded by Maj. Dave Doyle of Westover AFB. "*You'd better get me out of here, Dave,*" he deadpanned. "*I don't think they like me much right now at Torrejon.*" To the contrary, the liberated folks at the base loved him, and his country would gladly have saluted him for the imperative task he had just performed quickly and efficiently, and without even raising his voice.

PROTESTING THE PREVIOUS WAR IN MASSACHUSETTS

Photo by Whitey Joslin

Anti-war protesters near the main gate

The Vietnam War suddenly percolated below the surface in western Massachusetts as Westover became a major war hub for Operation Desert Shield. The base now handled twenty missions per day instead of their prewar level of twenty per week. With its long runway and geographic position an hour closer to European bases than other active duty airlift bases, Westover provided the perfect jumping-off location for heavily laden C-5s headed for the war zone. All this activity and sudden notoriety quickly drew antiwar protest to Westover's gates.

This protest was not unexpected. Massachusetts, by reputation, is one of the most liberal of states and notoriously antiwar. Westover was also surrounded by a covey of historically liberal colleges and universities including the "seven sisters" women's universities of Mt Holyoke and Smith as well as Amherst College, the University of Massachusetts, and Williams College.

In this instance, however, the protesters committed the sin, usually reserved for military generals, of protesting the previous war, Vietnam, instead of the one in progress. They were joined in this error by the governor, Chicopee mayor, police force, and newspaper, the *Union News*.

Initial protests consisted of a handful of protesters carrying signs on the sidewalks outside the two base gates: the main gate and the industrial gate. A steady flow of fuel trucks came and went through these gates providing the thousands of gallons of jet fuel required daily by the base's greatly enhanced mission.

Base officials suffered the standard love/hate relationship with the protesters. While we vehemently disagreed with their political position and felt it terribly misguided, we also knew we served to protect their right to protest, regardless of our view of their position, to the limits of our ability. This is the marvelous contradiction that makes American marvelous.

Standing on a hill near the main gate watching the protests one night with my daughter, Jessica, she asked if I worried about this protest. I told her that, yes, I worried about the protests hindering the mission, but that I'd worry more if there were no protesters, and that someday she would understand why this was my greater fear. I had to applaud them as I was cursing them under my breath, to encourage their political protest for a position I abhorred.

The protests grew over the first few weeks, adding numbers and color as they did. Protesters now wore grotesque face masks with red paint poured over them to mimic war casualties, and chanted rehashed Vietnam war protests such as "*Hell, no, we won't go!*" although no one had asked them to. The most unusual protest had to belong to the "Mothers of the Earth," young and middle-aged white women who sat in a circle beating tom-toms and chanting while wearing sack cloth that seemed to be potato sacks.

By October, the protests had drawn enough participants that a platform had been erected outside the main gate to hold speakers, who would rail against the war and the military to cheers from hundreds of protesters. The protest was taking on a momentum and camaraderie that enhanced their message and standing in the media. It was the continuation of Vietnam War protests that the protesters felt, in retrospect, had been righteously correct in the 1970s, and would prove to be so again now in the early 1990s. Many academics who had missed out on the glory of protesting Vietnam hurried to Westover's gates to ensure they would not miss out on this one. They arrived with an enthusiastic headiness of reclaiming former glory, of Woodstock, of protesting the Kent State massacre, of being on the righteous cutting edge and having a flower to slide into a soldier's gun barrel for the cameras.

This new chutzpah proved fatal to the protesters' mission, however. With their numbers and influence growing, protest organizers made a fateful overstep in November 1990 at the industrial gate. One day the protesters crossed the line of legality and stepped into the street to block the gate. Eventually, some lay in the street, theoretically inviting the constant flow of fuel trucks to run over them to feed the war machine inside the gates. No doubt some saw themselves in the tradition of the famous lone Chinese civilian blocking the tank column at Tiananmen Square the year before.

Photo by Whitey Joslin

Protester lying in street blocking the Industrial gate

This illegal escalation brought terrible pressure to bear on all sides. The loss of fuel truck access would cripple the airlift effort and leave American forces outnumbered and vulnerable in Saudi Arabia. The gate blocking directly endangered American soldiers' lives in the desert, and endangered the protesters who lay in the street. While Westover shifted the fuel truck flow to the main gate, the protesters could threaten to block both gates and shut down the operation, and soon closed one or the other gate as they wished.

Gen. Walker immediately appealed to the Chicopee police, and to the mayor, Joseph Chessey, to enforce the law and remove the protesters from the street. Chessey, however, had made the political calculation that his best political move would be to side with the protesters and against the military, regardless of the law. No doubt at Chessey's behest, the Chicopee police waffled on taking action against the protesters for several days. When we challenged them on their lack of enforcement for an illegal action while standing at the industrial gate, one officer said: *"We're looking into that."*

Incensed, Walker took an action for which he would soon have to beg forgiveness; he wrote to Massachusetts Governor Michael Dukakis to demand restoration of rule of law at Westover's gate. Instead of intervening, one way or the other, Dukakis sent the letter to the Pentagon, suggesting Walker had gone outside his chain of command, and outside the military, to inappropriately petition civilian authority for action.

In short order, the Air Force Reserve sent Maj. Gen. Dale Baumler to Westover for a meeting with Gen. Walker and Mayor Chessey. The media coverage of the Westover protests had resonated poorly at reserve headquarters in Georgia, where Baumler was a commander. One headquarters staffer told me on the phone that headquarters was very displeased with the negative publicity Westover was creating, and that perhaps they should shut down the base to make it stop. It was from this perspective Gen. Baumler arrived to negotiate the gate blocking crisis.

Behind closed doors, Baumler apparently acceded to Mayor Chessey's position. He instructed Walker to stop complaining about the gate blockage, so long as only one gate was blocked, and to use the other gate for the fuel trucks. He also instructed both the mayor and the commander not to comment on the contents of their meeting to the press.

Not two steps out of the meeting room door, Chessey sniffed, in public, "*Well, I guess Walker won't do that again!*" Walker, stone-faced and grim, left without speaking and has never, in the years since, to the best of my knowledge, said what happened in that meeting or criticized Chessey or Baumler for what occurred behind that door. During that meeting, Baumler had apparently levied threat of significant sanction against Walker for his inappropriate foray into the political process.

While Walker had held his temper, for once, I was berserk. I saw Baumler's edict as a crass and weak-kneed capitulation to the protesters, allowing them to commit an illegal act in the name of protest that would likely lead to the eventual blocking of both gates. Or, they could block one gate and then shift their blockage to the other gate once the fuel truck flow had been shifted, effectively blocking both gates and wreaking mayhem on the fuel transportation line. I saw Baumler's compromise as an abject apology to the protesters for Vietnam, for Desert Shield, and for our actions. Worse, he was potentially crippling our efforts to resupply our outnumbered troops in Saudi Arabia. Where was his mind? He had played right into the politicos' hands (Dukakis and Chessey) who wanted to exploit antimilitary and anti-Vietnam sentiments in their constituencies for their own political gain. By appeasing the protesters and politicians, Baumler apparently wanted to reduce the negative publicity Westover was creating. The protesters rejoiced in their victory, where even illegal actions would be condoned in the name of "peace."

The next day, the local paper, the *Union News*, published an editorial slamming Walker for sending his "missive" to Dukakis, chortling over his apparent sanction by the reserve headquarters general, and comparing him to Iraqi dictator Saddam Hussein for trying to "outlaw" dissent.

Chicopee mayor, 1; U. S. Air Force, 0

After one of the early skirmishes related to the American presence in Saudi Arabia, the U. S. Air Force has lost and the mayor of Chicopee has won.

It was a major general with a common-sense approach and, perhaps, with an eye to public relations who helped settle the dispute.

Not a missile was fired, but a missive — a letter from Mayor Joseph J. Chessey Jr. to Maj. Gen. Alan G. Sharp, vice commander of the Air Force Reserve — played a part in ending the hostilities.

Letters also figured in bringing the antagonism between the city and the Air Force to public attention. Brig. Gen. Frederick D. Walker, wing commander at Westover, wrote to Gov. Michael S. Dukakis and Chicopee aldermen. He complained about the way Chicopee police were handling protests outside the Westover gates. Police, he said, were "coddling" demonstrators opposed to U. S. involvement in Operation Desert Shield.

In his letter to the aldermen, Walker wrote that police "are apparently prohibited by 'higher' authority" from acting."

Reacting to this, Mayor Chessey charged in his letter that Walker's action was "totally inappropriate for a person holding his rank and position."

Defending both the police and the rights of the demonstrators, the mayor said:

"I don't personally agree with the protesters, but they have rights and, in the general's mind, those rights should be denied. . . . This is America. This is not Iraq."

Chessey's statement is eloquent in its simplicity, and his conduct has been admirable.

After a meeting in Chicopee with Maj. Gen. Dale Baumler, commander of the 14th Air Force, who was representing Sharp, the mayor said police policy would remain unchanged.

That Walker is displeased by the continuing demonstrations is not surprising. The military is not famous for its patience with such matters. That he chose to direct his complaints through civilian, rather than military, channels is puzzling.

And that Chessey stood fast, supporting the guarantees of the Constitution despite harassment by a brigadier general, is heartening.

Union News

Union News editorial

But, then, Hallelujah! Local Massachusetts civilians rescued us from the clutches of our own command and the politicos. There was no announcement, and it didn't seem to be led by anyone in particular; it was citizens acting individually to express their own convictions and opinions.

They didn't demand any publicity, or look for any thanks, they just showed up at the industrial gate to say, quietly, *enough*! They were greatly outnumbered, initially, by the protest army, but soon were gaining numbers and claiming one side of the street from the antiwar crowd. Although they didn't know it at the time, and I have been loath to admit it since, I watched their efforts with tears in my eyes from inside the gate. The simple, square, middle-class workers and families were sticking up for us when, seemingly, all of officialdom had sided against us. This was not the last time local civilians would help rescue the military from itself, nor the last time I would have tears in my eyes watching their efforts.

Photo by Whitey Joslin

Pro-troop demonstrators

Another public segment spoke up, also, and from a most unexpected quarter. The media coverage of the college-age protesters lying in the street and blocking the gate had played very poorly in some local bars whose customers rode Harley-Davidson motorcycles and who took an exceptionally dim view of protests and protesters. It seems a group of "Angels" decided to exercise their right to ride on public streets, specifically, the street immediately in front of the industrial gate at Westover. One sunny morning, the rumbling roar of their machines resonated at the gate long before they were in sight, and demonstrators on both sides of the street fell silent in astonishment, wondering why a biker gaggle was approaching a military base.

Their intent would soon be obvious as they rolled up to the antiwar protesters lying in the street in front of the gate. I'm not sure exactly what they said to the protesters, or how much color their language contained, but the gate blocking ceased immediately. I'm sure they pointed out, in a most diplomatic manner, that riding a motorcycle on this street is entirely legal, while lying in the street to block the gate is not, so they anticipated exercising their legal right to ride here no matter how many "bumps" there might be. This may represent the nascent beginnings of the "Rolling Thunder" motorcycle armadas now prevalent on Memorial Day celebrations in Washington, DC.

With the growing pressure of pro–military action supporters across the street, and Hell's Angels routinely patrolling the street in front of the gate, the protesters never again blocked either of the gates. Rule of law restored, compliments of Hell's Angels, of all people. The Air Force would not clear the gate, nor would the governor, nor would the mayor, nor would the local police, nor would the local newspaper—so the Angels did it. Thank you, Hell's Angels, the troops salute you.

Public opinion had now shifted away from the protests and, after the Westover gates had been unblocked, the resurgent pro-military public view would hold sway, even in this cradle of American antiwar sentiment.

CHAPTER FIVE: DESERT SHIELD

C-5 CRASH

In October I got an imperative call at home about 10 pm from our command post. A C-5 had crashed at Ramstein. I slumped against the wall next to the phone in despair. I had thought the C-5 impervious to crashes. Whenever one of many C-130 crashes over the years had made the news, my mother always flew into a panic that it might be me since she couldn't keep airplane designations straight. I told her to count the fingers on her hand to recall which one mine was, and it never had been. But this time it was a C-5, and I was shaken.

Maddeningly, details were missing. Whose aircraft, whose crew? Aircraft and crews were hopelessly mixed in the system. We only knew there were many crew casualties. It would turn out to be a Travis aircraft with a Kelly crew, but we didn't know that initially. The plane crashed shortly after takeoff, rolling to the left and falling wing-first into the ground a half-mile off the end of the runway. For years I could see the swath the wing had cut through the row of pine trees on the airfield perimeter. The accident investigation blamed an un-commanded extension of the #1 engine thrust reverser that caused an unrecoverable leftward rolling motion. Several crew and passengers in the rear compartment survived, but all crewmembers in the front of the plane died.

At the beginning of the Desert Shield effort, I had called MAC headquarters schedulers to make sure the active duty would not cut us out of the action. That turns out to have been a laughable concern, in retrospect. But then something else happened that somewhat doused my enthusiasm for flying into a war.

A few days after beginning the effort, we received a casualty notification video from MAC to instruct us on notifying the families of casualties of their death. As a senior operations officer, that meant I would be a prime candidate to deliver such notifications, if they became necessary. After viewing the tape, I wasn't sure I could handle this duty, to be the officer dressed in my Class A uniform getting out of a staff car in front of a house to relay devastating news to a family. Sadly, the family would know my mission as soon as they saw me exit the vehicle.

In the Mel Gibson movie, *We Were Soldiers*, about the Vietnam War, the notification officers at Ft. Benning were so overwhelmed and distraught over performing this duty, they defaulted by sending telegrams to the families delivered by taxi drivers. This led to terror any time a taxicab pulled up to a house on the post.

Since we didn't know whose crew had been flying the plane, I had to prepare for it being a Westover crew. I drove in to the command post for a long night waiting for details. I viewed the notification video again and shuddered at the possibility.

When we found out it was a Kelly crew, I was relieved for myself, but devastated for my Kelly counterparts who would now be performing this dreaded duty. I also kicked myself for my eagerness to launch, figuratively and literally, into a war. Fool, didn't I know what the other ramifications would be?

Whitey Joslin

Local Marine Alan Auger returning home, 1991.

Sound track: "Swing Low, Sweet Chariot" by the Robert Shaw Chorale

By the time Desert Shield kicked off we had moved to our new command post across the parking lot from the flying squadron. Built to specifications as a combination base operations and command post, it was a fine layout…for a sleepy reserve base managing their own fifteen aircraft and twenty missions a week. As a major C-5 stage base with twenty missions a day, however, it proved cramped and inefficient.

The command post provided a miniaturized version of the big-boy headquarters, command centers. A lower floor of phone banks and status boards run mostly by enlisted controllers was overseen by a raised-tier, glass enclosed commanders' section that could be sealed off for classified discussions and briefings. The command section was not really large enough for all commanders and deputies to inhabit comfortably at the same time, as was required for discussion of secret communications from higher headquarters. We brought in extra chairs and sat almost on top of each other for secret discussions. One laughable feature had a scrawny little table lamp someone brought in from home with a red bulb in it that we used to signify to ourselves, and to the lower floor personnel, that we had "gone secret" and not to interrupt us.

Working full-bore, 24/7, put a heavy strain on the command post operation even with all our personnel activated and available. Continuity among the three shifts presented problems, as corporate knowledge of the current situation walked out the door every eight hours. No matter how well we thought we'd briefed the following shift, disconnects arose.

A favorite joke at standup each day was the "janitor" explanation for screw-ups. When we tried to find out who had made some apparently harebrained decision that no one would fess up to, Gen. Walker shook his head and said, "It seems the janitor picked up the ringing phone as he passed by and made this decision."

A few times when I was running the show behind the glass on the upper deck, I'd watch Susan on the floor below and my mind would…wander. Once she was talking to someone just inside the inner cypher-lock door and proceeded to more tightly tuck in her blue long-sleeved uniform shirt. As it stretched tightly across her breasts, I thought the fabric might unravel under the stress or perhaps cause the most severely stressed blouse button to break loose and fire itself across the room. Argh. I'd close my eyes and put my head down, slowly pounding it against the table. Why does she torment me so, I lamented?

This got worse, at the command post and all over base, when the preferred uniform during the summer allowed the women to remove their heavy upper fatigue shirts, leaving them in, if not wet T-shirts, at least tight T-shirts. Is there no end to this torture?

LOBSTER DELIVERY BOY

During the height of Desert Shield, Gen. Colin Powell, Chairman of the Joint Chiefs of Staff, decided to send a present to his commander in the AOR, Gen. Norman Schwarzkopf. That present would be two Maine lobsters – and the delivery boy would be Lt. Col. Lacklen from Westover AFB, MA. My orders said to jump from aircraft to aircraft as necessary to reach Gen. Schwarzkopf's underground bunker in Riyadh, Saudi Arabia as fast as possible and to deliver the two lobsters *alive* to his personal chef.

I boarded a C-5 at Westover and stayed with the plane through Ramstein all the way to King Khalid Military City in northern Saudi Arabia. The whole way, I checked frequently on my two buddies ensconced in a bed of moist seaweed. They continued to gurgle bubbles from their mandibles to show me they were still alive. I informed them if they died, I would too!

From Military City I jumped a C-130 to Riyadh. Apparently the command at the air base had been advised of my imperative mission and I was driven to the building above Schwarzkopf's bunker. I took the elevator many floors underground and was escorted into his inner sanctum. I met his valet, who had a newly pressed set of desert fatigues on a hanger with "Schwarzkopf" emblazoned above the left breast pocket. The valet tried to take the lobsters, but I informed him I wanted to personally hand them to the chef. The chef soon appeared from further inside the complex. I opened the lobster box and had him certify the two critters were alive, and he assured me they were. Mission accomplished. I never saw Schwarzkopf, but I hope he enjoyed his Maine lobsters. I did leave a letter from my daughter Jessica for him, and he graciously answered her with a return letter. I thought I might get a lobster delivery medal, but never did.

MERCKER STEPS DOWN

In the middle of Desert Shield during the fall of 1990, Larry Mercker suffered several family problems that demanded time off to manage, something Gen. Walker did not want to allow. I could see both sides of the argument, but felt Walker was being somewhat unreasonable in his position. If he "rode Mercker hard," as he later admitted he had, Larry would resign as functional DCO and Walker would lose him as a manager altogether. If he gave him his requested time off, I would manage in his place until he overcame the family stress, the preferable solution. Walker, however, kept the pressure on Larry long enough that he did resign as DCO and returned to the squadron as a pilot scheduler to allow himself the latitude to rescue his family situation. That left me to take his place for the rest of Desert Shield and all of Desert Storm. I thought Larry and I made an excellent team and felt this was one call Walker had blown.

CHAPTER SIX: DESERT STORM

When Desert Shield turned into Desert Storm on January 17, 1991, it didn't make much difference to us at Westover; we continued running at full speed at the stage base. Days off were rare. We joked about someone at reserve headquarters mentioning no one was available due to a three-day weekend. Our response: "*What's a weekend?*"

Westover maintenance performed miracles during this time, fixing aircraft quickly and well to keep the flow going. Our safety officer had to warn the maintenance teams against pouncing on the arriving aircraft once they shut down engines. So frantically did the teams swarm the plane, the safety officer feared collisions among the groups. The primary ramp officer, Capt. Cam Leblanc, seemed to be everywhere at once managing the many maintenance projects on line. He seemed never to go home, and I knew this because I seldom did either.

This maintenance performance, despite significant personnel shortages compared to the other stage bases, and having only recently converted to the C-5, is the *primary factor* in Westover's success during this war. Ops played an important part, but maintenance providing airplanes to fly won us accolades from the command. I would provide details of this stellar performance, but I was not a part of it and lack specific knowledge of it. I can only say: hell of job, maintenance guys!

At the command post I heard from our crews that other bases were harassing and brow-beating crews to get on-time takeoffs, often refusing to let them eat before preflighting. We had not done that and we seemed to have the best on-time performance among the stage bases. I decided to double-down against the prevailing stage procedures.

In my arrival package given to crews after landing, I told them they were the best crews MAC had ever seen and I wanted them to get off on time, their way. If they wanted to go eat, go to the plane first and let maintenance know if they had imperative items that must be fixed, then go eat. Also, I advised them to try to stay on the maintenance timeline, or to catch up with it. I told them I, personally, would eat the late takeoff if they did it their way and it didn't work. In three months I only had one crew invoke that escape clause and it was a tanker guy I had known at Loring AFB in SAC years before. Shame on you, Bruce!

I also told the crews that if something was not right with their crew rest at Westover, to call me in the command post and I would hot-wire them to the full colonel responsible so they could complain, whether ops, maintenance, or base commander. I only had to make one call, that one to the base commander, Col. Hargis, because a flight lunch on a just-departed plane didn't have any eating utensils. Just as Col. Hargis answered his phone, the crew sheepishly said never mind, they found them.

As Desert Storm progressed, Westover routinely had the best on-time performance among the stage bases and the most accolades from system C-5 crews.

In the middle of Desert Storm we had a very close call at Westover. One of my buddies from Dover, Maj. John Hazard, had dropped by the command post to say hi while filing for his flight to Ramstein. We reminisced about our time together at Dover, and he left for his aircraft.

About two hours later, and just after he had taken off, I heard his call back to the command post. He said, in almost a leisurely voice, that he had lost an engine and was returning to the base. I imagined he must have lost oil pressure, or some other minor reason, by the tone of his voice. I tied up a few loose ends I was working on, grabbed my command radio and started out the door to observe his landing. As I had one foot out the door, Hazard radioed that he was on the deck and taxiing to parking. I was incredulous he had gotten back on the ground that quickly. I soon learned why.

Very shortly after takeoff his aircraft encountered a flock of sea gulls over the Springfield dump. The collision with them had taken out one engine and left another on fire. This could have been catastrophic since he took off at maximum takeoff weight. He had horsed the plane around and landed immediately. I had no idea he was in such straits or I'd have bolted out the door initially.

Hazard was put in for the Distinguished Flying Cross, entirely appropriately in my view. But, allegedly, a fighter pilot in charge of the AFRES review committee downgraded it to a lower level medal.

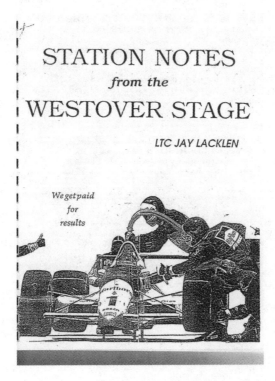

Photo by Jay Lacklen

Westover stage notes

NOTES FROM THE WESTOVER STAGE

WELCOME TO WESTOVER!

20 Feb 91

We want you to enjoy your stay here. If, at any time, any service is not supporting you to your satisfaction, contact the SOF
on Casino Royale or -3571. You can cut through all red tape and
beating around the bush by hot wiring yourself to the SOF. He
has hot lines to all wing deputies and he is not shy about buzz-
ing them.

1. YOU ARE GUINEA PIGS: in a novel experiment. We are running
this stage with an entirely new premise in crew control. We are
betting that if we treat each and every crew member like a DV,
make his stay as comfortable as possible and his job as easy as
possible, we will have the highest on-time reliability in the
system.
   Do you approve of this premise? Do you wish other stations
would adopt this attitude?
   If you agree with the above statements and would like to see
the last statement come true: GET OFF ON TIME!
   If Westover continues atop the reliability charts (as it has
for the past three months) the other bases will have to fight
back somehow. And that "somehow" is to start treating the crews
as Westover does. This has already begun to occur. (Have you
seen new crew cages anywhere recently?!).
   So keep up the good work and let's turn the whole system
around. Nothing gets a MAC commander's attention like trailing a
Raggedy Ass Militia reserve base in departure reliability.

2. TRUST THE CREWS: The command post will give you a timing
sheet when you show for your mission. Mx will try to hang a
broken airplane on the crew if you are behind this schedule when
the glitch occurs. We have adjusted our attitude on this:

    A.   That sheet is advisory, catch-up as soon as you can.

    B.   If you need to go eat, drop your bags off at the plane
         and check the forms. If you're going to have a cow
         about a write-up, have it early so mx can work on it.
         Then, go to the chow hall and eat if you need to.

    C.   You are the best airlift crews this command has ever
         seen. Do your best to get off on time, your way, and if
         it doesn't work, the DO will eat the crew delay.

1

Photo by Jay Lacklen

D.   Two suggestions: first, if possible, call the stage office thirty minutes before your LFA. If it looks like you'll get alerted, GO EAT! (By the way, don't worry about bugging the stage office. They are there to give you information, you are NOT bothering them.) Second, if possible, get your engineers to the plane by 2:45 prior, or into their preflight 2:30 prior. That is 1:45 after your alert so it should be possible. If you make this deadline, any problems found in the preflight will not be hung on the crew. Failing all else, try to start engines :40 prior and, again, you are off the hook.

3.   CREW KUDOS: Maj John Hazard and crew (709th DOV) for a quick VFR pattern with 2 and 1/2 engines, heavyweight, after taking multiple sea-gull hits in engines #3 and #4. Both engines were a loss, but #4 made it around the pattern, barely. This could easily have been a real catastrophe. Nicely done, guys.

LTC Batty and Maj Burkette, both AGAIN for heroic efforts to launch on time. LTC Batty (3rd DOV) was again cited by the mx weenies for exceptional efforts which resulted in saving their hides with an on-time takeoff. Maj Burkette rode one mission until it died two hours after scheduled takeoff, then voluntarily lept onto a second mission for which there was no crew.

4.   INTEL SHOP: We have one and they do a bang-up job. Stop by for a briefing at the command post when you file.

5.   THE BUS IS IN THE MAIL AND THE CHECK IS IN MY MOUTH: If something isn't happening when it should--TELL US!
Also, don't blow your cork on a non-performer. Call us and let us blow OUR cork on him. YOU are leaving. YOU can't make the appropriate deputy (even the DO) sweat for poor performance in front of the wing commander. We can. Lower echelon personnel will forget your tirade ten minutes after you take off. Tell us so the heat will stay on and justice will be done.

6.   THANKS: for a professional job under horrible circumstances. Just in case no has told you recently.

2

Photo by Jay Lacklen

HOW THE GULF WAR ENDED

American and coalition troops swept into Kuwait and southern Iraq from the west to defeat the Iraqi army. As the Iraqis capitulated, the road to the Iraqi capital of Baghdad lay open to coalition forces. However, the H.W. Bush administration wisely declined to attack Baghdad to dethrone Saddam Hussein. Bush insisted their mission to liberate Kuwait had been accomplished.

I strongly, and wrongly, disagreed with this policy. If we didn't depose Saddam now, while we had our larger army in the field, we would probably have to return to fight his regime again, I thought. I wanted to get it over with right then.

George W. Bush did return twelve years later to depose Saddam and inadvertently displayed why his father, wisely, had not "finished the job" in 1991. As Secretary of State Colin Powell, who had been Chairman of the Joint Chiefs in the Gulf War, warned, "If you break Iraq, you own it and have to fix it." Fixing Iraq, in addition to having politically destabilized the entire Middle East by deposing Saddam, led to great expense in blood and treasure. The region remains in turmoil today, thirteen years after the 2003 Iraq War.

The bizarre personality at the middle of this quandary, Dick Cheney, explained precisely and correctly why we should not topple Saddam in 1991 as Secretary of Defense. He used the same rationale Colin Powell used later about having to fix it if we broke it. However, ten year later, as Vice President, he led the charge into Iraq after 9/11 and reaped the whirlwind he had warned about in 1991.

VIETNAM WAR, GULF WAR COMPARISON

Retrospective comparisons of the Vietnam War and Gulf War (Desert Storm) in 2016 often take a positive view. The American military took years to recover from damage done to it in Vietnam and succeeded in reinventing itself as an all-volunteer force by the Gulf War. That much is true. Vietnam savaged the draft based military while the all-volunteer military performed admirably in the Gulf War.

But the truth is more complex. The two conflicts owed their outcome more to their circumstances than to troop differences. Vietnam proved a far harder slog than the Gulf War for a list of reasons:

- The involvement or proximity of two other superpowers severely constrained U.S. actions, provided sanctuary zones for the enemy, and removed the option of invading North Vietnam.
- The NVA and Viet Cong were dedicated nationalists willing to accept horrendous losses to prevail.
- The indigenous nature of the Viet Cong insurgency, and thick jungle foliage of much of Vietnam precluded large scale, conventional, battles the U.S. could easily have won. Instead, the NVA could attack when at an advantage and retreat to sanctuaries in Laos and Cambodia when at a disadvantage.
- The hot war in Vietnam lasted eight years, twice the length of WWII.

In contrast, Desert Storm proved a relative cake walk. This was an unequal war on many levels.

- No other superpowers existed to swing the balance toward the Iraqis.
- The Iraqis had no sanctuaries.
- Beyond the often first rate Republican Guard, the Iraqi army was demoralized, poorly led and surrendered by the thousands at first contact.
- The open terrain and lack of foliage allowed U.S. forces free range with tanks on the ground and planes in the air to crush the Iraqis in open conventional warfare. No contest.
- The length of hostilities lasted just over five weeks.

External circumstances evened the enemy odds in Vietnam and destroyed the odds for the Iraqis.

If soldiers could have been swapped out from one war to the other, the results of each would have been the same.

WELCOME HOME CELEBRATION

Photo by Whitey Joslin

Welcome home crowd

After Iraqi forces had been swept from Kuwait and defeated on Iraqi soil, hostilities ceased on February 28, 1991. The C-5 flow direction reversed and Westover became the first U.S. destination most returning troops would encounter.

Gen. Walker thought this a marvelous opportunity to provide a grand welcome home for the Gulf War troops and, collaterally, for those who were also Vietnam veterans who, in Walker's view, had never received a welcome home.

He was adamant. No soldier returning from the desert should pass through Westover without an elaborate welcome home. I found out how adamant he could be when he discovered such a soldier who had not been welcomed. Well, hell, the trooper hadn't told anyone he was from the desert, so the crew didn't warn us! Somehow Walker found him and I paid hell for it. After that I told the crews to interrogate their passengers if they were not sure if they were from the desert. I didn't need Walker roasting me again.

Walker found exceptional cooperation from the local community. As the flow through the base accelerated, local town folk reported to the base hangar to provide a crowd to welcome the troops. Since the flow continued nonstop, 24 hours a day, seven days a week, huge numbers of volunteers were needed. The many local groups participating, and individuals and families, provided welcome-home greeters for all shifts, every day. The crowd could vary from 50 or so in the early morning to 500–1,000 for known daytime arrivals of units stationed in the area.

One gloomy rainy night about 2300, a crew landed with a full load of troops. As their crew bus left the ramp I told them on the radio to swing by the command post and pick me up. As I boarded I saw they were tired and anxious to get into crew rest. I told them I'd like them to make one more stop with me. As we rolled up to the massive base hangar, a light showed through a single normal, room-sized door that was open in the large closed hangar doors. I told them, *"You are about to experience something you will remember for the rest of your lives, believe me."*

They looked at each other, curious, but still aggravated that I had shanghaied them for an extra stop.

I led them off the bus, stepped through the door, and moved aside to let the crew enter. The troops they carried had entered thirty minutes before them and stood on the far left side of the hangar.

As the aircraft commander stepped through the door, a cheer arose from several hundred local folks as they applauded energetically from a long line formed to the commander's right and bending into a horseshoe shape fifty yards away with welcomers two or three deep the entire length. Over a loudspeaker, the haunting opening musical chords of Lee Greenwood's song "God Bless the USA" boomed across the hangar floor, and the cheers increased.

The aircraft command stopped, stunned and amazed, seemingly unsure who all this celebration was for, all these people, all this hoopla, in the middle of the night, for him and his crew? Could it be? Quickly he realized it was. He walked forward to eager hands that reached for him as if he were a Super Bowl quarterback.

Photo by Whitey Joslin

Crew member starting down the welcome line

He and his crew moved slowly down the line, shaking hands and getting hugs across the rope line separating the welcomers from the welcomed. About halfway down the line they encountered a special group that called themselves "The Military Mothers," most in middle age, who would hug the troops and hold on briefly. For a regular few, this embrace caused them to break down emotionally. Perhaps they had a difficult time in the desert, perhaps they were

Vietnam veterans who had never had a welcome home. From deep inside them, a knot of past injury would erupt and not be suppressed by any measure of self-control. For these troops, the mothers would guide them behind partitions to let the tears flow.

As Lee Greenwood belted out his song, the crew continued down the line, bowled over by the attention, and received a beer at the end of the line. Most thought me correct; they would never forget this welcome home. They were not this crowd's soldiers, but they received a welcome as if they were.

VICTORY PARADE

In the spring of 1991, Chicopee planned a grand welcome home parade for the troops. Incredibly, Mayor Joseph Chessey, who had told local police not to remove protesters illegally blocking the base gate, and rejoiced at Gen. Walker's verbal reprimand by AFRES headquarters, wanted to lead the parade. No way, mayor, you jerk.

I wrote an editorial comparing Chessey's actions, and the disparaging *Union News* editorial, to actions in the fairy tale of "The Little Red Hen." The Little Red Hen wanted help baking bread and asked others, the cat and the pig, for help with the task. They both declined. Once the baking was complete, however, they all wanted to help eat the bread they had refused to help bake. The Little Red Hen told them to take a hike. Chessey and the *Union News* represented the cat and the pig, sticking it to us when we needed help, but then wanting to lead the parade (eat the bread) that we had baked. You've got to be kidding me!

Laughably, the *Union News* refused to print my editorial. The paper, which had chortled over Walker's reprimand by headquarters and that had likened him to Saddam Hussein in trying to suppress the right to protest in an editorial, didn't want me to point this out on their pages. Instead, I had it printed in a smaller local paper that was only too happy to oblige.

CHAPTER SEVEN: POST-WAR

BACK ON THE ROAD

With the war over I could get back on the road, something I had sorely missed during the previous five months. On my first mission into Kuwait I got a first-hand view of the carnage Iraq had visited on that country. First, on descent to the Kuwait City airport, I saw dozens of oil wells the Iraqis had torched and left burning, unattended, that sent dark columns of smoke into the air. This made an apocalyptic visage of the desert terrain.

Wikipedia Photo

Kuwaiti oil fields burning

After landing, I saw that many of the revetments and concrete walls bore pockmarks of small arms fire and the smoke from the oil well fires left a smog overcast. The Kuwaitis were very glad to see us, however, so that made up for the post-war weather pall that lay over the terrain.

MT. PINATUBO AND THE DEMISE OF CLARK AFB

On June ninth and tenth, 1991, Andy Lockhart of the U.S. Geological Survey Office and Maj. Gen. William Studer, a high ranking Pacific commander stationed at Clark AFB in the Philippines, flew over nearby Mt. Pinatubo in a helicopter. The volcano had given seismic indications it might erupt and Studer had to decide if he should order an evacuation of the 14,000 base personnel.

This would be a dicey and momentous call. If Studer ordered the evacuation and the volcano did not erupt, there would be hell to pay. If he did *not* order the evacuation and the mountain did blow its top, there would be hell-times-ten to pay.

Studer and Lockhart decided, after the second flight on the tenth, to evacuate immediately. While base personnel had been told to plan for possible evacuation, they now got the order. Do it, and do it now with urgency. On June tenth and eleventh, the evacuation took place. Studer and Lockhart remained on the base with a small emergency action team and waited for the mountain to validate their decision, or not. As the hours ticked by, the volcano continued to make its ominous rumblings, but did not erupt.

On the twelfth, Lockhart began to calibrate his reputational hit if he had blown this call. Similarly, Studer considered what explanation he could give his superiors if he had made a ghost town of a major Pacific Air Force installation for no reason.

And then the first powerful eruption occurred, sending a towering column of ash into the stratosphere. They had called it right. Studer asked Lockhart if that was "the big one," and Lockhart responded it was not, just the preliminary warning. He knew more was coming, but he didn't realize the extent of the coming catastrophe.

The major eruptions began on June fifteenth with a force ten times larger than the previous significant volcanic eruption of Mt. St. Helens in Washington state in 1980. This time the ash column reached 100,000 feet, drifted around the globe and dropped tropical temperatures by over one degree Fahrenheit in the next year.

But there was more to come. Four days after the initial eruption, a typhoon scored a direct hit on the area, raining ash mud onto the entire central Philippines, a miserable combination that led to 500 deaths, the dislocation of tens of thousands, and devastation of thousands of acres of local farmland.

Clark AB was buried under six inches of ash mud, the weight of which collapsed many base buildings. A later inspection team decided the base was not worth restoring. Subic Bay Naval Base was also significantly damaged and, although repaired, had its American lease revoked by the Philippine government, ending 100 years of U.S. military presence.

The beautiful tropical base I so enjoyed on the way to Vietnam in 1972, and rediscovered in 1990 as it had just been refurbished, would be no more except in my memory.

Mockba (Moscow)

In December, 1991, we were tasked with a mission to the soon-to-be-history Soviet Union. Walker leapt on the mission as his last grand adventure before retiring. I flew in command. We crew-rested at Rhein-Main and picked up a Russian navigator as backup in dealing with Soviet air traffic control and as a general interpreter. Then we flew east into the former forbidden zone of the Soviet Union.

It was as surreal a scene as I would ever experience. In these final winter days of the Soviet Union, my American air crew and I stood on the tarmac at Sheremetyevo airport outside Moscow intermingled with a cadre of a hundred Soviet soldiers, dressed in their full-length Peter the Great coats, as they manually downloaded our C-5 cargo aircraft.

Each group feigned total disinterest in the other, yet none could have failed to grasp the incredible irony of the moment. We had been each other's evil empire, the dreaded enemy we had spent our careers preparing to fight and defeat, and now we were working together at the same task on a frigid winter night in Moscow.

After several minutes of haughty posturing and faux disinterest I eye-locked with one of the Russians and could not let go, nor could he. What were our stares telling the other? As I thought about it afterward, his eyes seemed to say: "*So you are an American? You are what I prepared for? My reflex is to warily prepare to contest you, but now we need only ponder each other, and what was, and what is no longer. Our struggle could have ended civilization, but now we are fellow soldiers who will probably never fight, or perhaps may be on the same side. I had prepared to meet you my entire career, but with the intent to kill you. And now, here you are, and I find you so curious a creature I cannot release my gaze.*"

As the download continued, two behemoth refueling trucks arrived. The USAF has large refueling trucks, even though it still takes three or four to fully refuel a C-5, but these Russian trucks dwarfed anything I had seen before. They were enormous dinosaurs belching diesel exhaust and lumbering around hugely and menacingly, monstrous creatures from a mechanized nightmare, terrible machines searching for humans to crush. They presented one more bizarre feature to the surreal airport experience.

Our pilot group set off for the terminal with our Russian navigator to speak with someone in authority to arrange for support equipment and for security for the airplane. We circled the terminal in these very early morning hours only to discover the Soviet Union had shut down and gone home. There was no one in the terminal and every door was locked. Not only had the Russian Aeroflot flight crews parked their airplanes haphazardly in any available plowed spot and left, but the airport authority apparently had left also. Someone had sent the refueling trucks and soldiers, but we had no idea who.

We returned to the plane as our flight engineers were closing it up and shutting it down. Our Russian navigator asked around and found our transportation to the hotel. We piled into large, clunky Russian buses and left for the heretofore forbidden city of Moscow.

Moscow Elementary School

It was a ridiculous plan, to visit a Moscow elementary school in 1991, two days before the Russian flag replaced the Soviet flag over the Kremlin. I had no idea how I would get away with it, or how many "escorts" I might have with me as I did. However, I had planned nonetheless. My oldest daughter, Jessica, was in second grade at the time, so I enlisted her class to write letters to their Russian counterparts for me to deliver. I also took pictures of her class and hoped to return with pictures of the Russian class.

The visit to this randomly selected school near our hotel proved both the utter similarity of eight-year-olds the world over while also providing a wistful, poignant, and fascinating embrace of the "enemy" from the dreaded culture we had been prepared to obliterate in a nuclear winter.

The hotel concierge, a stunningly attractive young woman who spoke excellent English, looked at me with slightly perplexed annoyance at my question: Could she locate a local elementary school for me to visit, right now, and make arrangements? She ran her finger down a phone book column and found a suitable choice by the address. She then called and had the incredible conversation with a probably incredulous school principal.

I waited to be told this would not be allowed—I, in my American Air Force flight suit with a bright American flag patch on the shoulder, could never be allowed to roam a Moscow grade school without the highest authority, that I did not have.

Instead, the concierge wrote down the address of the school, the name of the teacher I would meet, and asked if there would be anything else (you bizarre American!). Ah, yes, could you call for a taxi for me? I asked.

I couldn't believe it! I was in! She could not possibly have alerted any authorities to my plans, and she was already busy with another customer, having moved on from my interaction. I picked up my VHS camera, my care package from the American school kids, and headed for the door to await the taxi.

Enroute to the school I kept looking behind the cab to see if we were being followed, but if we were, I could not tell. It certainly seemed not, and we were not, as it turned out.

In about five minutes I arrived. A small contingent of school officials waited on the front steps for me. It would be impossible not to recognize me in my flight suit and they all turned as I got out of the cab.

I'm sure I could not have been more fascinating had I been a Martian stepping from a space ship, an American military officer in uniform about to enter a Russian grade school. The principal's eyes were wary, half in wonder, half in trepidation this might be some sort of sinister test by the authorities.

I looked behind me one more time for any unannounced escorts. There were none.

After handshakes all around, the principal took me into the school where we took a right turn down a hallway to my selected classroom. And there she was, standing properly and formally just outside the first classroom on the right, Anna, the fiftyish, slightly gray, slightly stout teacher of the second grade class.

As the principal introduced us, it occurred to me Anna had been preparing to meet me her entire life. She had seemingly anticipated an impossible encounter with a forbidden American, whose language she had dedicated her life to learning, and which she spoke fluently. Her eyes sparkled with enthusiasm as she welcomed me. She showed me into the classroom and took me to stand beside her desk. She seemed to have no animus against me, as if we were friends long before we met, and against all propaganda from both sides that we should not be.

The students interacted as all second graders the world over must. The boys teased the girls and pushed and shoved each other. A gaggle of girls gossiped in a corner and giggled while stealing sly looks at the male objective of their conversation. The prettiest girl in the class, Ayla, sat alone, ignoring the surrounding bustle and keeping to herself. A male classmate grinned and tugged at her hair, then retreated. She turned and scolded him, but seemed not really to be angry.

All the children were nicely dressed and well-coiffed, as if someone cared about them and ensured they had what they needed. These someones, who were they? Were they the savage Soviet menace I spent my active duty military career training to subdue? Something terrible began stirring within me.

The bell to commence the class was still a few minutes away, but the students slowly showed awareness that some aura had descended on the room, almost like they were, somehow, in a church. The teacher stood silently before them with some manner of reverence with a man in a strange uniform they had never seen. Perhaps the flag patch on the shoulder suggested he was someone from far outside their experience. The students also noticed school administrators and teachers quietly filing in by the rear classroom door to stand silently to observe something, but what? What was going on?

Anna clapped her hands and announced the opening of a door to a new universe. She told them (she told me later) they could not really appreciate what the person standing next to her represented, but this would be a day they would remember all their lives. Who could I be, they must have wondered. Was I a party official? A lion-tamer from the Moscow circus? Some sort of celebrity? Who could this be to send adult school personnel into such a curious frenzy?

Anna explained to the children I was going to introduce them to a new world and they could ask questions when I was through. She said I was an American military officer and that this would be a new day for them, and for me.

Then she turned to me, with moist eyes, and stood ready to translate.

The terrible thing stirring within me now began to overwhelm. I remembered, as a second grader, hiding under my desk in a nuclear alert drill, preparing for the Soviet pilots who would be coming for me. Now here I was, the American pilot speaking to a new generation of Russian second graders.

The import of the moment crushed me. I looked at the children giving me rapt attention and began to choke up. Anna patted the back of my arm gently, telling me it would be all right, and slowly I found my voice. I never told her I spent years of my life sitting nuclear alert in a B-52 bomber ready to annihilate her and all these beautiful smiling faces before me. How could I have done that? What madness had I willingly pursued?

The children were now curious about what could be so significantly affecting all the adults in the room, their teacher, this man, school adults crammed into the rear of the room and listening from the hallway; what in the world was the problem? A few looked around at their classmates for a clue, but found none.

"*My name is Jay Lacklen,*" I began, pausing between sentences for Anna to translate. "*I am an American Air Force pilot who is visiting Moscow for a few days. I live 6,000 miles (too late I remembered they used metrics, not miles, but maybe Anna covered for me by converting) away in the state of Delaware, fairly close to Washington, DC.*

"*I have a daughter, Jessica, who is in the second grade in America, so I thought I would visit a Moscow second grade to deliver some items from my daughter's class in America. My daughter and her classmates are very interested in how life is in Russia.*

"I know you will not understand, but just a few months ago I would not have been able to visit with you. I would not have been allowed to be here, but now I am allowed, and a new door has been opened between Russia and America. It is important that we get to know each other because terrible misunderstandings in the past have led to difficult situations between our countries. I think...I think we didn't really know who you were."

The terrible stirring began to crack my voice, against my best efforts, so I shifted to something easy. I reached for the boxes I had brought from Jessica's class and began showing and distributing the items, candies, pencils, Bic pens, and pictures of America the kids had selected.

I had deputized a young teacher to wield my VCR camera and he took great delight in the task, moving around the room, filming the students as they asked questions or received one of the small gifts.

After the distributions, I took questions.

The boys, true to form, wanted to know about American tanks and trucks. I said they were pretty much like Russian ones. They also seemed impressed with my description of the C-5. Although huge, I assured them, Russia had a bigger one with six engines.

A quiet girl asked about my house. I told her it is a four-bedroom, two-story with a garage and a fireplace. She looked slightly confused. Do you mean, she asked, that your house has four rooms? No, I said, four bedrooms, it has four other rooms downstairs. This sent a murmur through the room, I suppose because most of these kids lived in apartments where just four rooms would be a luxury.

Most of the questions and answers revealed the similarity between us. The kids got a full description of our pets and seemed especially pleased that people in this faraway land also have pets, go to school, and pull the girls' hair.

Anna then rounded all of them up for a picture session. Eventually, they would exchange letters and more pictures with Jessica's class.

As my time ended, Anna walked me to the school door to wait for the cab. As I usually find with women, Anna already knew much of what I had just discovered. She seemed to know just who I would be, that I would show up eventually in some form, and that I would confirm much of what she anticipated about people, Russians, Americans, and life.

Photo by Jay Lacklen

Moscow second graders, teacher Anna behind on right

Day Two in Moscow

The second day in Moscow, the last day the Soviet flag flew over the Kremlin, we went downtown to do some shopping. Our lists included Russian winter hats and lacquer nesting dolls, each of several layers encapsulating an identical smaller doll within.

We had dinner at the hotel and then took a taxi to Arbat Street near the Kremlin since walking across Red Square was a must-do item, especially for those of us who had served in the Strategic Air Command. Gen. Walker led the way.

Our cabbie displayed a no-nonsense but amicable demeanor and spoke excellent, if somewhat accented, English. He asked us questions, also, since Americans had been very rare in Moscow up to this point.

He dropped us off on Arbat Street and we asked what the fare had been in rubles. He shrugged and asked for payment in dollars. I explained we had been warned not to use dollars because the regime could cause problems if we were caught using our own currency. He said no one would know what he took, and he often dealt in dollars…so we gave him dollars. He avoided rubles like an Ebola infection.

In retrospect, I wish I'd had hours to talk with him. As with cabbies everywhere, he would know the present state of everything from politics to the culture to the location, cost, and relative risk of any type if debauchery you might seek. He knew Moscow and Russia, and I'd have paid dearly for his time to expound on his country for me. Maybe another day.

We started our stroll down Arbat in the frigid darkness, our breath turning to visible vapor on exhalation. Despite the conditions, the street teemed with vendors hawking almost everything. As we moved among them, I sensed we were being followed, and we were. All I saw was overcoats and hats, never a face, as they walked leisurely about twenty yards or so behind us, never threatening, but constantly there. They seemed to be going through familiar motions that had now become irrelevant as the Soviet regime had figuratively left town.

We found a Russian fur hat trader, and Gen. Walker and I each purchased one. The vendor knew from our dress and accents we were Americans and demanded payment in dollars, twelve per hat if I recall correctly. I explained we wanted to use rubles as per the rules, which meant some huge number of them to equal twelve dollars. Walker, in his personal fashion, screwed up his face like a petulant little boy, and said he'd pay as he wanted to pay, and fuck those guys following us. So he did, in dollars. I paid with rubles. No one ever called us on using the dollars.

Red Square was a short walk away so we put on our Ruskie hats and walked on to the huge plaza. I had only seen the square on TV with May Day parades including huge Russian ICBM rockets, tanks, and lots of very regimented soldiers. We walked out toward the middle of the square and drifted apart as we went, each contemplating the experience on his own. I marveled that I now stood at the heart of the evil empire I prepared to destroy while flying the B-52 bomber in the Strategic Air Command. I looked at the Soviet flag on the pole over the Kremlin, the last day it would fly there, incredulous that I was standing in that infamous square. This was the last place on earth I'd have been allowed to visit a year ago, yet here I was, a mind-blowing turn of events. When I was a child, Soviet Premier Nikita Khrushchev blustered at the United Nations that the Soviet Union would bury the United States. Now here I was watching us bury the Soviet Union after wearing them down during the Cold War.

I looked toward the stairs to a subway station on the edge of the square. One of the overcoated ones watched me while smoking a cigarette whose red glow brightened as he took a drag. He seemed to be going through familiar motions and not really to be interested in doing his accustomed job. I imagine he might have been distractedly wondering how he would make a living now that there was no government to send him out on his practiced mission.

The soon-to-be Russian leader, Boris Yeltsin, seemed an accurate symbol of what Russia would become in the days after the Soviet Union collapsed. His demeanor had changed from an in-control apparatchik to a reeling, often inebriated, off-balance, ex-Soviet official who didn't know how to control himself and didn't know precisely where he, or his country, was headed.

When we assembled in the hotel lobby the next morning, I said there must have been some sort of business convention at the hotel the day and evening before. I had seen scores of attractive, smartly dressed women in the lobby so that must have been the explanation. Some of the enlisted snickered at me, telling me they were "business women" all right, and several had conducted "business" with them last night. One of the crew chiefs claimed he had conducted business with four of them, in fact, for $10 apiece!

YEREVAN

Departing Moscow, we proceeded south to the city of Yerevan with a plane full of medical supplies for local hospitals. The city lay just east of Turkey in Armenia and Mt. Ararat was visible, the reputed last resting place of Noah's Ark.

Armenia is relatively recently renowned for the WWI Turkish genocide of perhaps two million Armenians and the expulsion of many more from their homeland. This was carried out by the "Young Turks" regime that arose in the Ottoman Empire. The term has endured to identify standouts of a rising generation without appreciation for what the actual Young Turks did to Armenia, an atrocity Turkey refuses to admit even today. The Young Turks' actions, for which they were never held to account, places them in the same league of 20th century genocides as Pol Pot in the Cambodian genocide of 1975–1979. Upon my return I spoke before the local Springfield, MA, Armenian community. They and I were near tears by the end of my presentation recounting my favorable report from the homeland that many of their ancestors had fled for their lives.

Our four-hour Yerevan stop proved very interesting. First, just outside the ugly concrete Soviet designed terminal, a short stout babushka (grandmother) sold shot-glass sized sips of a local potato based alcoholic spirit something akin to vodka. We still had to fly, but to be sociable, and for improved international relations, ho, ho, I downed one of the samples. It wasn't bad, actually. The dollar I gave her was ten times what she expected so she was very pleased to have seen me.

On the way back to the C-5 we walked directly next to a Soviet Tupelov airliner about the size of an American DC-10 airliner. On a whim, I asked a female flight attendant at the base of the entry staircase if we could go on board to say hello. She smiled and said "yes" in English. I bounded into the passenger compartment just behind the cockpit and found other flight attendants blocking the first aisle inside the door, so I went to the second to greet the sixty or so passengers seated in the front passenger section. I made sure my shoulder displaying the American flag patch was turned toward them briefly as I waved to them. Almost to a person they smiled and waved back.

We then flew back to Rhein-Main for crew rest and then back to Westover. This had to rank as the most interesting mission of my career.

DEATH OF GAY BROTHER

In 1992 I got the news that jolted my view on homosexuality. My ten years' younger brother, Kevin, was dying of AIDS. I knew he was sick but he had guarded the diagnosis closely until it became obvious he was dying. My mother broke the news to me. "*Kevin has AIDS*," she said. She did not have to elaborate; we both knew what that meant. He was gay and he was terminal.

This fell much more heavily on my mother than it did on me. She had to admit to her friends why her son was dying, and her generation had near zero tolerance on this issue. Facing this almost broke her, a cherished son dying of the "love that dare not mention its name."

My generation was not much more tolerant than my mother's. Fag jokes were standard fare in the squadrons to which I belonged. There were no openly gay pilots, although, after some left for San Francisco, we discovered their true orientation. I remember noting the fact when I was told, but did not bear any ill will toward them or think any less of them.

Two aspects of the gay rights societal shift were crucial. First, the false presumption that sexual orientation was elective had to be demolished. It seems this should have been self-evident. None of us selected our orientation after reviewing options from a sexual smorgasbord of choices. As we reached puberty, our orientation revealed itself from within us. Nothing was taught to us, it just blossomed along pre-programmed lines. We were wired from birth. Anti-gay prejudice insisted gay behavior was learned after initial blossoming of heterosexual orientation while denying the possibility of innate homosexuality.

Having established orientation as genetic and not as a choice makes gay rights a civil rights issue, not a social preference referendum. If being gay is as innate as being black, or red-headed, then discrimination on that basis violates civil rights, whether we like it…or not.

As I considered the repercussions of my new view, I admit I had qualms. While I would not comment on two male officers dancing together at a formal military banquet, it would cause me deep angst. I would defend their right to do it, but I would have trouble embracing it. My only escape from this dilemma is knowing when my generation passes, those that follow will have a far more favorable, and proper, view of this issue, and for that I rejoice.

Second, AIDS, while doing its terrible work, freed gay men, and collaterally gay women, from the taboo they had lived under. Many "soldiers" died in the AIDS war, but they defeated the notion of sexual choice and proved the gay case in society's eyes.

It revealed the truth when persons we already revered were unmasked by the disease as gay. If my brother, or my friend, or celebrities I revered, died in the AIDS war, then I had to accept the premise that orientation is not a choice, and is irrelevant to my feelings toward them. If I revered them before I knew, then I had to revere them afterwards, also. If it didn't matter before, why should it matter after?

I was scheduled to fly to Atlanta for Kevin's final days. Before I took off, my mother called to say he would die that night. I hurried as best I could, but arrived too late to the hospice. I stood next to his body and put my hand on his stone-cold forehead. He did not "die of AIDS" directly; he died of AIDS-induced pneumonia. We faced a perplexing dilemma that day. He could have been saved, this time, from this bout of pneumonia, but it would have been a temporary victory. In his weakened condition, pneumonia or some other ailment would soon claim him, so we had to let him go even as we had the means to bring him back briefly.

Now that the truth be known, I rue my previous treatment of the many gay people I knew, but did not "know," for my shabby attitude toward them. For the fag jokes and deprecation of their, unknown to me, orientation, I offer an abject apology. I did not know, even though I should have, or could have.

I am profoundly sorry for these actions.

"Ski"

In early 1992 Westover received a new commander to replace Gen. Walker. "Ski," a full colonel, met the management team with Gen. Walker a few days before Walker retired and left the base. Walker had at least briefly mentored Ski in past assignments and spoke well of him, although Walker must have realized what would be unleashed on us with Ski. Disarmingly mild-mannered and soft-spoken, Ski had commanded the reserve unit at Charleston AFB when a hurricane scored a direct hit on it. He also reportedly had a string of Congressional investigations of incidents during his tenure there.

Walker must also have known what Ski represented, the dreaded headquarters bureaucratic rank climber who cared about HHQ's opinion of him greatly and about his subordinates' opinion of him not at all. With Walker off the base, Ski issued his new marching orders: no more innovative or creative solutions to problems. We would do things as HHQ wanted them done without fail. Headquarters had been apoplectic at Westover's actions during Desert Shield and Storm, but had to bite their tongue since we garnered high accolades from MAC for running the best stage operation in the entire system with no previous experience (actually an advantage for us) and significant shortages of personnel and equipment.

I got a personal warning from him. There would be no more freelance epistles to the command from outside channels, as my Isandhlwana pamphlet had been. Everything would go through Ski first, did I understand? This was not actually new. I ran the pamphlet by Walker well before I distributed it widely throughout AMC and AFRES, but did not inform him I was sending it far and wide. He had officially frowned on my doing so, but I think he applauded the act that trumpeted the handicaps the command had forced on us during the war. Ski let me know nothing like that would happen on his watch.

I had always despised loud, inflexible, paranoid screamers for commanders, but in some ways Ski was worse. He almost never raised his voice and usually spoke softly and mildly. But the message he usually conveyed was strict adherence to command policy so he would look good in the eyes of the generals at headquarters. That meant he expected us to forget and abandon all the valuable lessons we had learned under Walker. Ski would forever be the "customer" in relations with subordinates, and we should never forget that. The wing mission was enhancement of Ski.

The best example of this relationship would be his audacious attempt to do away with "double TPs" or double training periods, to save the command money (and to earn himself a gold star from the generals) at the expense of the reservists.

Double training periods allowed reservists to earn two days' basic pay for one eight-hour training day. This is the same pay scale awarded for drill weekends and it makes up for reservists' expenses to travel to and from the base from their home. While active duty "man-days" allowed such travel pay, training periods did not. C-5s flew four-hour training sorties in the local pattern, twice the time of smaller aircraft, and thus the allowance for double pay. With an hour pre-briefing, two hours of preflight and one hour of debrief, these eight-hour double pay days were prized by reservists to make it worthwhile to train.

So when Ski proposed this brilliant idea, he said local flights would stop after two hours and would replace the first period reservists with a new set so each would get only two hours' flying and thereby receive only one day's pay. Ski graciously allowed the instructors at each position to bag a double pay day if they stayed on the plane throughout, a factor that did not endear us instructors to our trainees. We seemed to be in cahoots with Ski to screw the reservists, a real morale crusher created to make Ski look good at the expense of everyone else.

And then, the crowning insult to injury only Ski could have provided. He visited the squadron one day and pulled me aside. "*Jay,*" he said, "*I know this is going to look bad, but I need to log a double TP tomorrow. I haven't flown enough hours for the quarter that ends Friday to qualify for flight pay, so I need the full four hours and I need it tomorrow because it's the only day I can do it.*"

"*Yes, sir,*" I said, trying not to let my face reveal the revulsion I felt, "*That will look very bad.*"

"*Well,*" he responded, "*that is how it has to be, so arrange for it.*"

Another episode occurred at the MAC "Rodeo" competition among airlift crews held at McChord AFB, WA. One of the events is a difficult obstacle course competition among security police personnel. By tradition, and wing commander edict, the flight crews are supposed to "fall out" by 0800 to cheer on our security police (sky cops) on the course that includes vertical wall climbs, swinging rope obstacles and other strenuous challenges followed by a three-mile run. I was exhausted just watching these poor guys run the course.

On this wing competition, Ski's first, Rodeo team leader Lt. Col. Dave Moore had a problem. All the pilots stayed in the bar too late and failed to show up to cheer our team at the obstacle course competition. He knew Ski would feel greatly embarrassed in front of the other commanders whose pilots had (grudgingly) shown up. But, as the competition began, Ski did not seem to notice the absence of the Westover pilot corps. Moore breathed a sigh of relief that he had not been chewed out over the pilots' absence. But, as he later related it to me:

"At exactly the nanosecond I thought I had gotten away with it, at that very instant, Ski suddenly appeared just beyond the end of my nose with eyes bulging and asked, derisively and threateningly, "What's the matter, Colonel, are your pilots too good to come out to support our cops?" Although, in this case, I admit Ski had a valid case.

There would be one episode where I actually felt badly for Ski. This time he would meet a fellow bureaucratic bonehead equally as obtuse as he, but who, with two stars, outranked him. Bummer!

The general flew on a local and found old, moldy potato chips under one of the pilot seats. For this transgression he upbraided Ski and declared this airframe grounded until it had been sent through the C-5 interior refurbishment currently in progress. Using such a ridiculous pretense for taking the action, the general wanted to embarrass Ski before the command. He did the same to several other airframes he thought improperly cared for by Ski's wing that drastically limited our training flights for months. After his public scolding by the general, I wanted dearly to ask Ski how it felt to be browbeaten by a pompous, self-centered jerk who outranked you, a feeling we subordinates of his knew all too well.

HURRICANE ANDREW

By the summer of 1992, Ski had pretty much driven innovation and curiosity out of the Westover force. He had picked fights with virtually every one of Walker's team members and caused most to transfer to another base or crouch into a purely defensive mode. I'm sure he relished Westover's newly acquired quiescent demeanor that would please HHQ—and that was his entire career objective, to please HHQ so they would be pleased with him, his "bullets" always securely fastened and accounted for.

Alas, for Ski, an ominous event approached that would vividly display the real-world drawback to his methods and these standard military methods in general.

In late August, Hurricane Andrew, a soon-to-be Category 5 storm, approached lower Florida. This was of absolutely no concern to officialdom at Westover since the storm would never come near us. The remnants of the Westover Walker team, specifically me and MSgt. Ronnie Robins, saw an opportunity.

Walker had encouraged us to think broadly and outside the box, in the current vernacular, and we had. As Andrew began churning toward Florida, we developed a plan. We knew that the primary problem after a hurricane was a lack of ability to inspect and survey damage in the immediate aftermath of the storm. Those who had been hit would be too shell-shocked to report, power and communication would be disrupted, and no one would have thought to have the means to inspect in the immediate aftermath. Thus it had been previously, and, seemingly, would always be, as Hurricane Katrina in New Orleans showed thirteen years later.

We at Westover did have the means, however. On the weekend prior to Andrew hitting Florida on Monday, August 24, we had a FEMA communications van and technicians sitting in a Westover parking lot on a separate training mission. We had Massachusetts National Guard helicopters and pilots available, and a C-5 aircraft to carry the van and the chopper to Florida, as near as possible to the affected area, as the wind subsided. (We were already a "Joint Base" with assets from multiple services, the alignment currently in vogue with the military in 2016.)

Had we been able to execute this mission, we could have put knowledgeable eyes into the skies over Homestead, Florida, and been able to relay their reports back to national authorities immediately through the FEMA communications van. This was precisely what was needed at precisely the right time, which ensured no one would think it plausible. In retrospect, it is amazing

Ski didn't get wind of this and stomp on it immediately. He did stomp on it, but not until almost every other bureaucracy involved had already done so.

As we coordinated the plan, we had to say mother-may-we to several bureaucratic monstrosities, most of whom initially shrieked that we could never be allowed to do such things. The first stop, however, started well. The Massachusetts Army Guard gave permission to use its helicopter and pilots, but warned that the Massachusetts Guard commander would have to ask for permission from his Florida counterpart to operate in Florida airspace.

While we awaited word on that front, we petitioned the FEMA workers to get permission from Washington to allow us to use their van, and them, for the mission.

The final requirement would be to have AFRES allow the use of a crew and C-5 to transport the helicopter and van to Florida. Since Andrew was nearing its target, a crew would have to be put into 12-hour crew rest very soon. Then, by serendipity it seemed at the time, TACC, the new AMC command center, called and asked us to put a "Bravo" (standby) crew into crew rest for possible Hurricane Andrew relief. Well, at least someone was thinking more than two steps in front of them. While appreciated, this seemed to be reactive, instead of proactive planning, by TACC.

While things looked promising at this point, the torpedoes were already in the water for us.

When the Massachusetts Army Guard commander spoke with his Florida counterpart, the counterpart exploded. He sputtered derisively at some other state having the audacity to want to operate in his airspace instead of his forces doing so. He would handle any hurricane relief requirements, thank you (and fuck you!), and didn't need any help from us! However, within 24 hours, his choppers would be twisted pretzels sitting upside down in trees and his forces would be in utter disarray for weeks after the storm. Homestead AFB would be largely obliterated by Andrew and of no use in recovery efforts. With no Florida Guard or active duty choppers available, there would be no military helicopters in the skies over the disaster area for days, and therefore no realization of the disaster's scope.

Next, FEMA regional and national headquarters reported that they could not find anyone on the weekend to approve the plan; therefore, we did not have permission to use the FEMA equipment or personnel. This dumbfounded us. The very mission for which the FEMA trailer and workers had been created and funded to perform would not be performed because no one would give permission. The FEMA team had permission and funding to train for disaster, but could not get permission to participate in the approaching actual disaster. One wonders what the training was for if they would stand down precisely when needed?

I again thought of the Brits pondering the impenetrable cartridge crates as the Zulus approached. The perfect, planned for, solution to the problem sat before them (thousands of bullets), but they could not get to them. We had the perfect solution before us, but we could not get permission.

At Monday standup at Westover, the very day Andrew tore up Florida, Ski made it three out of four bureaucracies who invalidated themselves by failing to perform the mission they had been funded to perform. As with the others, AFRES would cover up its delinquency instead of correcting the problem.

Background is required to fully outline the utter imbecility of AFRES procedures in this fiasco.

The reserves operate on man-days, or funding for one person for one active duty day. Each unit begins the fiscal year with enough man-days to last them through the spring. For some reason, Congress withholds the final man-day allocation until the proper resolutions are passed. If this legislation is held up, it creates a man-day shortage. Reportedly, the AFRES commander has been threatened with severe repercussions if he allows any excess man-day usage before the final package is passed.

This creates the yearly, artificial man-day crunch. Even though it happens every year, commanders gravely intone, every year, that, although this has happened before, this time they really mean it! This time the wolf is really at the door and there will be *no* man-days for *anything* extra until October 1. Simulators will be canceled, minimum numbers of crew members will be sent on missions, training curtailed, and no one will be authorized a man-day without explicit authorization by a full colonel or above.

After several weeks of no man-days, we are suddenly flooded with almost half a year's worth of man-days we must now use up before the end of the fiscal year. And we *must* use them up, or we may not get an equal number next year. Now there are man-days for mowing lawns, painting rooms, picking up trash, and piling crew members onto missions. The man-days eventually show up every year, yet every year we are told that this time the brass really means it, and they will not. The colonels know the panic isn't valid, we know it isn't valid, yet everyone carries out the charade as if it were. Thank God there are no Zulus lurking around the main gate. "Sorry, we can't fight today, no man-days."

Hurricane Andrew arrived in the middle of such an artificial man-day crunch.

When I authorized the Bravo crew, the word somehow got to AFRES headquarters, and holy hell broke loose. Without realizing TACC had requested the Bravo, AFRES and, therefore, Ski, thought I had done it on my own. I'm sure Ski endured his most dreaded fear—HHQ displeasure—on my behalf. Later, when I talked to a man-day manager at AFRES, he fairly screamed into the phone at me: "There will be hell to pay for this!!" There would be hell to pay, all right, but not the kind he envisioned. An entire string of officials, from President H. W. Bush on down, would be asked why they had their bullets bound up in impenetrable wooden cases with Hurricane Zulu running amok in Florida.

So, at standup on Hurricane Andrew Monday, Ski set me up and cut me in half in front of the assembled multitude of staff members.

"Colonel Lacklen, I understand we have a Bravo in crew rest," he said.

"*Yes, sir, we put them in crew rest last night...*" I said, starting to explain the call from TACC.

Ski suddenly cut me off as he made a horizontal slicing motion with his hand and fairly hissed: "*Bringing up your own personal Bravos again, Lacklen?*" This represented a severe public rebuke for an action he had failed to investigate or understand. As always, this did not impede him from hacking to pieces his supposed culprit.

Ski then launched into a long recitation of the near criminality of awarding unwarranted man-days against regulation. By the time he finished, all present must have been thinking I'd be on the next C-5 bound for austere Camp Red Cloud, Korea, to become the club officer.

After Andrew had passed over Florida, an ominous silence enveloped the entire area. No one knew anything: not how bad the damage was, not how many had died, nothing. There was no word from the devastated area for two days. Most attention then shifted to the second landfall forecast for Louisiana. I kept looking for damage reports from Florida, but there were none until late Wednesday.

Finally, word began to dribble out of the area. The Category Five storm had literally flattened Homestead, Florida and several other communities. Andrew had gone through the area as a near-tornado ten miles across. Over sixty people were dead, 25 billion dollars of damage had been done, and the survivors were desperate for water and medical aide. The survivors, news commentators, and Congress demanded to know where the government had been for two days while southern Florida was dying. Andrew had inflicted the most expensive natural catastrophe in American history, yet it took two days for America to even realize it.

Thursday standup at Westover had a decidedly different flavor to it. Ski, now in desperately humble awe of the catastrophe, assured all the staff members that Westover would spare no expense to contribute to the recovery effort in Florida. Then, as I knew he would, he turned to me.

"Jay, I want you to offer AFRES all the Bravo crews we can spare and I have been assured there will be as many man-days as we need for this effort." He even managed to keep a straight face while he said this. Hell was now being paid and this was our small piece of it.

He must have seen the fire in my eyes, however, because he looked away quickly. I wanted to slice my hand through the air and ask if he wanted the same type of Bravo crews he had publicly slammed me for bringing up on Sunday. You know, when they might have done some good, might have saved people in Florida, and might have saved the president from the ferocious public opinion flogging he was now taking. *Those* kind of Bravo crews, sir? And, of course, the previously nonexistent man-days now rained upon us a few days early.

The Zulus were disemboweling officials up and down the line from Florida to the White House, and now, *now*, Ski wanted to open the cartridge crates and provide the bullets. I'm sure his next efficiency report would gloat over his tight management acumen for parsimonious use of man-days, and brag of all the money he had saved the government. This, just as the British armorer, had he not lain disemboweled on the field of battle, could have pointed proudly to all the unused bullets he had saved for Queen Victoria at Isandhlwana.

Apparently the AFRES mission is to save money, not to fight wars or rescue people in natural disasters.

STEPPING OFF THE PROMOTION LADDER

A month or so after the end of Desert Storm, when most of the troops had come home and system activity had largely returned to normal, I heard that Dover would soon need a new Deputy Commander for Operations. Since my family had recently returned to Dover to live in the house we owned there, I wanted to follow them and take the same position I now held at Westover. Ordinarily, this would have been an easy transfer to make. I had moved to

Westover leapfrogging my Dover contemporaries to the ADO position, and then taken over as acting DCO at Westover replacing Larry Mercker. I would be moving again which was ordinarily required for promotion to 0-6. And, I had already performed as a DCO at an Air Force Outstanding Unit Award wing for wartime performance. In addition, I wanted out from under Ski's thumb.

I had created a problem, however. In the aftermath of the war, I had written an epistle (Isandhlwana) critiquing the performance of AFRES, MAC, and several unnamed individuals at AFRES Headquarters. It covered most of the incidents related on these pages during Desert Shield and Desert Storm. While I had shown the twenty-page booklet to Gen. Walker, who lauded it, I had also sent it far and wide up the chain, to include CINCMAC, Gen. H. T. Johnson, without informing him. This did not seem to bother Walker except that he expressed to me he was taking heat from his superiors for a "loose cannon lieutenant colonel he could not control." He did not seem upset by this, however. I suspect he thought they all richly deserved critiquing and privately applauded my effort.

At AFRES headquarters, the two-star generals were apparently apoplectic over the epistle, but they had to hold their fire because the MAC four-star commander, Gen. Johnson, sent me a laudatory letter acknowledging that things had not gone well initially (such as at Torrejon) in Operation Desert Shield, but that I and others had made it work. He also reminisced over our time together at Castle AFB in the late 1970s and said he appreciated all Gen. Walker, I, and the Westover team had done.

While the AFRES hierarchy could not smite me directly, they could indirectly, as I was about to find out in my attempt to transfer for the Dover DCO position. The reserves were reverting to a bureaucratic peacetime structure. Innovative, nimble loose cannons were to be loathed and crushed (until the next war, of course). The bullets must remain securely fastened into their crates.

I called Col. Kosikowski, the Dover wing commander's executive officer who had hired me at Dover in 1981. I asked for an interview with the Dover wing commander, whom I did not know. This colonel, whom I will call "Dantley," had a reputation as something of a scatterbrain from the few inquiries I had made about him. But I had seen worse, so I just wanted to see if he would hire me as his DCO.

Colonel Kosikowski welcomed me on my arrival at the commander's office and we spoke briefly before he ushered me into Dantley's office for my scheduled 1330 appointment. The colonel seemed cordial and friendly as we discussed the DCO position I had come down to interview for. As an aside we discussed country music, which I had been told he liked and which I, generally, did not. But I did like a current song, "Two Dozen Roses," by Shenandoah, despite it having everything I didn't like in country music, syrupy guitar twanging and cowboy laments. I just loved that song despite these features and I told him so. I thought the interview went well with no discordant conflicts of opinion and I thought I might get the job.

Little did I know. In addition to the long knives out for me at headquarters, I had my previous nemesis, Lt. Col. Sea Gull, apparently bad-mouthing me to Dantley. At all costs, Sea Gull did not want to work for me, especially after stripping that ASEV accolade out of my OER years before. He, who had never carried a command radio, never talked down a crippled aircraft, never fielded a 3 AM phone call for an emergency, never commanded a wing flying operation, seemed determined I would not command one over him.

I got the bad news from a senior Westover officer who attended an AFRES conference at 14th AF at Dobbins AFB outside Atlanta. He recounted Dantley's recitation about Lt. Col. Lacklen interviewing to be Dover DCO.

Reportedly, Dantley informed the assembled senior officers that I had arrogantly entered his office (I did not), and claimed I, instead of Walker, had made Westover a success during the war. (I absolutely did not. Even if I thought that, I would not tell Dantley, who would immediately relay this to Walker.)

Next Dantley told the group I not only had walked in arrogantly, but, further, he didn't know me from Adam. (Ludicrous, I had set up the meeting with his exec, who was expecting me and must have informed Dantley of having scheduled it. Further, his exec had written to me specifically asking for a copy of Isandhlwana for Col. Dantley. I sent a copy with a cover note for the commander that I saw on the Sea Gull's desk with numerous red comments on it.)

According to the colonel, I said that Dover was "*all screwed up and only I could fix it.*" This probably came from my explanation for why Westover got the AFOU, because we made the crews the customers instead of threatening them as Dover had. I foolishly thought Dantley would like to have a favorable outcome in his operations sector on a par with Westover's. Silly me. I presented this as reason to hire me, my past performance at Westover. If you are hiring a professional football coach, you want to know his won/loss record from his previous position.

Dantley further said he had asked around the Dover reserve headquarters building asking what others thought about hiring me and that "*several said they would not like to see that.*" I presume he means Lt. Col. Sea Gull as the one person who said that; I got along well with everyone else in the building to include Col. Kosikowski.

And, finally, the greatest abomination, Dantley told the commanders at headquarters, "*The negative feedback on Lacklen was such that I would not like him back in any capacity whatsoever.*" (What? Not in any capacity? Not even as a squadron scheduler? I had been acting DCO at an AFOU award unit during a war and there is no position I would qualify for at Dover?)

I had grossly underestimated what a thorough job the system would do on me, or how obsequiously Dantley would fall for it, or accede to it. If he had all these alleged problems with me, he should have confronted me with them at our meeting, but he mentioned none of them. He was all smiles and cordiality, and we both liked "Two Dozen Roses." I had no opportunity to defend myself from the hatchet job.

When I sent Isandhlwana to the system, I presumed it would accelerate me rapidly, either upward or downward. I had hoped AFRES commanders would read the critique as Gen. Johnson had, as constructive, heartfelt and arguably correct, but that was not the case. The direction would be downward. Further, I had hitched myself to a retiring, out-of-favor, one-star in Walker.

Ironically, my letter from Gen. Johnson, used as an endorsement on my OER, resulted in my promotion to full colonel at the next promotion board in 1993. Lt. Col. Lacklen, who Col. Dantley declared unfit for any position at Dover, had survived an extremely selective selection process and been promoted to colonel. Apparently the AFRES promotion board members had not yet gotten the memo on me.

Unfortunately, I had to turn down the promotion. If I had accepted it, I would have six months to find a full colonel position, or billet, or I would be forcibly retired and unable to draw retirement for ten or more years. Given my apparent accelerated downward reputation within the command, I feared I would not be able to find such a billet, so I declined full colonel. By the next promotion board, the members had apparently received the Lacklen memo, and they would not make the "mistake" of promoting me again.

Accepting defeat, I called the 709th, my previous squadron at Dover, and begged for a job. They did not have any. I then begged the 326th, the sister reserve squadron, and they said they'd love to have me, but they had already promised the next position to someone else, but after that they would hire me. That took so long that I spent 18 months at Westover while the family lived in our house in Dover that we had rented out during our Westover years. When the tenants moved out a few months after Desert Storm in 1991, I moved the family back in, presuming I'd get the selection as Dover DCO. When it all came apart, I was stranded at Westover, a painful and wrenching family dilemma inflicted as a result of my actions and misperceptions about the command.

I can't recall how it happened, but I ended my Westover tenure as acting DCO, ADO, chief of the command post and flying squadron ops officer while new officers were brought in. Quickly, a new DCO arrived that took one of the jobs off my hands. Then a new ADO arrived, leaving me as squadron ops officer and command post supervisor until I departed for Dover in June 1993.

SIGONELLA PICKOFF

In November 1992, my Westover C-5 crew got "picked off" from our scheduled mission to fly another mission. The original mission was a standard Navy run to Rota, Spain; Sigonella, Italy; Bahrain; and return by the same bases to Westover.

When we alerted at Sigonella for our next leg, the command post offered us another mission. It seemed a Travis AFB active duty crew was in delay at Sig and their flight engineer was going non-current for a check ride and could not complete the mission. They asked if we would assume that mission instead of continuing our own.

The new mission would take us around the world, eastbound, through Pakistan, Australia, Samoa, and Hawaii. Had this been a crew with standard reservists, who needed to be home on time for their "real" jobs, we could not have taken the new mission. But this crew consisted of reserve bums (no other job) and ARTS. If I'd had a standard reservist crew, when asked if they would volunteer, they would have said "*Hell, no!*" But the bum/ART crew said "*Hell, yes!*" So around the world we would go. This would be my final mission hurrah at Westover.

Unfortunately, our suitcases contained winter clothing, sweaters, long-sleeved shirts, and heavy jackets that would be excess baggage in Australia, Samoa, and Hawaii. But we could always buy swimsuits and short-sleeved shirts along the way.

The first leg would be a max crew-day body wrecker: Sig to Bahrain; to Islamabad, Pakistan; to Diego Garcia in the middle of the Indian Ocean. We took off late in the afternoon from Sig, quick-turned Bahrain for fuel around midnight, and arrived overhead Islamabad just before sunrise.

I hoped for daylight because we would be within 20 miles or so of the Himalayan mountain chain and its 20,000-foot peaks. I didn't want to fool around in the dark at an unfamiliar field with towering mountain peaks. Thankfully, the early predawn light allowed us to see the mountain outlines as we began our steep penetration to the field.

Our approach went routinely until we departed the final approach fix. I then saw as bizarre a sight as I have ever seen. In the dim predawn light, a heavy smoke fog rose from dozens of individual chimneys used to make bricks. These were apparently personal kilns for small family-run brick businesses, and even in the dim light I could see smoke rising that gave the area the look of an industrial ecological disaster, a dark sooty landscape that might have appeared similar to thermal vents on some alien planet inhospitable to humans.

In another surprise, about an hour later, the sun rose above the mountains and revealed an entirely different view. The Pakistani air base seemed Mediterranean in its climate. Warm air from the south provided short-sleeved shirt weather, and colorful flower gardens surrounded by verdant grass covered the base campus. We could have been back in Sigonella.

The base seemed a typical military outpost; cadets marched in formation and uniformed Pakistani Air Force personnel went about their tasks as we do in the States. After this second quick turn, we took off in bright sunlight headed south down the Indus River valley to the Indian Ocean enroute to Diego Garcia, about five and a half hours south.

Again I found the unexpected while flying down the Indus Valley. The river's shores were barren, as was the entire valley. At least the Nile had a ten-mile, or so, wide strip of green along the river, but the Indus had none. It seemed to run through a barren desert, a landscape unchanged by its presence.

I had stayed awake the entire mission thus far, almost 20 hours, and I was winding down hard as we approached the Indian Ocean. My two fellow pilots, Keith Guillotte and Craig Peters, had taken sleep breaks previously, so I told them they had the leg to Diego and I hit the bunk to sleep like a dead man.

Diego Garcia finds itself strategically located in nearly the exact center of the Indian Ocean. Discovered and named by a Portuguese explorer in the 1500s, this coral atoll had its original inhabitants removed by the British in 1971 when they leased the island to the United States to build a military base. If you are not military, don't expect to visit the island.

Diego bears a geographic similarity to Ascension Island in the South Atlantic Ocean as a military base in the middle of an ocean at about the same latitude. The major difference is Ascension's volcanic creation compared to Diego's as a coral atoll.

The other pilots rousted me out of my slumber cave in the forward bunk room prior to descent late in the afternoon on a sunny tropical day. After landing and getting our rooms, we visited a beachcomber style bar and grill that provided a marvelous view of the ocean waves breaking on the reef about a mile away, as picturesque a tropical view as I've seen. Unfortunately, that is about all there is to see on Diego.

The island now operates as a bomber base with B-52 and B-2 aircraft for operations in Southwest Asia. I fear I might go mad if I had to spend more than a month on the island if I were still a B-52 pilot. As a transport pilot I have the good fortune to say "hi and bye" to Diego as I passed through, which I did three or four times in the C-5.

Late the next afternoon, we alerted for the second leg of our eastward journey, about 2,500 nautical miles and six hours to Darwin on the north shore of Australia. We flew this segment almost totally at night, and rarely have I felt more alone in the universe, with no signs of land or humans for hours on end over the East Indian Ocean.

My only connection with civilization, the HF radio, made communications, as mentioned previously, sound as if I were calling Oceanic Control from Mars from my spaceship.

Finally, the lights of Darwin appeared far in the distance surrounded by nothing, the outback to the south and the Indian Ocean to the north. I'd report to you on Darwin except I saw almost none of it except base operations at the air field. We refueled, filed our flight plan and ate in about three hours. Then we launched south across the Australian continent for the three-hour flight to the isolated radar tracking station of Woomera, 300 miles north of the south coast port city of Adelaide. On the way we would pass almost directly over Alice Spring in the interior.

Midway in our climb to FL 330, the earth below us went black with no signs of human habitation. The view remained this way for most of our cross-continent trek across the outback. The only comparable view I had seen of land with no one on it was flying south out of Berbera, Somalia in the 1980s, zero lights, nada, none as far as I could see in any direction.

After a while at cruise, I sat alone as Keith and Craig slept. Checklists were complete and there was no chatter on interphone. I experienced silence and darkness for long stretches of time, except for the stars. The stars! I remembered the Crosby, Stills & Nash song "Southern Cross" and my promise to finally see this constellation mostly invisible from the Northern Hemisphere.

I didn't really know what I was looking for—something the size of Orion or the Big Dipper? There was something of a moon lighting the sky so only bright stars shone brightly enough to be seen as I scanned the cosmos. After a few moments I looked up and there it was, a large four-point cross in the southern sky, four bright stars rising above me. I stared in awe at this symbol from heaven that southern mariners had used for thousands of years to guide them. This seemed a near-religious moment, and I felt as if I were in a celestial cathedral with a soaring aria needed to complete the moment.

We landed in morning sunshine in Woomera for a stay of several days. On landing rollout, however, we got a "Det Fail" light on our annunciator panel telling us one or more of our 24 wheel brakes was free-wheeling and not providing any braking action. Sometimes this malfunction can be cured by adjusting the wheel hubs, but sometimes it cannot and more extensive maintenance is required. Except there was no maintenance in Woomera and such a fix might require a week or more to fly in from Travis AFB in California. We adjusted the hubs and hoped that would be sufficient, something we would not know until takeoff roll.

I had anticipated Woomera providing an outback showcase of the Australian interior, a hiking opportunity and photo bonanza. As soon as I exited the plane, however, I met the scourge that would hound us over the entire crew rest, leave us cowering inside buildings in self-defense and longing for an opportunity to leave this hell hole.

This scourge gave me a glimpse of what the Egyptian Pharaoh must have experienced when Moses sicced hordes of locusts on him; in this case the culprit was the tiny outback fly. These pests have but one goal, to relentlessly invade every head orifice in search of moisture: eyes, ears, nose, and mouth. When outdoors we constantly employed what the locals term the "Woomera wave," or a flapping arm motion in front of your face in a futile attempt to hold the creatures at bay.

As the only targets for miles in any direction, we became the hunted prey for these outback denizens as they invaded Woomera in huge swarms. Being indoors provided some relief, although the pests had penetrated even this space to a minor extent. Outside excursions around the small town that covered only a few dozen acres were limited to the local bank to cash checks (debit cards were still ten years or so in the future) and grocery store.

My one unrequired foray to the modest zoo on the edge of town left me longing for a hat with mosquito netting. I employed a constant Woomera wave while quickly reviewing the caged kangaroos, koalas, kookaburras, and parrots before fleeing back to the hotel.

After a few days in this purgatory we launched for Sydney. At 60 knots on takeoff roll, the "Det Fail" light again illuminated – and no one said a word. Technically this would demand an abort call and termination of the takeoff, but that would mean perhaps a week in Woomera waiting for a maintenance team from the States to fix the problem. No way, Jose, we were leaving this place!

On landing roll at Richmond AFB in Sydney a few hours later the "Det Fail" light again illuminated and immediately all three of us shouted *"Det fail light!"* We told the station manager he'd have to fly in a Maintenance Recovery Team from the States to fix this gear malfunction. He said he had a C-141 due in the next day and could do that. Drat! The next day? However, when I called in the next day, the manager apologized profusely that Travis had sent the wrong parts! *"Oh, no!"* I replied, smiling. *"Call us when you have the parts,"* I continued. *"We'll be roaming Sydney until you do!"*

This good fortune could not be fully exploited, however, because much of the crew, to include all three of us pilots, were coming down with head colds. This had been precipitated by several grueling crew days that impaired our immune systems and would crimp our forays around Sydney to allow us extra sleep time to fight the malady.

On a trip to a local pharmacy for meds, I encountered a phenomenon I've only experienced twice in my Air Force travels. As I stood in line to pay for my purchases, and not contemplating anything in particular, I became aware I didn't know where I was. What country was I in? Sydney was so similar to the States that I had to stop and think about where we were. Rolling, green forested hills to the west of the city provided substantial, but not total, relief from the cursed flies, but seemed similar to Pennsylvania just west of Philadelphia. The pharmacy on a strip mall seemed utterly familiar, and the Aussies, until they spoke, were identical in facial features and dress to Americans.

The only other time I suffered this confusion was while eating at a McDonald's in a large mall complex in Tel Aviv, Israel. Again, being slightly spaced-out from lack of sleep during crew rest, I had to recalibrate where I was because all the visual clues said I was still in the States. A pair of spectacularly attractive Israeli women in their early twenties walking by snapped me out of my confusion. I savored the sight briefly before realizing they each had an Uzi submachine gun slung on their shoulder. That brought home the difference between Israel and America and reminded me I wasn't "in Kansas" anymore.

We spent three days in Sydney, mostly nursing our head colds. What a waste, to finally get to Sydney and then get sick for most of the stay.

Our next trip segment promised to be exotic in a South Pacific manner, five hours to Pago Pago in American Samoa and about another five hours to Hickam AFB, Hawaii. We took off in early morning sunshine and stayed in it all the way to Hickam.

Pago Pago proved as marvelous as I anticipated, a small speck of green on an endless blue ocean, about twenty miles long east to west and ten miles wide north to south. The runway seems built on the ocean, as waves break almost on the edges of the concrete.

Just to the north the highest island peak rose 2145 feet above the Pago Pago harbor. That is about as much of the island as we saw. We spent our three-hour turn time in a large open-air thatch roofed arena where Samoan dancers performed for us.

I kept trying to imagine the island in the 1700s when European explorers discovered it in its raw nature, green, abundant, and welcoming. I can't imagine the joy in the ship's crew when this verdant ocean oasis appeared.

We had to be on our way, unfortunately. My cold had gotten worse as it threatened to close my right ear's Eustachian tube and cause an ear block on descent. I kept my sinus spray at the ready as we took off and climbed out to the north toward Hawaii, five hours away.

I knew from flight surgeon briefings and from experience not to use the nose spray on the way up. The air pressure in my inner ear would soon be greater than cabin pressure and would blow congestion out of the ear tube. About thirty minutes prior to descent I would use the spray and hope it dampened Eustachian tube inflammation and prevented the ear block. This rarely worked, however, because the spray only briefly passed by the Eustachian tube entry into the throat and had limited effect. And, sure enough, my right hear blocked on descent into Hickam. However, this would be a relatively mild block that cleared a few minutes after landing. It did ground me for three days, something my squadron mates back at Westover found suspicious. Yeah, sure, you get yourself grounded in Hawaii, what a fairy tale! The other two pilots were also grounded for the same style head cold, so they provided me with cover.

Departure for Dover

In July 1993, after 18 months living in a studio apartment in Chicopee, I finally secured a technician position with the 326th AS in Dover. While I welcomed the return to family and our house in Dover, I recognized I would suffer an unfortunate downgrade in professional status, taking a large step backward in career digression until retirement ten years or so in the future. I didn't anticipate how painful and aggravating this digression would be.

The time frame of this book encompassed two positive, rewarding events: the dissolution of the Soviet empire and the successful removal of Saddam Hussein from Kuwait. The first of these had been a primary objective my entire career during the Cold War, flying in Vietnam and sitting nuclear alert in the B-52. The Gulf War, in retrospect, was the only laudable hot war I experienced during my career, with the possible exception of the upcoming Afghan War. Yes, that means Vietnam, Grenada, Panama, and the 2003 Iraq War were not laudable or necessary on the scale they were pursued. I can still see the justification for launching into Vietnam in an attempt to replicate a partitioned country in the pattern of Korea, where a capitalist south would shame a communist north. By 1969, however, it became apparent this would not be plausible and should have led to an armistice with the promise of substantial foreign aid as leverage. Finally, we could have bought them instead of bombing them. Had that happened, and the military draft evaporated, I probably would have been a high school history teacher and football coach.

On the dispiriting side, the Gulf War showed the awkwardness of shifting from the Cold War to a hot regional war on short notice. I do not absolve myself from this awkwardness, but I do feel the team at Westover made the transition quickly and somewhat successfully with positive results. B/G Mike Walker provided this success by allowing us to proceed as we thought necessary as long as we produced desired results. The glorious welcome home provided to the troops by the Westover community doubled as a celebration of Walker's command ability and the results he had produced. This was validated when Gen. H. T. Johnson, CINCMAC, came to Westover to present the base with the Air Force Outstanding Unit Award for its Iraq War performance.

Welcome Home Montage

All Montage Photos by Whitey Joslin

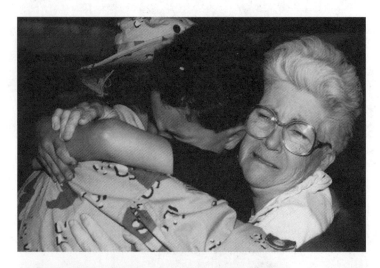

AFTERWORD

I now returned to Dover expecting a quiet, leisurely path to retirement. I could not anticipate I would twice appear on the CBS News show *60 Minutes* opposite the Air Force, followed shortly thereafter by being activated for 9/11. Finally, I would approach retirement under threat of court-martial and jail time in an orange jumpsuit at Leavenworth over the Anthrax Inoculation Program (AVIP).

I would live this final career decade in interesting times, as I will detail in book three of the series.

Photo by Nate Tarleton

C-5 air-refueling at sunset

SOUND TRACK TO ACCOMPANY BOOK

I have included "Shanties" of our British brother cargo carriers from the sailing ship era. They, similarly, traveled the world to many different ports and had many of the same concerns—weather, ship maintenance, and captains who occasionally went astray in their duties. I dedicate the final shanty, "Swing Low, Sweet Chariot," to airlift crew members who have passed on and remain only in our memories.

I lived   One Direction (Song to accompany book cover)

"Sea Shanties" by the Robert Shaw Chorale:

What Do We Do with a Drunken Sailor?

Blow the Man Down

Spanish Ladies

Haul Away Joe

Swansea Town

Whup! Jamboree

Lowlands

A-Roving

The Drummer and the Cook

Swing Low, Sweet Chariot

Arabian Arias

Ancient Egyptian Music – The Nile River

Songs of the Era:

Don't Stop Believing	Journey
Amarillo Sky	Jason Aldean (Altus AFB, OK)
Oklahoma	Movie soundtrack (Altus)
Midnight Blue	Lou Gramm
Kyrie	Mr. Mister (Aircraft liftoff)
Appalachian Spring	Arron Copeland (Hagerstown)
Lady in Red	Chris de Burgh (Bea's anthem)
Panama	Van Halen
I Can't Hold Back	Survivor (Susan's song)
Massachusetts	Bee Gees, in Melbourne, 1989
Hold on Loosely	.38 Special
Nothing Is Going to Stop Us Now	Starship
I Wanna Dance with Someone	Whitney Houston
I Should Have Known Better	Richard Marx
Down Under	Men at Work
Southern Cross	Crosby, Stills & Nash (Australia)
God Bless the USA	Lee Greenwood (Welcome Home)
Two Dozen Roses	Shenandoah (Dantley interview)

ACKNOWLEDGMENTS

I owe a great debt to many of the same people who helped me self-publish book one. These include Hillcrest Media for overall coordination of the process, Marta Tan, my unofficial editor, and Pam Nordberg, my official Hillcrest editor, both of whom provided excellent service. My wife Eleanor provided proofing in addition to allowing me to disappear into my man cave to write for hours on end. I also received helpful, and sometimes emphatic, feedback from Facebook denizens who commented on many of the book segments I posted on military pages. I appreciate even the hostile comments that helped me avoid many factual errors prior to book printing.

Finally, I owe Colonel Whitey Joslin immense thanks for providing his extensive collection of Westover photos taken during the Gulf War. These help provide an indispensable visual record of Operations Desert Shield and Desert Storm at Westover AFB.

Photo by Whitey Joslin

Col. Whitey Joslin

ABOUT THE AUTHOR

Photo by Whitey Joslin

Jay Lacklen, March 1991, Westover AFB, MA

Jay Lacklen is a retired Air Force Reserve, Lt. Col, pilot with over 12,000 military flying hours. He entered the service in 1970, retired in 2004, and flew in all conflicts from Vietnam to the 2003 Iraq War.

Jay flew 330 hours in the C-7 Caribou out of Cam Ranh Bay, RVN. He flew 2000 hours in the B-52 D,F,G and H models from Loring AFB, ME, Castle AFB, CA, Andersen AFB, Guam, and U-Tapao AB, Thailand. He led the last Arc Light cell formation out of U-Tapao in June 1975. He flew 9,500 hours in the C-5 Galaxy with the reserves from Dover AFB, DE and Westover AFB, MA. At Westover he performed as Deputy Commander for Operations for Operation Desert Storm. After retiring, he taught pilot training simulators at Columbus AFB, MS, from 2005 to 2014.

Jay appeared twice on the CBS News program "60 Minutes" opposite the Air Force, in 1998 on TCAS procurement, and in 2000 on the anthrax inoculation program. Lacklen is currently writing the third volume of a three-volume memoir, "Flying the Line, an Air Force Pilot's Journey," from his home in Vienna, VA.

He is married with four daughters and one granddaughter.

INDEX

Page numbers in **bold** indicate photographs.

A

C

G

H

L

Y

Z